Cultural policy and urban regeneration

Cultural policy and urban regeneration

The West European experience

edited by
Franco Bianchini and Michael Parkinson

MANCHESTER UNIVERSITY PRESS
MANCHESTER and NEW YORK

distributed exclusively in the USA and Canada by ST. MARTIN'S PRESS, New York

Published by Manchester University Press
Oxford Road, Manchester M13 9PL, UK
and Room 400, 175 Fifth Avenue,
New York, NY 10010, USA

Distributed exclusively in the USA and Canada
by St. Martin's Press, Inc.,
175 Fifth Avenue, New York, NY 10010, USA

British Library Cataloguing-in-Publication Data
A catalogue record for this book is available from the British Library

Library of Congress Cataloging-in-Publication Data
Cultural policy and urban regeneration : the West European experience
    / edited by Franco Bianchini and Michael Parkinson
        p.   cm.
    Includes index
    ISBN 0-7190-3556-2 (hardback)
        1. Europe–Cultural policy. 2. Urban renewal—Europe.
    I. Bianchini, Franco, 1959- . II. Parkinson, Michael, 1944– .
    01055.C82   1993
    306.4'094—dc20   92-29426

Paperback edition published 1994

ISBN 0 7190 4576 2

Typeset in Joanna
by Koinonia Limited, Manchester
Printed in Great Britain
by Biddles Limited, Guildford and King's Lynn

Contents

Tables

Illustrations

Plates

Figures

Editors and contributors

Franco Bianchini is Reader in Cultural Planning and Policy and course leader for the M.A. in European Arts and Cultural Policy at De Montfort University, Leicester. He was Research Fellow at the Centre for Urban Studies, University of Liverpool, from 1988 to 1991. Amongst other works he is the author of the 'Urban cultural policy' discussion document for the National Arts and Media Strategy (1991) and of the study 'Cultural policy and urban development' carried out within Urbanisation and the Functions of Cities in the European Community, a report commissioned by the European Commission from the Centre for Urban Studies, University of Liverpool (1992). He is also the co-author of City Centres, City Cultures (Manchester, CLES, 1988, with M. Fisher, J. Montgomery, K. Worpole) and of Out of Hours: A Study of Economic, Social and Cultural Life in Twelve Town Centres in the U.K. (with Comedia Consultancy, London).

Michael Parkinson is Professor at the European Institute of Urban Affairs, Liverpool John Moores University. He was formerly Director of the Centre for Urban Studies, University of Liverpool. He has lived and worked in the city during the past twenty years but spent several years in the 1970s as chairman of an Urban Studies Programme in the United States. He has written extensively about the problems and prospects of Liverpool. He has been working on problems of comparative urban regeneration, funded by the Leverhulme Trust. He is currently leading two major research projects. For the Department of the Environment, in conjunction with University of Manchester, he is making an assessment of the impact of government policies upon Britain's inner cities during the past decade. For the European Commission he is conducting an international research team across Europe assessing the future of European cities during the 1990s. He is the author of, amongst other things: Liverpool on the Brink; Reshaping Local Government; Regenerating the Cities: the U.K. Crisis and the U.S. Experience; and Leadership and Urban Regeneration: North American and West European Experience.

Jude Bloomfield is lecturer in Political Science (Modern European Studies in the German Department, University College, London. Her doctoral research on 'Theories of Fascism and Strategies of Resistance in the 1920s in Italy and Germany' is to be published. She researched and produced with Roy Peters and Brian Homer an exhibition on the post-war reconstruction of Birmingham, 'Imagining the city' and contributed to the film 'Paradise Circus' on women and the city. She has done research on European cities, the left and cultural policy for a forthcoming book Staging Revival: Cultural Policy in Four European Cities, and is currently working out a research programme on the emergence of European civil society.

Peter H. Booth is a qualified planner and a lecturer in the Centre for Planning,

University of Strathclyde, Glasgow. He is the co-author (with D. Harding) of *A Strategy for Public Art in Glasgow City Centre* (Glasgow Action, 1987) and the author of *Art in the Environment* (North West Arts, 1989). He acted as consultant on public art to Glasgow District Council's Festivals Unit during the 1990 European City of Culture Year.

Robin M. Boyle is Chair and Professor for the Department of Geography and Urban Planning at the College of Urban, Labour and Metropolitan Affairs, Wayne State University, Detroit. He is the co-author of *Privatism and Urban Policy in Britain and United States* (with T. Barnekov and D. Rich, Oxford University Press, 1989).

Jens S. Dangschat is Professor in the Department of Sociology, University of Hamburg and director of the Centre for Comparative Urban Research. He has published numerous articles on comparative urban development in western and eastern Europe, residential segregation, new household types, gentrification and urban development of Hamburg. He is the author of: *Social and Spatial Disparities in Warsaw*; 'Displacement by culture? Causes of the instrumentalisation of culture and its impacts', in R. Ebert, F. Gnad and K.R. Kunzmann (eds) *New Forms of Co-operation of the Local State and the Regional Economy in the Cultural Sector*; *Gentrification – Indicator and Result of Economic Restructuring, Social Change, Local Policies and Shifts in the Inner City Housing Market*, and is co-editing three books on gentrification (on Hamburg, Germany and Europe).

Jurgen Friedrichs studied Sociology, Psychology, Philosophy and Economics in Berlin and Hamburg. He took his Ph.D. at the University of Hamburg in 1968 where he became Professor in 1974 and Chair of Sociology in 1978. In 1981 he founded the Centre for Comparative Urban Research. Since 1991 he has been Chair in Sociology at the Faculty of Economics and Social Sciences at the University of Cologne and is Director of the Research Institute of Sociology. He is co-editor of the *Kölner Zeitschrift für Soziologie und Sozialpsychologie*. His major publications include *Methods of Empirical Sociological Research* (1971, 15th edn, 1990); *Urban Analysis* (1977, 4th edn, 1991); *Urban Change in Capitalist and Socialist Countries* (ed., 1985); *The Changing Downtown* (with Allen C. Goodman, 1986); *Affordable Housing and Homelessness* (ed., 1988); *Sociological Urban Research* (ed., 1988).

Julia M. Gonzalez Ferreras studied History and Geography at University College, Dublin, and Urban Geography at St Hugh's College, Oxford. She is at present Director of International Relations at the University of Deusto, Bilbao, Spain. She is lecturer at the Department of Leisure Studies and the Programmes of European Leisure Studies (PELS). She has taken part with other authors in the research on *Leisure as a Transforming Factor in Bilbao, Leisure Research in Europe* and *Leisure Policies in Europe* – presently in press.

Maarten A. Hajer is Research Fellow in the Leyden Institute for Law and Public Policy, University of Leyden, Netherlands. He studied Political Science and Urban and Regional Planning at the University of Amsterdam and Politics and the University of Oxford. His main publications are *City Politics – Hegemonic Projects and Discourse* (Avebury, Aldershot, 1989) and *De Stad als Publiek Domein* (Amsterdam, WBS, 1989).

Patrick Le Galès is a Research Associate, Observatoire Sociologique du Changement (CNRS/FNSP), Paris. His publications include: *Villes et économie: l'invention des politiques locales en France et en Grande-Bretagne* (Paris, L'Harmattan, 1992); 'New directions in decentralisation and urban policy in France: the search for a post-decentralist state' in *Government and Policy (Environment and Planning)*, January 1992; 'Les facteurs sociaux d'une politique de developpement local a Coventry', *Sociologie du Travail*, April 1991.

Emmanuel Negrier is a CNRS-funded researcher at CEPEL, at the University of Montpellier. He is a contributor to *La Communication Politique*, Paris, Les Presses Universitaires de France, 1992. His main research interests are public policy towards cable TV in France and the relationship between the regional and the European level in telecommunication policies in southern France.

Foreword

The recognition of the growing importance of cultural policy as a strategy contributing to the regeneration of cities induced us to organise two events on this topic in the course of the life of the Centre for Urban Studies. The first event, held in Liverpool in October 1989, was The Art of the City, a seminar for Liverpool decision-makers from the public and private sectors, led by Robert McNulty, the President of Washington-based Partners for Livable Places, and by leaders from cities from across the United States. The theme of the seminar was how – indeed whether – Liverpool could learn from the American experience and begin to exploit effectively the potential of its cultural resources to spearhead regeneration.

The second event was the academic conference on which this book is based, held in Liverpool in October 1990 and sponsored by the European Commission. This initiative was inspired by the Centre's growing interest in research about West European urban development and strategies. We also felt that while – at least since Arts and the Changing City, a conference highly influential among policy-makers, organised by the British American Arts Association and held in Glasgow in October 1988 – the British public had been relatively familiar with American models of the use of cultural policy in urban regeneration, there was virtually no discussion of the European experience in this field. We therefore decided to commission for our conference studies of cities in Britain, the Netherlands, Germany, France, Spain and Italy, arguably the six countries in the European Community which have been most active in the urban cultural policy field. The case studies selected do not pretend to be a representative sample of the varied range of uses of cultural policy by decision-makers in different types of European cities. The book is rather a first attempt to outline an agenda for future research, and begin to fill a rather large gap in theoretical and empirical knowledge about urban development strategies in contemporary western Europe. The city case-studies are preceded by an introductory chapter which sets the historical framework within which the evolution of urban cultural policies in western Europe must be understood. The concluding chapter explores the controversial implications arising from the recently established use of cultural policy as a vehicle for urban regeneration, raises a range of questions directed at both policy-makers and researchers, and speculates about the future of cultural policy in the urban Europe of the 1990s.

Franco Bianchini and Michael Parkinson,
Liverpool, December 1991

Remaking European cities: the role of cultural policies

Franco Bianchini

Introduction

During the last twenty years cultural policy has become an increasingly significant component of economic and physical regeneration strategies in many west European cities. The chapter provides a context for this book by discussing the factors which have placed culture more firmly on the urban development agenda in western Europe. One should be careful when generalising about the evolution of urban cultural policies in western Europe because of the scarcity of comparative research in this area and the great diversity in the definitions of 'culture' adopted by national and city governments. Equally there are differences in their ideological backgrounds, levels of financial resources and powers, and in the nature of relations between the public, private and voluntary sectors in cities in European countries. Despite this diversity, however, a number of common trends in the evolution of urban cultural policies can be identified.

One of the key trends, common to most advanced industrial economies, is the decline in working time and the increase in the proportion of disposable income spent on leisure activities. This led city governments to increase expenditure on culture and create specialised bureaucracies and policy-making bodies, to enhance their provision of cultural services to cater for growing, more sophisticated and differentiated public demand.

More specifically, the cultural renaissance of European non-capital cities such as those in this collection was encouraged by national policies for the decentralisation of powers from central to regional and local government, the emergence of grassroot and social movements raising new kinds of cultural demands, and the need to adapt to the social and economic transformations caused by the processes of economic restructuring of the 1970s and early 1980s. Economic change affected different cities and regions in different ways. However, many city decision-makers saw the development of cultural policies as a valuable tool in diversifying the local economic base and achieving greater social cohesion. They paid new attention to expanding economic sectors like leisure, tourism, the media and other 'cultural industries' including fashion and design, in an attempt to compensate for jobs lost in traditional industrial sectors. A lively, cosmopolitan cultural life was increasingly seen as a crucial ingredient of city marketing and 'internationalisation' strategies, designed to attract mobile international capital and specialised personnel, particularly in the high-tech industrial and advanced services sectors. Participation in cultural activities was promoted also as a way of integrating unemployed young people, new residents, immigrants and social groups displaced by economic restructuring into the local community.

In terms of the strategic objectives of cultural policy, the most important historical trend is the shift from the social and political concerns prevailing during the 1970s to the economic development and urban regeneration priorities of the 1980s. During the last decade, a shift to the right in the political climate in most west European countries and growing pressures on the financial resources of local government helped downgrade the earlier emphasis on the importance of access to culture, especially for disadvantaged groups. It also undermined the view of culture as a contested political issue and of cultural policy as an alternative to traditional strategies for political communication and mobilisation. The strategies of the 1980s emphasised political consensus, the importance of partnerships between business and public sector agencies, the value of 'flagship' cultural projects in promoting a city's image and the contribution of culture to economic development. In fact, the case studies in the book reveal that the direct impact of 1980s cultural policies on the generation of employment and wealth was relatively modest, in comparison with the role of culture in constructing positive urban images, developing the tourism industry, attracting inward investment, and strengthening the competitive position of cities.

The consolidation of cultural policy's function as a strategy for economic development, city marketing and physical regeneration does not mean that older arguments for interventions in this area of policy-making have been abandoned. Rather, old and new, social and economic, community and elite-oriented, arguments coexist, often uneasily, within the agenda of city governments. This cohabitation obviously gives rise to contradictions and tensions, which are explored in the chapters on different cities in this book and in the concluding chapter.

The diversity of the West European tradition of urban cultural policy-making

Interventions by city governments in the cultural field are affected by a number of factors, whose importance vary in different national contexts. These variables include: national attitudes to culture and cultural policy, to the ideologies of political parties in power locally and nationally; levels of local autonomy; the commitment of the 'investor class' to provincial cities; the configuration of the geography of national cultural economies; the size and nature of the local market for cultural activities; and the influence of external models of policy-making.

During the last two decades there were in urban Europe considerable differences in the notions of 'culture' upon which the policies were based. The English, for instance, have traditionally been more uneasy than continental Europeans with the terms 'culture' and 'cultural policy', and have tended to use the narrower 'the arts' and 'arts policy'. The broadest definitions of 'culture' and 'cultural policy' adopted by west European city governments encompassed a variety of elements, including not only the 'pre-electronic' performing and visual arts (theatre, music, painting and sculpture) but also contemporary 'cultural industries' like film, video, broadcasting, advertising, electronic music, publishing, design and fashion. At the outer reaches, the phrase 'cultural industries' included also the tourism, heritage and leisure industries. In this heterogeneity of definitions, there were nebulous distinctions between a variety of concepts such as 'art', 'arts', 'communication(s)', 'culture', 'entertainment', 'heritage', 'leisure', 'media' and 'recreation'.

The nature of urban cultural policies was affected also by the ideological characteristics of political parties in power at national and local level. There was, for example, a substantial difference between the British Labour Party and other west European Socialist and Social Democratic parties, such as the German SPD, the French PS, the Spanish PSOE, the Italian PSI and PDS and the Greek PASOK. The Labour Party's ideological tradition is, in essence, a blend of Fabian utilitarianism and trade union economism. The combination of these two influences meant that the party's mainstream concentrated mainly on narrowly defined economic and social policy questions and was until very recently more reluctant than its continental counterparts, whose ideas had been much more influenced by Marxism, to formulate broader strategies and visions of the future encompassing questions of culture and cultural policy.

The levels of autonomy, the financial resources, the powers and the statutory responsibilities of municipal governments also had an impact on cultural policy-making. In the cases of Greece, Portugal and Ireland the limited financial independence and powers of municipalities was a serious constraint on the development of urban cultural policies outside capital cities. Cultural policies also tended to be more stable in countries like Germany, where cultural expenditure is a statutory duty of local authorities, than, for instance, in Britain where no such requirement exists.

The geographical distribution of production, distribution, marketing, management and training infrastructures in the cultural industries (in commercial music, film, TV, publishing, advertising and fashion, for example) – which are traditionally concentrated in the capital cities in Britain, Ireland, Denmark, France, Spain and Greece, and more decentralised in Germany and Italy – is an important factor affecting the ability of provincial cities to successfully implement production-oriented strategies for the cultural sector. One example in this book is Liverpool, a city richly endowed with indigenous cultural talent, which has traditionally been exploited by commercial cultural industries based mainly in London.

The scope and ambitiousness of municipal cultural policies is influenced also by the size of the local market for cultural activities, which in turn is related to the social and educational profile of urban populations and to the standards and characteristics of arts education in particular. The chapter on Bologna, for example, shows that levels of personal expenditure on the performing arts by local residents were very high, at about twice the national average. This enabled the Council to develop much more wide-ranging and ambitious arts policies than those implemented, for instance, by its counterpart in Liverpool, a city of similar size but with a considerably lower educational profile.

The degree to which the 'investor class' – developers, banks, other major financial institutions, companies of national and international significance – is committed to the city is equally important. This factor is influenced by the extent to which the structure of capital in different European countries is decentralised, and it affects the potential for the development of public–private partnerships for the implementation of cultural policies. In Britain, a country with a strongly vertically and internationally integrated economy, cultural policies during the 1980s have been used also as a way of rekindling the commitment of the investor class to provincial cities. Such commitment is relatively low by the standards of countries like Germany, France, Italy and Spain.

The extent to which different municipalities have been influenced by regeneration strategies in American cities in the 1970s and 1980s also contributes to the diversity of the European experience of urban cultural policy-making. In many US cities, the interests of arts organisations seeking new homes and funding coalesced with those of politicians attempting to relaunch downtown areas, and developers wishing to use arts venues, museums and leisure facilities as a means of adding value to office, housing and retail schemes in central districts. The US experience probably influenced the 1980s debate about the role of cultural policy in the urban regeneration process more strongly in Britain than in any other European country, partly because of political affinities between the Reagan and Thatcher governments. The American influence, however, was felt also in industrial cities in other west European countries like two in this collection – Rotterdam and Bilbao – which attempted to use cultural flagship projects to break cycles of decline. Many waterfront regeneration projects with strong cultural components, such as Rotterdam's *Kop van Zuid*, were heavily influenced by American models like Baltimore's Harbor Place, Boston's Quincy Market and New York's South Street Seaport.

Despite considerable national variations, it is possible to identify a common trajectory in the development of cultural policies in west European cities. Cultural policies tended to expand as a result of the decentralisation of cultural funding and responsibilities from central to regional and local government in the 1970s and the 1980s. They also became more politicised over the same period, in response to growing pressure from urban social movements and increasing awareness among many city politicians of the need to extend their political communication and mobilisation strategies to the cultural arena. During the 1980s there was a clear shift in the policy rationale from social/political priorities to economic development objectives. This shift was caused primarily by the increasing pressure national governments applied on city governments to justify their interventions on economic grounds, and by the need for cities to respond to the structural socio-economic changes which the recessions of the early and late 1970s had brought about.

Decentralisation and the growth of urban cultural policies

One of the most important factors encouraging the cultural renaissance of provincial cities in western Europe was the decentralisation of powers from central to local and regional government – particularly in Italy, Spain and France. In Italy the growth of urban cultural policies in the 1970s was related to a reform at the beginning of the decade, which created a comprehensive system of regional government, with a new tier of regional capitals. These included cities like Turin, Milan, Venice, Genoa, Bologna, Florence, Naples and Bari, which could now draw on the resources of municipal, provincial and regional councils to finance their cultural policies. Expenditure on culture by Italian municipalities grew from 302 billion lire in 1980 to 800 billion lire in 1984 (Bodo, 1988) and there was a noticeable increase in the number of specialised officers working in the cultural policy field. In the cases of the Provincial Councils of Florence, Turin and Milan – for example – the number of officers responsible for cultural matters increased from 4 to 17, 6 to 14 and 1 to 40 respectively between 1975 and 1984 (Marchetti, 1987).

New constitutions approved following the establishment of democratic regimes in Greece (1975), Portugal (1976) and Spain (1977-78) created varying degrees of decentralisation. This was especially significant in Spain. The responsibilities of municipal government in the cultural policy field were widened, and seventeen cities – Barcelona, Valencia and Seville amongst them – became capitals of new regions (autonomous communities) with extensive powers and considerable resources.

After their electoral victory in 1981, the French Socialists introduced a wide-ranging decentralisation programme between 1982 and 1986. The state transferred to the ninety-five *départements* responsibilities over public welfare and social services, and to the twenty-two regions adult education, training and school building, as well as important aspects of road building, cultural, tourism and industrial policy. Under the Socialist Minister of Culture, Jack Lang, a new *Direction du Développement Culturel* was created, which stipulated 'cultural development agreements' with regions, *départements* and municipalities. In 1982 and 1983 the Ministry of Culture stipulated agreements with as many as ninety-one towns and cities throughout France, including the two French cities in this book, Montpellier and Rennes (Forbes, 1987). The agreements were crucial in providing opportunities for the development of cultural policies. They were exploited particularly by the mayors of regional capitals like Bordeaux, Toulouse, Montpellier, Lyon, Strasbourg and Rennes, who could draw on financial and technical resources at all four levels of government. Bordeaux, together with Grenoble, was the municipality with the highest cultural expenditure, with over 1,400 FF (about £140) per inhabitant in 1987. Cultural expenditure as a percentage of municipal budgets was highest in Lyon and Strasbourg (over 20 per cent), followed by Brest, Lille, Grenoble and Bourdeaux, all spending between 15 per cent and 20 per cent. Per capita expenditure on cultural policy by the municipalities of French cities with over 150,000 inhabitants grew from 601 FF in 1981, to 789 FF in 1984, and 905 FF in 1987 (*Développement culturel*, July 1989).

In Britain the 1980s were characterised by a process of erosion of the powers of local and metropolitan authorities, which run counter to trends towards decentralised government and enhanced regional autonomy in most west European countries (Crouch and Marquand, 1989). One of the most spectacular manifestations of the centralisation process under the Thatcher governments was the abolition in 1986 of the Greater London Council (GLC) and of the metropolitan councils of the six largest urban areas in England (MCCs). The trend towards centralisation was apparent in most areas of policy-making, ranging from local finance to education and training, housing and economic development (Travers, 1989).

However, cultural policy was a partial exception to this trend. The contributions from the Arts Council of Great Britain to Regional Arts Associations (RAAs) in England increased as a percentage of the Arts Council's total expenditure from 14.3 per cent in 1983-84 to 23.5 per cent in 1988-9 (*Cultural Trends*, March 1990). This was in line with the strategy outlined in 1984 by the Arts Council in *The Glory of the Garden*, a document setting as one of its priorities to redress the bias towards London-based institutions in cultural funding, by distributing new funds to the regions. The *Glory* strategy did not achieve this central objective because many of the cultural funding responsibilities of the abolished GLC were transferred to the Arts Council after 1986. The concentration of Arts Council expenditure in London was thus further reinforced. Such expenditure in 1984-5 was 5.5 times higher than the average regional spending, while by 1987-8 it was 6.3 times greater (Pick, 1991).

Despite the continuing London bias, a wide-ranging reform initiated by Conservative Arts Minister Richard Luce in 1988 transferred many of the direct grant-aiding responsibilities of the Arts Council to new Regional Arts Boards (RABs). These new policy-making bodies are more powerful and, in some cases, larger than the old RAAs. Their policies and strategies are often not adequately co-ordinated with those of city governments, partly because the representation of local authorities on RABs is lower than it used to be on RAAs. This lack of co-ordination is a problem because local authority expenditure on culture has become increasingly significant over the last twenty years. Net revenue expenditure on 'arts support' from local authorities in England and Wales grew from about £20m in 1976-77 to just over £100m a decade later (Feist and Hutchison, 1990). Notwithstanding these increases, however, expenditure per head on the arts and museums by local and regional government bodies in the UK in 1987 was £4.5 – considerably less than in Germany (£23.7), France (£17) and The Netherlands (£10.5) (*Cultural Trends*, March 1990).

Growing municipal expenditure is only one indicator of the growing importance of cultural policy at urban level since the early 1970s. Municipal policy-making bodies in our field rapidly multiplied since the early 1970s. In many west European city governments, new departments and committees responsible for cultural policy-making were either newly created or separated from larger administrative units within which cultural affairs had traditionally occupied a minor position. The quality of the political personnel in charge of cultural policy improved and the profile of cultural policy issues grew, as witnessed by increasing coverage in the local press, radio and TV. All these signs point to the growth in the political status of cultural policy, a trend whose origins must be traced back to the early 1970s.

The politicisation of urban cultural policies

Urban cultural policies in western Europe during the 1950s and 1960s were relatively unimportant, non-controversial areas of local policy-making. They were largely based on the narrow identification of 'culture' with the pre-electronic 'arts'. They typically made few connections between a city's cultural resources and their possible exploitation for urban renewal, tourism, image or economic development purposes. Municipal committees in charge of cultural policy were often political backwaters, attracting politicians with no particular abilities, often nearing the end of their careers.

However, a range of factors in the early 1970s made cultural policies politically more important and controversial. The most innovative and high-profile initiatives in Italy, France, West Germany and Britain were developed since the mid 1970s by left-controlled local authorities, which broke away from the tradition of attributing a relatively neutral, non-political value to cultural policy. The emergence of these new cultural strategies was related to the rise of the post-1968 urban social movements – feminism, youth revolts, environmentalism, community action, gay and ethnic/racial minority activism – whose activities had a clear cultural dimension, in two distinct respects. First, these urban movements were often closely associated with an 'alternative' cultural sector encompassing experimental theatre groups, rock bands, independent film-makers and cinemas, free radio stations, small publishing houses, radical newspapers and magazines. This cultural universe challenged the traditional distinction between 'high' and 'low' cultural forms – generally accepted by the national leaderships of left parties – and adopted a very broad definition of 'culture' combining in imaginative ways old and new, highbrow and lowbrow elements. Second, the new urban social movements saw cultural action and political action as inextricable. It was impossible to define boundaries or priorities between the two. The movements largely rejected the subordination of cultural needs and issues to wider political and economic priorities, which characterised much of the west European left's traditional ideology and practice.

The elites which introduced the most radical cultural policy experiments in west European cities in the late 1970s–early 1980s were often influenced by both the style and the substance of the politics of the new urban social movements. Many of these politicians had absorbed the wide definition of 'culture' adopted by the new movements, and recognised that cultural development formed an integral part of the agenda of urban policy and politics. Unlike the leaderships of their respective parties, 'new left' politicians like Renato Nicolini, the councillor in charge of cultural policy in Rome City Council from 1976-85 – a period during which it was controlled by the Italian Communist Party (PCI) – and Tony Banks, the first Chair of the GLC's Arts and Recreation Committee under the left-wing Labour administration led by Ken Livingstone (1981-86) devolved powers and resources to grassroots groups, recognising that the new urban movements were entitled to a generous degree of political and cultural autonomy.

Cultural strategies were used by this new breed of local politicians and policy-makers to achieve different social and political objectives. They radicalised the traditional welfarist objective to promote individual and group self-expression and widen access to cultural facilities and activities for all citizens. Equally common was the use of cultural policy to encourage forms of public life accessible to all residents and not just to the privileged. In response to increasing differentiation in urban lifestyles and growing socio-economic inequalities within cities, policies on culture and leisure were also used to encourage face-to-face interaction and promote community rebuilding. This was in part an attempt to counteract trends towards social atomisation and the domesticisation of cultural consumption by reasserting the function of the city centre as a catalyst for civic identity and public sociability. It also involved rediscovering and celebrating, as a reaction against the negative effects of functional zoning in land use planning, physical features of the pre-industrial city like density, 'walkability' and the overlapping of social, cultural and economic uses.

The organisation of arts festivals and other forms of cultural animation helped consolidate opportunities for participation in public life for people of different ages, social classes, genders, lifestyles and ethnic origins. Animation initiatives were used also to give life and meaning back to the use of time by the elderly and the unemployed, even if such time had no economic recognition or market value. They often served to revitalise not only 'dead' time but also 'dead' space, such as industrial buildings made redundant by economic change. Animation initiatives were especially successful when combined with other municipal policies. These included urban design strategies to create new public spaces and make the city more attractive and 'legible', pedestrianisation and traffic calming measures, and the provision of evening and late night public transport, good street lighting, community policing and childcare. These strategies often were a response to public desires to 'reclaim' the city centre for community use, particularly at night. These aspirations had been expressed in Italian cities by the symbolic occupations of public squares organised by the youth 'Movement of 1977' − whose impact on cultural policy-making in Bologna is examined by Jude Bloomfield in her contribution to this book − and the feminist 'Reclaim the Night' demonstrations in the late 1970s.

Cultural policies were often part of strategies developed by left parties in many cities to respond to the decline of their traditional industrial working-class constituencies, and to establish a new political base with the new urban social movements and emerging social strata like the public sector middle classes. Cultural policy was useful as an alternative form of political communication and mobilisation, responding to the decline of the mobilising power of traditional left ideologies and increased public disaffection with conventional party politics. The popularity of the Estate romana, the summer cultural animation programme initiated by the PCI-controlled Rome City Council, probably contributed to the consolidation of the PCI's relative majority at the local elections of June 1981, as the party suffered heavy losses everywhere outside Rome. By 1982, influenced by the electoral profitability of the Rome experiment, a large number of municipalities in the 'red belt' of Italy, covering the PCI-dominated regions of Emilia-Romagna, Tuscany, Umbria and the Marches, had set up departments in charge of cultural policy (assessorati alla cultura). Between 1980 and 1982 municipal expenditure on cultural animation events and activities grew in real terms by 69 per cent in the red belt, and by 30 per cent and 36 per cent respectively in the north-eastern and southern regions, dominated by the Christian Democrats (Felicori, 1984; Bianchini, 1989).

In short, local politicians often launched new, high-profile cultural policies as a symbol of the break with the political styles and programmes of the past. This was certainly the case in many major Italian cities after the local elections of 1975 and 1976, when the left took control, ending three decades of rule by the Christian Democrats. Cultural policy was often seen by many local politicians in Italy in the second half of the 1970s as a flexible and cheap vehicle to project political images. It allowed politicians to take centre stage, and to gain or maintain visibility, often with no need to create a specialised bureaucracy (Dente, 1988).

The shift from social and political to economic priorities in the 1980s

In the course of the 1980s, the shift towards neo-conservatism and neo-liberalism by most national governments in western Europe was accompanied by a squeeze in local government finance and, subsequently, expenditure. Indeed the emergence of urban cultural policies during that period has been interpreted by one commentator as a partial compensation for the inability of local authorities to continue the expansion of traditional social policies (Dente, 1988). In cities in the UK, Ireland, Denmark, Germany, France and Italy local authorities' share of public expenditure decreased in the 1980s (Wolleb, 1989). This meant that the trend towards the decentralisation of functions from central to local government was not matched by the expansion of local finance. On the contrary, both local fiscal autonomy and national government contributions were reduced.

In the field of cultural policy, as in many other policy areas, the changing national political climates and the pressures to reduce local government expenditure led to a strategic shift from social to economic objectives. This was initially a defensive strategy aimed at preserving existing levels of cultural expenditure. It was accompanied by efforts to encourage private sector sponsorship of cultural events and activities, to monitor more effectively local cultural resources and to improve the administration, management, delivery and marketing of cultural services. Later, however, some cities began to realise that the process of urban economic restructuring following the recessions of the early and late 1970s provided opportunities to forge more positive arguments for expanding expenditure on culture. The 1970s emphasis on personal and community development, participation, egalitarianism, the democratisation of urban space and the revitalisation of public social life was replaced by a language highlighting cultural policy's potential contribution to urban economic and physical regeneration. The language of 'subsidy' was gradually replaced by the language of 'investment'. Community access, popular creativity and grassroots participation became less important, for example, than the role of prestigious flagship cultural projects in promoting a city's positive image, or the development of sector strategies aimed at maximising the economic potential of local cultural industries.

Socio-economic change and the emergence of cultural policy as an urban regeneration strategy

In the 1980s European city governments had to adapt to two related phenomena which during the 1970s had caused profound changes in urban socio-economic structures: the globalisation of corporate profitability strategies and the crisis of the 'Fordist regime of accumulation', which is characterised by large-scale production of relatively homogeneous commodities for mass markets. Technological change gradually made it possible for transnational corporations to shift unskilled and semi-skilled parts of the production process to newly industrialising countries, particularly in the Pacific Rim and Latin America. European urban areas whose economies were based on heavy industrial sectors, on mass consumer industries using mature technologies and on distributive services related to declining sectors were hit particularly severely. These processes produced reductions in traditional manufacturing employment. They also created polarisation in urban labour markets between, on the one hand, the better paid and more secure employment in the managerial, professional and technical fields and, on the other, employees – many of whom were women and ethnic minorities – in less skilled, low paid, low status and often part-time service occupations. Macro-economic pressures created by the recessions of 1973 and 1979 forced national governments to introduce public expenditure cutbacks, with negative effects on levels of public sector employment and welfare benefits. By the 1980s city decision-makers in western Europe realised that they had to develop their own strategies to respond to the economic and social problems generated by the restructuring. Cultural policies emerged in many cities as an element of these strategies.

The use of cultural policy as a response to the socially traumatic consequences of economic restructuring has been interpreted pessimistically as 'a carnival mask' (Harvey, 1989) used by local and national politicians to conceal growing social inequality, polarisation and conflict within cities, or, optimistically, as a 'social glue' for integrating new immigrants, encouraging social cohesion and shaping new civic identities. Local decision-makers also exploited the potential of cultural policy to modernise and diversify the economic base of cities. Cultural facilities and activities have increasingly become part of what cities are expected to provide as an element of the local 'quality of life', if they want to have a chance of success in the intense inter-urban competition for mobile international capital and high income strategic functions.

Prestigious arts festivals, major sports competitions and other high-profile cultural events were organised by urban policy-makers to support 'internationalisation' strategies, and to enhance the cosmopolitan image and appeal of their cities.

Cultural policies became more important also as instruments for direct interventions in expanding economic sectors such as tourism, sports, recreation, the arts and the media. The fact that innovation in the cultural sphere is one of the driving forces of urban economies was clearly grasped by cities – such as Glasgow, Paris, Rennes, Montpellier, Barcelona and the Ruhr cities – seeking to consolidate their position as centres for R&D and design-intensive industry, and advanced services. The quality of urban life and, more specifically, the liveliness of urban cultural milieux are increasingly seen by European urban policy-makers as important elements in innovative capacity.

In those cities which failed to adapt their policies to the urban regeneration and economic development priorities of the 1980s, cultural policy tended to become more marginal, losing political status and financial resources. This process can be exemplified by contrasting the fortunes of the cultural policies developed by Rome City Council from 1976-1985, which failed to adapt to the economic and political realities of the 1980s, with those implemented by the municipalities of Hamburg and Sheffield in the same period, which successfully adapted to the changing economic and political climate. Rome City Council intervened very imaginatively and successfully in the field of cultural consumption, through the provision of popular entertainments and the revitalisation of public spaces. But it failed to link this with cultural production and distribution strategies. This failure meant that after the left coalition lost power at the 1985 local elections the new Christian Democrat-controlled administration could quickly dispose of the cultural policy legacy of its predecessors. Programmes for the development of local cultural industries survived radical political shifts in Hamburg and Sheffield. Cultural industries strategies in these two cities continued to receive support mainly because of their symbolic impact: they associated the city's image with the media, design, fashion, high technology and other expanding economic sectors.

As some of the contributions to this book make clear, the direct impact of cultural policies on the creation of wealth and employment was relatively small. In the 1980s cultural policies gave their most significant contribution to urban regeneration by helping to construct urban images able to attract tourists, skilled personnel and investors, to diversify and strengthen the local economic base.

The 1980s: cultural policy as an image strategy

In the 1980s, cities with different economic functions in the European urban hierarchy profitably used cultural policies to improve their internal and external images. Prestigious cultural projects acted as symbols of rebirth, renewed confidence and dynamism in declining cities like Glasgow, Sheffield and Bilbao, which were dependent on obsolete economic sectors and struggling to find for themselves new economic niches and functions. They acted as symbols of newly acquired elegance, sophistication and cosmopolitanism in wealthier cities like Frankfurt, anxious to consolidate their competitive advantages by filling the gap between their high economic status and their often relatively low cultural standing. Cultural policies were used as symbols of modernity and innovations in cities like Montpellier, Nîmes, Grenoble, Rennes, Hamburg, Cologne, Barcelona and Bologna that wished to develop sectors of the economy such as fashion, crafts and design-based manufacturing and high-tech industry, that depend for their success on cultural inputs. They were used as symbols of reconciliation in cities like Berlin and Derry, with a high potential for social conflict between older residents and migrant minorities, or different political and ethnic groups respectively. Cultural 'flagships' like the Burrell collection in Glasgow, the Albert Dock in Liverpool, Centenary Square in Birmingham, the Antigone district in Montpellier, the Museum quarter in Frankfurt, the 160 new public squares created in Barcelona in the build-up to the 1992 Olympics all became powerful physical symbols of urban renaissance.

At the 'global city' level, Paris under the Mitterrand presidency carried out a series of prestigious cultural projects to enhance its credentials as the future 'economic and cultural capital of Europe', including Mitterrand's *Grands Chantiers*: the Orsay Museum, the Museum of Science and Technology at La Villette, the Louvre Pyramid, the Institut du Mond Arabe, the Opera at La Bastille. By contrast, the fragmentation of cultural policy-making in London after the abolition of the GLC in 1986 contributed to the relative decline of the image of the city as an international centre for cultural and economic innovation (Kennedy, 1991). The absence of an elected strategic authority, able to speak on behalf of the whole city, prevented London from capitalising on its considerable strengths in, for example, theatre, street fashion, electronic music and ethnic cultures. Without the GLC it became more difficult to co-ordinate cultural with transport and planning policies, to form public–private partnerships to implement projects and to organise festivals and other large-scale events which would celebrate and make more accessible to residents and visitors the cultural strengths of the city.

One of Europe's 'aspiring global' cities, Frankfurt in Germany, probably did most during the 1980s to enhance its international image though cultural policy. The city's financial centre and airport are among Europe's busiest, but until a decade ago its cultural life was under-developed and its overall image poor. The city was dubbed Bankfurt, Krankfurt (*krank* meaning 'sick') or even G'stankfurt (from *stinken*=to stink). It was associated with *Geld, Porno und Krawallen* (money, pornography and riots) or *Mörderer, Millionären und Marxisten* (murderers, millionaires and Marxists). But under its chief officer for cultural affairs Hilmar Hoffmann, working closely with the mayor, Walter Wallmann, the municipality developed a strategy to enhance the city's cultural status. Expenditure on cultural policy increased from 6 per cent of total municipal expenditure in 1970 to 11 per cent in 1990. In the 1980s, about 1 billion DM was invested in high-quality cultural buildings, converting a derelict opera house into a concert hall and creating thirteen new museums on the banks of the River Main.

The Netherlands' second city, Rotterdam, similarly improved its image, traditionally that of a dull industrial centre dominated by petrochemical works and the port, through cultural initiatives, including the creation of a new Museum of Architecture and the organisation of new jazz and film festivals.

Glasgow, Bradford and Birmingham, cities severely hit by the decline of manufacturing industry during the recessions of the 1970s and early 1980s, achieved substantial changes in image through their use of cultural policy. Glasgow's image only a decade ago was associated with razor-gang street violence and urban decay. The city, however, was able to gain substantial benefits from a cultural upgrading strategy including environmental improvement initiatives, the opening of the prestigious Burrell Collection in 1983, the launch of the successful 'Glasgow's Miles Better' advertising campaign, and the organisation of a coherent annual programme of cultural festivals. Glasgow's efforts culminated in its nomination as 'European City of Culture' for 1990. As Booth and Boyle point out in their contribution to this book, it is still too early to accurately measure the impact of the 1990 celebrations, but 1990 certainly enhanced the credibility of Glasgow-based arts organisations and the city's national and international image, particularly in tourism terms.

In Bradford, the city marketing campaigns co-ordinated by the Council's Economic Development Unit, known as 'the Myth-breakers', were crucial in the success of a strategy linking tourism policies and cultural flagship projects. The most important was the National Museum of Photography, Film and Television, opened in 1983 in a redundant theatre building in the city centre. The impact of cultural policy in Bradford has not been systematically monitored. But it is clear that the opening of the National Museum enhanced the city's reputation in media industry circles. Bradford is currently one of the cities competing for the headquarters of Channel 5, Britain's fifth national TV channel. The museum also rapidly became a major tourist attraction. It was visited by about three million people in its first five years of existence (Hunter, 1988) and contributed to improving the overall appeal of Bradford as a tourist destination.

In Birmingham's case the city centre, because of a series of postwar planning disasters, was regarded by local policy-makers as the main problem to be tackled to strengthen the city's position in international business circuits. The City Council built a new International Convention Centre incorporating a fine concert hall for the City of Birmingham Symphony Orchestra, organised a series of annual arts festivals, encouraged London-based arts organisations to relocate to the city, and enhanced the distinctive features of city centre districts. These initiatives followed an overall urban design strategy, and were co-ordinated with policies on public art and the re-use of the city's canal system.

In short, the mobilisation of culture to the cause of city marketing is one of the most recent ways in which cultural policies have become an established and legitimate part of urban regeneration strategies in western Europe. Cultural facilities and resources are not regarded by local decision-makers as more important in determining a city's appeal to investors than local educational and skills levels, the quality of local schooling and of the local environment. They have, however, become increasingly important complementary factors in the competition between cities possessing similar advantages.

Conclusions

The establishment of cultural policy as a strategy contributing to urban regeneration does not mean that older arguments and justifications for policy-making in our field are no longer valid. The evolution of the rationale for urban cultural policy-making has not followed a process of simple progression, with each new argument replacing the traditional ones. Despite extensive debates during the last four decades, the basic aim of 1950s urban cultural policies of promoting high-quality art and widening access to it remains one of the reasons for cultural funding at municipal level. Equally, the 1970s objective of endowing community and marginalised social groups with an independent cultural voice retains much of its validity. Some of the contributions to this book explore the tensions and conflicts which arise from the existence within the agenda of the same city government of 'old' and 'new' rationales and priorities for cultural policy-making, often championed by different agencies.

There are conflicts between the goal of maintaining prestigious facilities for 'high' culture marketed to wealthy visitors which emphasise 'exclusiveness', and of opening up popular access to them. Even more problematic is reconciling the need to develop elite 'flagship' schemes to enhance urban competitiveness with decentralised, community-based provision of more popular cultural activities, targeted in particular at low income and marginalised social groups. In the attempt to attract financial support from central government and the private sector, city decision-makers have often concentrated their resources on the former, at the expense of the latter. Lastly, there are tensions between the use of cultural policy as an ingredient of internationalisation strategies and the need to protect and develop indigenous local and regional identities, and the cultures of often socially and economically disadvantaged immigrant communities.

City governments have tried to address these problems by progressively widening the definitions of 'culture' upon which their policies are based, and by developing the function of the city centre as a focus for public social life genuinely accessible for all citizens. Despite these efforts, the chapters in this volume show that the balancing of different priorities, interests and pressures in cultural policy-making is a difficult art indeed.

References

Ardagh, John (1990) France Today, Harmondsworth, Penguin.

Bianchini, Franco (1987) 'GLC R.I.P. Cultural policies in London', New Formations, 1

Bianchini, Franco (1989) 'Cultural policy and urban social movements: the response of the 'New Left' in Rome (1976-85) and London (1981-86)', in Bramham et al. (1989).

Boden, Trevor (ed.) (1988) Cities and City Cultures, Birmingham, Birmingham Film and Television Festival.

Bodo, Carla (1988) 'La spesa culturale degli enti locali: un'analisi quantitativa', in Salvati and Zannino (1988).

Bramham, Peter et al. (eds) (1989) Leisure and Urban Processes: Critical Studies of Leisure Policy in Western European Cities, London, Routledge.

Centre for Urban Studies, University of Liverpool (1992) Urbanisation and the Functions of Cities in the European Community.

Crouch, Colin and Marquand, David (eds) (1989) The New Centralism, Oxford, Blackwell.

Dente, Bruno (1988) 'Politiche culturali e amministrazione locale', in Salvati and Zannino (1988).

Feist, Andrew and Hutchison, Robert (1990) Cultural Trends in the Eighties, London, Policy Studies Institute.

Felicori, Mauro (1984) 'Feste d'estate: indagine sulla politica culturale dei comuni italiani', in Parisi (1984).

Forbes, Jill (1987) 'Cultural policy: the soul of man under socialism', in Mazey and Newman (eds) (1987).

Harvey, David (1989), 'Down towns', *Marxism Today*, January.

Hunter, Jean (1988), 'A national museum in an inner city role', in Boden (1988).

Kennedy, Richard (ed.) (1991) *London: World City. Moving Into the 21st Century*, London, HMSO.

Marchetti, Aldo (1987) 'La cultura delle province', in *Ikon*, 14.

Marchetti, Aldo (1988) 'I soggetti e le finalità della spesa per la cultura: una ricerca dell'Istituto Gemelli', in Salvati and Zannino (1988).

Mazey, Sonia and Newman, Michael (eds) (1987) *Mitterrand's France*, London, Croom Helm.

National Physical Planning Agency (1989) *Cities and Culture*, The Hague, Ministry of Housing, Physical Planning and Environment.

Parisi, Arturo (ed.) (1984) *Luoghi e misure della politica*, Bologna, Il Mulino.

Pick, John (1991) *Vile Jelly. The Birth, Life and Lingering Death of the Arts Council of Great Britain*, Doncaster, Brynmill.

Salvati, Mariuccia and Zannino, Lucia (eds) (1988) *La cultura degli enti locali (1975-1985)*, Milan, Angeli.

Travers, Tony (1989) 'The threat to the autonomy of elected local government', in Crouch and Marquand (eds) (1989).

Wolleb, Enrico (ed.) (1989) 'La crise des villes en Europe', Paris, mimeo.

2

See Glasgow, see culture

Peter Booth and Robin Boyle

On the night of 31 December 1990 Glasgow passed the baton of European City of Culture to Dublin. A traditionally Scottish hogmanay party in the city's George Square ended a year-long cultural extravaganza that stretched from Pavarotti to the Rolling Stones, from the Berlin Philharmonic to Frank Sinatra, from John McGrath's *The Ship* to Peter Brook's *La Tempete*. Not surprisingly, this interpretation of the European designation, and the costs incurred in staging the events, aroused considerable local controversy:

1990 has been a year of fun, entertainment and enjoyment for the people of Glasgow and that's what we wanted it to be.

(Pat Lally, former leader, Glasgow District Council)

1990 was a year when an intellectually bankrupt and brutally undemocratic administration projected its mediocre image onto the city and ordered us to adore it.

(Michael Donnelly, one-time assistant museum curator,
People's Palace, Glasgow)

Our purpose here is not to explore the fine grain of Glasgow's extraordinary cultural pageant in 1990. We will indeed return to the broad issues raised by these quotations but we have no intention of entering into the cut and thrust of what, in essence, was a local argument. Rather, we seek to ask if Glasgow, a city with a deserved reputation for achieving urban improvement, has employed culture as an integral part of that regeneration. We also explore the extent to which 1990 was part of a longer-term strategy of using the arts as a means of achieving wider economic and social change. Although much of the data are still in the process of being collected, our analysis includes a tentative assessment of investing in culture and the impact this can have on the future prospects of cities, like Glasgow, searching for a new role in the late twentieth century.

Theoretical context

Detailed description of specific urban regeneration can play an important role in understanding the processes of urban change. But that same description can be translated into more valuable critical analysis if it is clearly located within a theoretical context. Moreover, that analysis becomes all the more powerful when the case-study model is set into the appropriate historical framework. For this review of contemporary cultural policy in Glasgow we have chosen to comment on three convergent urban theories that might usefully shape critical analysis.

1 The contemporary promotion of urban culture can be defined as one strand of local economic policy that is used to cushion the negative effects of the painful transition from an industrial to a post-industrial economy. In this model, culture is defined in the language of economics, with the attendant measurements applied to policy analysis: investment, leverage, employment, direct and indirect income effects, social and spatial targeting and so forth. Culture is then bundled up with business services, with tourism, with the leisure industries as part of a narrow definition of urban regeneration driven by the objectives of employment creation.

2 Cultural policy, be it defined as a formal policy or not, can be employed as part of a local response, perhaps as a strategy in its own right, to the globalisation of capital and the political necessity to marshal all available resources to attract and hold international investment. Cultural policy then becomes one strand of place marketing, with cities vying against the opposition (other cities) to flaunt their ownership of old masters, fine architecture, symphony orchestras or rock musicians. Depending on the audience, a city's culture is packaged and repackaged to become an incentive (perhaps the opera) for the potential inward investor; an 'urban flagship' (waterfront renaissance) to attract new property development; or simply good copy (floodlit Georgian facades) for urban advertising.

3 Alternatively, culture, in the context of urban regeneration, can be part of what has been called the 'mobilisation of the spectacle' (Harvey, 1989). Taking a negative perspective, culture as urban spectacle is crudely used to both justify and repay contemporary urban lifestyles. Here the 'city of luxury' or the 'gentrified city' (Marcuse, 1989: 703), often found close to the central business

district, needs the urban spectacle to reinforce residential choice. In a sense, it is the reward for upper- and middle-class commitment to the city. Choosing another perspective, the concept can be used to explore the premise that city authorities promote urban events from extravagant displays of urban sculpture to the conspicuous promotion of the theatre or music or indeed sport as symbols of unity to cement or patch-over class, racial or ethnic divisions. As with monumental civic architecture, promotion of the spectacle can be used as a demonstration of action but, 'it is a fragile and uncertain tool of unification, and to the degree that it forces the consumer to become a "consumer of illusions" contains its own specific alienations' (Harvey, 1989: 273).

We will return to these three theoretical positions in our analysis of the role played by culture in the Glaswegian version of urban regeneration. But before setting the historical context, it is useful to mention two further concepts of urban adaptation that may be particular to this case-study of cultural policy in Glasgow.

4 It is argued that the city of Glasgow has an internationalism not found in other provincial British cities. It is held that the pace, scale and impact of industrialisation forged urban heterogeneity that was to become manifest in an artistic community that combined the best of European, English, lowland Scots and Gaelic culture. Moreover, the commercial development of the nineteenth and twentieth centuries brought further cultural variety to the city, from eastern Europe, from Italy, from the United States; and most recently from the Indian sub-continent. So much so that as early as 1915 the town clerk spoke of the 'cosmopolitan' mix of the city (quoted in Daiches, 1977).

5 It is also held that the distinctive skills found in the city's predominantly working-class labour force, a legacy of the industrial heritage (mainly in metal manufacture and fabrication), have been transformed into the contemporary visual arts, not least in a new school of painting that has been termed 'social realism' and in new sculpture that both evokes and parodies the past. There is now an argument that this re-utilisation of working-class skills in the contemporary development of art in the city spreads culture across class and spatial divisions.

Historical and economic context

'The high, tragic pageant of the Clyde. (George Blake, 1935).

The economic and physical change that is now a feature of late twentieth century Glasgow is all the more stark because of the city's rich industrial heritage. First trade with the Americas in tobacco followed by sophisticated and profitable textile manufacture, linen and then cotton, was to see Glasgow prosper in the eighteenth and nineteenth centuries. The wealth created out of textiles and the attendant development of a scientific and physical infrastructure in the region was put to good effect as the city emerged as one of the heavy engineering capitals of the world.

The comparative advantage of the region was largely due to the local reserves of coal and ironstone. In the districts surrounding the city, iron smelting and its associated technology became the bedrock of the economy. Iron production and the skill-base of the workforce quickly led to the development of new processes and products: especially iron ships on the Clyde and railway engine manufacture in Glasgow.

It was through shipbuilding that Glasgow gained its position in the world economy and its reputation, real or imaginary, for left-wing political activism. Between 1870 and 1914, Scottish shipyards were responsible for one-third of the total British output and in the peak year of 1913 the thirty-nine Clydeside yards launched 750,000 tons of shipping, nearly one-fifth of the world's tonnage (Oakley, 1990). Some 60,000 men were employed in shipbuilding with another 40,000 in ancillary and related industries, giving Glasgow at the turn of the century the lowest unemployment rate of any British industrial region.

Hence, within living memory Glasgow had indeed been an industrial city of world standing. At the turn of the century, in addition to shipbuilding, marine engineering and locomotive manufacture, new industrial processes were started: sewing machine manufacture at the Singer Plant in Clydebank, motor vehicles (Arrol-Johnston, Albion and Argyll), specialised steel production (Colvilles) and integrated manufacturing, including armaments, as in Beardmore's parkhead foundry (Keating, 1988). The population of the city expanded accordingly, rising from 77,000 in 1801 to 300,000 in 1851, reaching 785,000 before the First World War. Indeed, by the early twentieth century Glasgow would boast that it had claim to the title 'Second City of the Empire', (Oakley, 1975).

Moreover, Glasgow developed a unique urban lifestyle centred around the tenemental form of housing. As the city expanded, developers responded to market demand for inexpensive housing, close to industry: to the south (the notorious Gorbals), to the west and on the River Clyde (Govan and Partick), in the north (Springburn and Maryhill), and – in the east – Calton, Bridgeton and Dalmarnock (see Horsey, 1990 and Smout, 1986). Private buildings created a dense, hard urban fabric of four-storey buildings, containing a range of generally small flats (called houses), often with the most primitive of facilities. Yet despite the poverty and misery that was to be generated by the sub-division of houses and the lack of investment, a distinctive urban culture emerged from the dark, smoke-filled 'closes' (common entrances).

Like the yards on the Clyde, the working-class culture of the close became inextricably linked with the city's history and out of it has developed a rich seam of urban mythology. For the memories of the tenement are selective. Gone is the disease, the cold, and the gloom. Instead, the tenement is often fondly remembered as a symbol of community that has been lost, as a symbol of sharing (of the good and the bad) that has been forgotten and as the symbol of a lifestyle sadly missed by so many: 'the community spirit of the tenement, the neighbourliness, was the thing that has been lost. Whole communities were broken up that had lived together in the tenements for years. Everybody knew everybody else.' (reminiscences of a Springburn resident, quoted in Faley, 1990: 169).

Glasgow's economic decline was less abrupt than its earlier ascendancy but the urban impact was just as telling. The post 1918 slump and the depression in the 1930s weakened the economic base of the city, exposing the vulnerability of its heavy industries to stagnation in world trade. Unemployment peaked at 30 per cent in 1930. The nadir in shipbuilding was reached in 1933 when output sank to 7 per cent of its 1913 peak. Not surprisingly, the steel industry was also affected. Of even greater concern was a failure of the Scottish economy to recapture its share of modern industry in the inter-war years. Moreover, Keating (1988) records that the 'entrepreneurial culture of the Victorian period all but disappeared with the attention of the remaining big industrialists concentrated on cartelisation, protection and monopolisation' (p. 7).

Sidney Checkland's famous study of Glasgow used the metaphor of The Upas Tree to illustrate what was happening to a city in decline.

The Upas tree of heavy engineering killed everything that sought to grow under its branches ... now the Upas tree, so long ailing, was decaying, its limbs falling away one by one. Not only had it been inimical to other growths, it had, by an inversion of its condition before 1914, brought about limitation of its own performance. (Checkland, 1981)

And it is widely held that the decline of the city was not assisted by a failure to develop new industrial relationships. Instead, Clydeside and Glasgow became synonymous with union militancy and defensiveness, protecting out-moded working practices. Equally at fault were the employers who clung to a belief in autocratic control with an antiquated conception of workplace management. Alan Massie's summary of decline makes for painful reading:

Clyde-built had been a synonym for quality; now the Clyde seemed to represent all that was worst in British industry: restrictive practices; obsolete ideologies; weak, unimaginative and increasingly desperate management; inefficiency; over-manning; short-sightedness; the absence of any intelligent sense of direction. (Massie, 1989: 102)

The decline of the city's economy continued in the 1960s and 1970s. Both shipbuilding and metal manufacture recorded dramatic falls in employment and by 1980 there was less than 13,000 people employed in shipbuilding on the Clyde. And this pattern was repeated across almost all manufacturing sectors. Between 1971 and 1983, manufacturing employment in the city fell by 45 per cent. Returning to the river as a barometer of decline, in 1990 only two shipyards remained on the upper-Clyde, employing less than 6,000 workers.

Key demographic and economic statistics for Glasgow in 1990 (with a Scottish comparison) are summarised in Table 2.1 below. The most striking statistic, and one central to the theme of this chapter, is the proportion of the city's employment in the service sector. Today, Glasgow has a lower proportion of people employed in manufacturing than the Scottish average. Contrary to a widespread belief, Glasgow is no longer predominantly a manufacturing city but is arguably the key business centre in Scotland.

Urban policies, programmes and projects

What the preceding statistics do not show is that in the 1970s Glasgow failed to capture additional service sector employment. While the proportion of jobs in services increased, the number of

Table 2.1 Glasgow: summary of demographic and economic statistics (with Scottish comparisons)

(1) Population	1975	1989	% change
	885,100	696,000	−23.1
	(5,206,200)	(5,094,000)	−2.2
(2) Unemployment (%)	6.5	10.9	
	(4.8)	(8.5)	
(3) Employment (%)	1976	1990	1995[a]
Primary	0.5 (4.1)	1.8 (4.4)	1.8 (4.4)
Manufacturing	31.9 (29.3)	17.8 (21.3)	15.4 (18.7)
Construction	6.7 (8.3)	7.3 (6.7)	7.8 (7.1)
Services	60.9 (58.3)	73.1 (67.7)	75.0 (69.8)

[a]Taken from projections constructed by Business Strategies Ltd.
Source: Baird and Walker, 1990. Glasgow District Council, 1989.

people employed in this sector actually fell from 250,000 in 1978 to 240,000 in 1986. However, the recognition of the shift in the economic base of the city triggered post-industrial policy development. In contrast to some forty years of divisive urban policy in the city, the pursuit of a new economic base helped to bridge political divisions, activate the private sector and eventually stimulate a measure of contemporary urban renaissance. This culminated in an attempt to fuse culture, especially promotion of the arts, with the policies and programmes of urban regeneration.

The evolution of Glasgow's urban renewal policies is both complex and confusing (Boyle, 1990; Keating, 1988; Checkland, 1981). In summary, the politics and the product of urban regeneration in the city have been dominated by the social problems of industrial decline, and in particular the urban legacy of high-density, low-quality tenemental housing. From 1940 to the mid 1970s city politics and urban planning were driven by a simple objective: to rehouse the working class in municipal housing on land purchased by the corporation. The resultant social structure and physical morphology of the city was dramatic. By 1980, more than 60 per cent of the city's households lived in rented accommodation owned by the public sector. Many families were relocated from the older slum tenements into a series of peripheral public-housing schemes encircling the city. Some were offered homes closer to the city centre in high-density, often high-rise, blocks built as part of a hugely ambitious comprehensive redevelopment programmes. Others were encouraged to leave the city, with the offer of homes in the new towns or in suburban communities through a formal 'overspill policy'. Owner-occupation was at best ignored. New private housing was often actively discouraged. The result was a heightened division between an increasingly working-class city and middle-class suburbs, outwith the city boundary.

The movement of people was mirrored by equally dramatic changes to the industrial structure and location of manufacturing in the city. Surviving industry was encouraged to relocate to sites on the edge of the city or, with the support of central government, to find a new labour force in the new towns. At best, policy was to facilitate industrial transition. As trade on the Clyde fell, the docks lay derelict or were gradually in-filled awaiting some future, but undefined, use. The central area remained important as Glasgow never lost its traditional commercial, service and retail functions. However, planning policy did little to initiate service sector expansion.

The outcome of Glasgow's urban renewal was not simply spatially divisive; it was also sterile. The ambitious plans for the development of 'communities' within the peripheral estates, each with a range of social and commercial facilities, proved impossible to achieve. The shopping centres in these schemes were very slow to develop; the promised public and private leisure facilities never materialised. The resulting social and physical environment was devoid of the life and soul of Glasgow made famous by its tenemental history. The product of housing renewal policies in the 1950s and 1960s was quantitative rather than qualitative, physical rather than social, utilitarian rather than enriching. Culture and the new Glasgow were miles apart.

During these two decades Glasgow sought to build a modern city but the results were all too often soulless. In the 1970s and 1980s the commitment to urban renewal was just as strong but the policies, the mechanisms and the product were worlds apart. Ironically, the dramatic shift in housing renewal policy, started in the late 1960s and continued through the 1970s, transformed not simply the physical appearance of the city but also the attitude of city politicians and officials.

By the late 1970s the success of the housing association movement in the city began to have an impact on the monolithic housing management department of the city council. Younger politicians and their officials sought an alternative to the crude municipalisation strategies of the old guard. When the Labour Party lost control of the city between 1977 and 1980, the Conservative administration, their officials and the younger Labour councillors in opposition found the opportunity to examine a new approach to the city's housing policies. On regaining control of the city council in 1980, Labour announced its 'alternative strategy', aimed at maximising the use of existing resources and encouraging the flow of private resources into housing. A significant proportion of grant aid was used to assist owner occupiers undertake tenement improvement but the housing department also sought to encourage new private sector development including the conversion of derelict city-centre warehouses and other properties.

This was supported by a relaxation of the city planning department's constraints on private residential development within the city centre. As early as 1981, the draft Central Area Local Plan identified the 'Merchant City' as a non-statutory 'Special Project Area'. By 1988, some 1,964 houses had been completed, 612 were in the pipeline and a further 1,120 were planned or under negotiation.

This gradual and often informal rediscovery of city-centre living was aided by a renewed confidence in the arts, not least in the development of theatre. In 1980, a small theatre club took ownership of the Tron Church in the heart of the city's decaying warehouse district. As the theatre gradually took shape, the 'Tron' and a small number of other attractions (principally the Cafe Gandolfi) began to attract middle-class attention. This new awareness of the possibilities of city-centre living, linked to the arrival of new cultural venues jointly stimulated modest 'back-to-the-city' movements. Hence, by the early 1990s, the Merchant City had become more than simply a gentrified housing area but laid claim to being an alternative cultural district with new galleries, studios, the (old) City Concert Hall, and a new experimental theatre being constructed in the crypt of a local church by the adjacent Strathclyde University.

The Merchant City was never planned as such but its success, as with other contemporary urban projects within Glasgow, was due in considerable measure to the funding and commitment of a government agency. Much has already been written on the subject (Boyle, 1990; Keating, 1988; Keating and Boyle, 1986; Lever and

Moore, 1986) but it is difficult to underestimate the importance to
the new Glasgow of the Scottish Development Agency, created in
1975 and, significantly, headquartered in the city. Charged with the
task of regenerating the Scottish economy, the agency was initially
reluctant to become involved in urban regeneration. Nonetheless,
bowing to intense political pressure, the SDA was asked to assume
responsibility for the 'GEAR' Project in 1976 (GEAR = Glasgow
Eastern Area Renewal) (see, Donnison and Middleton, 1987; Keating
and Boyle, 1986). The level of agency expenditure through the
GEAR project, £78 million by 1986 when the programme was run
down, had a significant physical and psychological impact on the
fringe of the city centre.

In addition, the agency's involvement across a series of property
initiatives was also important for the city. The SDA delivered
financial resources and a high profile to projects such as the
refurbishment of the disused Templeton's carpet factory, financial
packaging of the Scottish Exhibition and Conference Centre, land
assembly for the redevelopment of the St Enoch site as a major retail
centre and the co-ordination of the Glasgow Garden festival in 1988
(HMSO, 1991). At the finer grain of urban renewal, the SDA
activities in Glasgow and those of its promotional offshoot, Glasgow
Action (Boyle, 1989) were similarly important in terms of
supporting cultural activities: temporary exhibitions, development
competitions and community art projects. Its continued support for
landscaping, stone cleaning and floodlighting also served to
highlight the architectural strengths of the city.

Glasgow District Council had similarly developed urban regeneration projects in Maryhill, the Merchant City, in the Broomielaw and
Cathedral Precinct areas. The success of these initiatives led to an
attitude of flexibility within the agencies and a history of mutual co-
operation between the different parties concerned. This context of
collaboration was also translated into combined public–private
financing of urban redevelopment, a feature that was to be
harnessed, albeit in modest terms, during 1990.

This phase in the city's adaptation to a post-industrial world will
be best remembered for the council's vigorous approach to urban
marketing. In 1983 Glasgow District Council launched a campaign of
municipal marketing and unabashed self-promotion. With the
support of the city businesses and institutional interests, the slogan
'Glasgow's Miles Better' became the ubiquitous symbol of a changed

city. This proclaimed, for anyone bothered to notice, that Glasgow had found itself a new role in business services, in advanced education, in publishing and in the arts. As the Myerscough Report (Myerscough, 1988) was to demonstrate, in the 1980s far more people worked in the arts (c.14,000) than built ships on the Clyde.

It is important to appreciate that the Miles Better campaign was more than simply civic hype, but was built on an established belief that Glasgow should be proud of its artistic and cultural heritage and use it to the city's advantage. Long before the concept of the European City of Culture had been conceived, David Daiches, commenting on the plan for the housing of the Burrell Collection wrote, 'amid the fierce debates about high-rise flats and grandiose plans for urban renewal, Glasgow had been quietly establishing its right to be considered as a great city of the arts' (Daiches, 1977: 253). The early 1980s was a period when a series of individual projects and events matured at the same time, producing an important critical mass of cultural activity.

The opening of a new art gallery to house the eccentric but internationally renowned Burrell Collection was undoubtedly the catalyst that drew the different components together. This, together with the plans for a new Royal College of Music and Drama, and firm proposals to construct a new concert hall was sufficient for Daiches to suggest that 'Glasgow ... will have a place of rank as an art centre among European cities' (Daiches, 1977: 253). Hence Glasgow's cultural resources – the home of Scottish Opera and the National Orchestra, the Citizens' Theatre (see Coveney, 1990), and the largest municipal art collection outside London – became part of the marketing literature, joining references to the city parks, access to outdoor recreation and proximity to the Scottish Highlands, promoting the city for tourism, for inward investors, for business. Thus by the early 1980s culture held centre stage in the promotion of a post-industrial Glasgow.

Arriving at culture

Allowing the appointed advertising agents, Saatchi and Saatchi, to promote Glasgow as European Capital of Culture (emphasis added) reveals much about the objectives of the city's agencies in capturing the title. The promotional objective was to show 'a lively, thriving metropolis' to the world at large and also to the people of Glasgow. Hence 1990 was, from the outset, seen as a way of extending the city's image campaign launched in 1983 (Boyle, 1990). It seemed that whilst the prevailing rough and unattractive physical image of Glasgow held by outsiders had been shaken by 'Glasgow's Miles Better', the next step in image repair would be a demonstration of cultural richness. In this way cultural policy in Glasgow, at least for the period up to 1991, would be used to improve the city's international profile.

The annual event of European City of Culture was well suited to this purpose. The concept had been initiated by the ministers responsible for cultural affairs within the European Community. The nominated city could not only choose the form that the event could take but also could adopt the prestigious title of 'European City of Culture'. This is a far wider city marketing opportunity than the original educational intention which was 'to encourage an awareness of cultural links within the European Community's common cultural heritage' (Council of Europe, Strasbourg, 1983). Previous cultural cities on a yearly basis from 1985 had been Athens, Florence, Amsterdam, Berlin and Paris whose international reputations for cultural activities were already established. In contrast, Glasgow would use the title to further its establishment as an international post-industrial city with a growing cultural tourism appeal. The title of 'European City of Culture' was in Glasgow's case bringing the status rather than the status of the city bringing the title (Taggart, 1987). This implies a degree of strategic thinking in terms of city marketing, since the city did recognise that the event constituted a type of regeneration tool.

The logic of developing culture as a marketable commodity was substantiated by a timely research project. In 1985 Glasgow District Council, the Greater Glasgow Tourist Board (GGTB), Glasgow Action and the Scottish Arts Council had commissioned the Policy Studies Institute (PSI) to quantify the economic importance of the arts in Glasgow. The PSI report, published in 1988, showed that the arts in Glasgow was a £204,000,000 industry and employed 2.25 per cent of the working population either directly or indirectly. Thirty-six per cent of attendance at the arts in Glasgow was by tourists (approximately 500,000 in 1986) which generated some four hundred jobs. The cultural industries, defined as publishing, the art trade, designer trades, broadcasting, music, film, video and cinema created 54 per cent of these jobs and £174,000,000 income (Myerscough, 1988). The message conveyed was that further service sector jobs could be created as cultural tourism increased.

1990: the bid

The formal submission for consideration as European City of Culture was made by Glasgow District Council in April 1986. The submission was co-ordinated by Glasgow District Council and Glasgow Action and was backed by letters of support from all manner of cultural private and public organisations. Significantly, the submission referred to Glasgow's long history of staging highly successful exhibitions and events since the last century and also the positive experience within the city of inter-agency co-operation arising from the 1988 Garden Festival and the already established event of Mayfest, a month-long arts festival that had originated from a partnership between major trade unions and Glasgow District Council. The bid also highlighted the continuing support given to the arts and culture in general by the district council. Prior to 1990, this amounted to £18m per annum. In addition, the regional council was identified as a significant supporter of the arts in the city as was the Scottish Arts Council.

The objectives of attracting the designation of European City of Culture to Glasgow were identified as follows:

1 'To maintain momentum already generated by the image building initiatives and the marketing effort.
2 To provide a corporate marketing platform for the city's various artistic activities.
3 To utilise and build upon the existing organisational experience and co-operative effort within the city.
4 To stimulate increased awareness, participation and cultural developments in Glasgow.'

(Glasgow District Council, 1987a: 2-3)

Noticeably, the bid emphasised the importance to the city of developing cultural tourism. The goal of 1990 was that of a year-long, event-based programme and supported by the high quality of existing performance events, the number of Scottish arts companies, the number of high-quality galleries and the proposed building of a new concert hall. The bid documents identified Glasgow's established arts infrastructure as a strength. The Burrell Collection opening in 1983 had rapidly become the most visited attraction in Scotland other than Edinburgh Castle. Glasgow had established city galleries and other exhibition spaces such as the Third Eye Centre. It was the home of Scottish Opera, Scottish Ballet, Scottish National Orchestra, Scottish Theatre Company, Scottish Early Music Consort, the Citizens Theatre and other theatre companies such as 7:84 and Wildcat.

The strategy of the bid was clearly promotional and heralded the need for Glasgow to direct its thrust to international markets. The arts would be used as an additional strand of economic planning directly through the attraction of tourists to the big event and indirectly through supporting an attractive image that might bring inward investment and relocated headquarters. The background of an improving environment and a history of initiatives used as pacers for regeneration made such a logic easily accepted. Glasgow was successful, defeating Bath, Bristol, Cambridge, Cardiff, Edinburgh, Leeds, Liverpool and Swansea. The mere fact of winning the title inevitably conferred a comparative advantage upon Glasgow through the recognition of its cultural specialisation.

Shaping cultural policy

The need for the 1990 Year of Culture to be high-profile, event-based and attractive to cultural tourism was consolidated by the pressures to produce the programme quickly and to complement the existing tourism strategy for the city. The use of the event as a focus for cultural tourism had been a fundamental feature of the marketing strategy adopted by the Greater Glasgow Tourist Board (GGTB)which had been established in 1983. Its initial analysis of the city's strengths, coupled with that of the McKinsey Study commissioned by the Scottish Development Agency in 1984, identified the breadth of cultural provision and a policy of promoting the wealth of activities and the high quality of the facilities was adopted.

It seemed to the GGTB that existing travel companies bringing visitors to Scotland were not coming to Glasgow *per se* but that the city did have potential as an emerging conference destination. There was already a range of high quality attractions but none that had an international appeal to complement Mayfest. To this end the Inter-

national Jazz Festival, the Choral Festival and the Festival of Folk Music
and Dance were initiated to be held annually between May and
September to spread the visitor season. Existing organisations such as
the Scottish National Orchestra, the Theatre Royal and the Citizens'
Theatre also reviewed their programming to cater for seasonal visitors.

The succees of the Glasgow Garden Festival in 1988 further
changed perceptions of the city among UK visitors. In 1989 the
city's museums had 2,800,000 visitors, out-performing those of any
other city in the UK apart from London. The establishment of the
Scottish Exhibition and Conference Centre and of the Greater
Glasgow Convention Bureau allowed the city to host conferences
which brought some £33,000,000 of business in 1989. In 1982
some 700,000 visitors had come to Glasgow. By 1989 this had
increased to 2,300,000 with the prospect of over 3,000,000 in
1990. The accommodation provision increased in response. Since
1988, twelve major hotel projects have been announced with an
estimated value of £116,000,000 and five of these hotel have been
completed (Glasgow Economic Monitor, GDC 1990).

1990: making it happen

A Festivals Unit was established within Glasgow District Council in
1987 with the task of co-ordinating events for 1990. Given the need
for city promotion, the Festivals Unit inevitably used a series of
prestigious events in the 1990 programme to raise the international
profile of Glasgow. The objectives of the Festivals Unit built upon
perceived existing strengths and aimed to: develop a visible, high-
profile programme of cultural activities in 1990, marking Glasgow's
designation as European City of Culture; strengthen and develop
organisations and facilities that already existed in the city beyond
1990; introduce new projects into the cultural life of the city and
create an expanded base of activities, audiences and participants.

The intention was to address both the local and the universal. The
emphasis was upon endeavour rather than high or low art. The
implementation of the programme had two strands: to support local
artists and groups on their own terms and organise a broad cultural
programme that would raise Glasgow's profile in Europe and
beyond. This required a definition of 'culture' which was all encompassing. It would include lifestyle, forms of cultural production,

values and beliefs and it led to the inclusion in the events programme of activities ranging from sport, education, science and food through to the more conventional forms of artistic expression (Palmer, 1988).

Whilst the Festivals Unit developed a programme of cultural activity it did recognise a further requirement to strengthen infrastructures which would have longer-term positive impacts on Glasgow's culture, social and economic environment after 1990. The 1990 programme therefore was seen not as an end in itself but as a means by which other objectives could be achieved (Palmer, 1988: 7). However, since these objectives were never made explicit, it is not difficult to identify linkages between 1990 and wider cultural and economic development objectives. The uncertainty is compounded by the different objectives held by the many public and private organisations who formed partnerships to implement initiatives. Strathclyde Regional Council, for example, participated by spreading the events to the region as a whole, focusing upon social and educational benefits. One event they sponsored was the European Special Olympics, demonstrating clearly that their intentions were to increase access, participation and enhance social welfare (SRC, 1988).

In 1991 total expenditure on the 1990 celebrations was still not computed and the value of ticket sales taken into account. But total costs were of the order of £53.5m; £35m was contributed by the district council.

Table 2.2: Expenditure on the 1990 celebrations

Resourcing 1990	£m
Glasgow District Council	35.0 (£15m from special arts fund established for 1990)
Strathclyde Regional Council	12.0
Private Sponsors	5.5
UK Office of Arts and Libraries	0.5
European Community[3]	0.5
TOTAL	£53.5m

Sources: Correspondence with Robert Palmer, Festivals Unit; Scotland on Sunday, 23 December 1990; Glasgow 1990, Fact Sheet no.8.

The wider, long-term benefits of 1990 have yet to be calculated but the first indicative data made available by the tourist board illustrates the marked short-term impact of the Year of Culture. As table 2.3 shows, the city attracted considerable numbers of additional tourists, with accommodation bookings through the city-centre bureau increasing by 80 per cent.

Table 2.3: Indicative visitor data, 1990 (based on bookings through the Greater Glasgow Tourist Board and Conference Bureau)

Measure	Number	Increase over 1989
Visitors to GGTB	605,065	+ 44%
Telephone requests	77,973	+ 71%
Bed-nights booked	57,828	+ 81%
Value of accomm. bookings (£)	71.32m	+ 80%
Value of ticket sales (£)	63.42m	+ 364%

Source: Greater Glasgow Tourist Board, 1991.

Table 2.4 presents slightly more robust data in terms of hotel and guesthouse occupancy data collected by the Scottish Tourist Board. Again this shows a substantial increase from 1989, with bedspace occupancy increasing by 39 per cent and room occupancy increasing

Table 2.4: Occupancy rates (%) 1990 and (1989) (based on Greater Glagow Tourist Board area)

Month	Bed spaces	Rooms
January	40 (38)	56 (49)
February	46 (30)	63 (49)
March	54 (40)	62 (47)
April	64 (44)	65 (48)
May	69 (47)	71 (53)
June	65 (43)	67 (48)
July	59 (41)	63 (47)
August	72 (57)	66 (50)
September	69 (49)	67 (51)
October	63 (46)	58 (40)
November	62 (43)	61 (39)
December	43 (29)	36 (22)
1990	58.8 (42 25)	61.25 (45.25)

Source: Scottish Tourist Board, Occupancy Survey 1990.

Table 2.5: Attendance figures, 1990. Year total attendances for principal exhibition venues, excluding Glasgow's Glasgow

Galleries	1989	1990		Difference (%)
Burrell	490,572	878,772	+ 388,200	+ 79.1
People's Palace	345,559	466,697	+ 121,138	+ 35.1
Kelvingrove	1,041,392	1,016,921	− 24,471	− 2.3
Third Eye Centre	279,893	445,335	+ 165,442	+ 59.13
Hunterian Gallery	56,686	108,641	+51,955	+ 91.7
Transport Museum	633,551	535,938	-97,613	− 15.4
Pollock House	146,900	161,405	+14,505	+ 9.9
McLellan Galleries	N/A	129,731	N/A	—
Haggs Castle	39,787	41,091	+1,304	+ 3.3
Provand's Lordship	121,709	134,892	+13,183	+ 10.8

Source: Glasgow Museums, 1991.

by 35 per cent. Accepting the limitations of these data, the early indications are that the policy of targeting cultural tourism was successful. Table 2.5 illustrates the impact 1990 had on museum attendance, with some of the major venues recording visitor increases ranging up to 92 per cent.

Cultural controversies

The organisers of 1990 attracted criticism, firstly, for the manner in which the city's culture programme failed to relate to the citizen. In particular, one group calling itself 'Workers City' (McLay, 1988), maintained that much of the 1990 programme had little relevance to the working-class cultural heritage of Glasgow. They were particularly critical of the way in which Glasgow's economic, social and political history was represented in 'Glasgow's Glasgow', a major exhibition of the city's history staged during 1990. This single most expensive event in the Year of Culture, costing £4.6m, attracted extensive criticism for its original policy of charging a £4 entry fee, exorbitant by Glasgow standards for museum entry. It also failed to attract projected visitor numbers. The financial management of the project engendered considerable public debate, with responsibility being traded between the District Council, the private company that staged the event and its accountants. But it also attracted serious criticism for the way that the exhibition handled Glasgow's industrial and political history. Its critics argued that the industrial history of Glasgow was reduced to a series of tableaux, that lacked coherence and critical awareness, 'a ragbag of artefacts presented with the cacophony of noise in a claustrophobic space' (Kemp, 1990: 22).

Similarly, the story of the Clyde and shipbuilding figured prominently in a wide-ranging debate as to how the city's heritage should be explained, interpreted and displayed during the Year of Culture. It was argued that a powerful mythology about the river, the yards and their working-class communities served to exaggerate shipbuilding's economic, political and cultural importance. This debate came to a head during 1990 when one of the largest theatrical events in the city, receiving public sponsorship of £900,000 was a nightly re-enactment of the construction and launch of a ship on the Clyde. The conflict between the critical and the public reactions to this play illustrate both the deep-seated images of shipbuilding in the city and the problem of using theatre to critically examine an urban myth. While generally well received, The Ship was criticised in the press for being sentimental, superficial: 'reek(ing) of easy options and intellectual laziness ... exploit(ing) that appetite for the past by twanging easily on the heart-strings and the memory-cells' (McMillan, 1990). Yet The Ship was a sell-out, its run was extended and offers to take The Ship on tour (!) were received from a number of sources. Rather than using theatre to critically examine the past, The Ship served to reinforce important urban memories: a sense of purpose, craft, skill, community, pride and the remnants of a socialist ideal.

However, the criticism of Workers City needs to be seen in the context of an extensive community events programme that attracted widespread support during 1990. With the financial assistance of the public agencies and the Scottish Trades Union Congress, a range of more than five hundred exhibitions, local gala days and theatrical events brought the Year of Culture closer to the public, especially into the peripheral public sector housing schemes that lacked an indigenous, well-established, arts community.

There was, secondly, criticism that an opportunity was missed in 1990 to link urban regeneration and economic growth with cultural development. Whilst there have been physical improvements in the fabric of the city and increases in the number of tourists, it is not certain that these have been reflected in employment opportunities or in the strengthening of the commercial and manufacturing sectors (Hayton, 1990). Perversely, it has been suggested that in relation to economic growth, the deliberate policy was to have no policy on the understanding that choice and adaptive management are only possible once the qualities of the city had been effectively identified and marketed. Cultural richness would be the pump-primer and the next stage would be to diversify the regeneration policies to create employment. This approach required the city to initially invest heavily in the arts infrastructure as in the case of the building of the Royal Glasgow Concert Hall and the Burrell Gallery. The use of a programme of events meant that any development of the cultural industries was largely overlooked and led to a concentration upon cultural tourism.

Third, Glasgow District Council made extensive use of the Year of Culture as an opportunity for image promotion. Building on the 'Glasgow's Miles Better' campaign, Glasgow Action advocated the requirement for the city to have a new image that was 'available, open and accessible' (Glasgow Action, 1985). Its policy was to reinforce the city's identity, to undertake physical improvements and to establish a momentum of change that would attract tourists and headquarter offices to the city. The establishment of a high-profile arts infrastructure, reinforced and advertised by the Year of Culture programme would demonstrate the improved quality of life in Glasgow, attracting corporate headquarters and encourage conference and cultural tourism. This in turn assumed that growth in these sectors stimulates a similar growth in banking, finance, public administration, construction and service sector jobs (Hamilton, 1990). Generally, arts venues such as theatres, concert halls, performance space and galleries would be stimulated to create growth in the tourism and leisure industries but the cultural industries that produce artistic goods and performances would be left to look after themselves and respond to market forces.

The linkage between 1990 and building the city's tourist market also produced discussion. Tourism has expanded but it gives rise to an emphasis upon the servicing of the visitor rather than the development of local talent and the cultural industries. It is certainly a creator of employment but the quality of the jobs created has been frequently questioned. Estimates of employment (full- and part-time) in the Glasgow area dependent upon the tourism and leisure industries show a growth from 14,785 in 1985 (Myerscough, 1988) to 25,000 in 1989 (Segal, Quince and Wicksteed in Hayton, 1990: 12).

The GGTB maintains that its policy has not been to sell culture to the tourists but rather to enhance those unique qualities of cultural life in Glasgow from which visitors and locals alike can benefit. It does this through the use of events and attempts to relate these to the development of local culture and skills. For example the Glasgow Jazz Festival endeavours to create long-term benefits by achieving four objectives. It brings international stars to the city to perform at the highest level. It allows good local performers a broader audience and range of venues. It enables newcomers to be enthused with jazz. Significantly, it also attempts to advance jazz music production through the sponsorship of new compositions and jazz residences.

Furthermore tourism is seen as contributing to regeneration through the creation of jobs in major showcase developments which create permanent visitor attractions. However, there has been little progress in this policy area. The McKinsey Study (1984) did identify a major aquarium as a development target and in 1990 the Clyde Ship Trust announced plans to establish a £20m Clyde Maritime Museum in Govan. The project forecast is for 500,000 visitors per year and to recruit fifty craft apprentices annually. But neither has started.

Glasgow's attempts at creating cultural industries have similarly not yet come to fruition. Indeed a number of initiatives have been caught in the property slump of 1990. For example, in 1986 the SDA announced a proposal to create a Glasgow Fashion Centre in the disused Courthouse in the Merchant City. It was founded on the idea of manufacturing and selling 'Glasgow style' to compete in the international fashion market. The building would contain all manner of fashion and apparel design, printing, manufacturing and retailing display connected with fashion production. The project became a flagship public–private venture in the city centre, critical to the completion of the Merchant City. In the autumn of 1990 the developer, Merlin International, withdrew its interest in the scheme, leaving the SDA without the critical private investor. The agency is again seeking a use for the building, courting another possible hotel development.

At a smaller scale, there have been many community-based projects and events but few have been formally linked with job creation as it appears that no one was given this task as part of the 1990 organisation. Local arts development has taken precedent over training and production considerations, not because of a lack of awareness about such needs but because of the lack of an appropriately funded policy.

Looking to the future

Despite the artistic success of 1990 and the attraction of short-run economic benefit, Glasgow lacks an integrated cultural policy. In part, this is a reflection of an ambiguity in the relationships between culture and the development process. But it is also caused by the predominant use of culture as an economic and city marketing tool. The evaluations of 'culture' as urban spectacle or simply as a party is only valid if they are rooted in achievement, whether this is a new production or the celebration of place that truly reflects its audience. In Glasgow the bridge between mainstream and local development has not been forged – nor have the mechanisms of promoting the local culture at the international level. To this extent there is either a gap in the marketing of the city or a lack of a product that could or should be marketed. The difficulty with attempts to use cultural qualities to emphasise the competitiveness of the city is the presupposition that there is a demand for them in the market place.

For Glasgow, cultural development has not been regarded as a single-stranded regeneration policy but as a core element in improving the quality of life. Conceptually, there is nothing wrong with a city celebrating and showing its confidence to citizen and visitor alike (Booth and Harding, 1987: 10). Such a strategy maintains the momentum of change created by the physical improvements and emphasises that Glasgow is an attractive and pleasant place (Hamilton, 1990: 13). The production of The Ship and the controversy surrounding 'Glasgow's Glasgow' may represent a localised false nostalgia but they served to focus debate and animate local identity. How this relates to urban regeneration or whether it represents value for money in terms of urban investment is a moot point.

The debate about how the city portrays its social history is symptomatic further of the recognition that art and culture are an integral part of the community and exert a powerful influence on the quality of life. As Palmer has written, 'the city has started to come to terms with its own living and changing culture' (1988: 2). This could not have been prescribed in policy terms since the linkages between cultural, economic and social planning are unclear. As a result, there is confusion about the nature of the next step in the regeneration process – whether it is further city promotion, cultural specialisation or some form of physical initiative. One view is that the time is now ripe for a more balanced approach. This would acknowledge the weaknesses of the manufacturing base in the city. It would recognise that the quality of the city's labour supply needs improving, otherwise citizens will not be able to obtain jobs, whatever industries are attracted. It understands also that too much emphasis upon cultural tourism or services may have an adverse effect upon job quality (Hayton, 1990: 21). In short, integration and diversification are required. Furthermore, there may be a problem of talent leakage from the city whilst these policies are put into place. One success of 1990 might have been the raising of awareness and the creation of city-wide talent. But the mechanism for developing this is not in place and funding is not available.

The concentration of cultural production into a year-long festival had other problems. Expectations were raised and local talent discovered. A strategy is now required that allows this talent to be nurtured, given training and support, and provided with accommodation in the city. Similarly, there is a need to establish a local infrastructure that can distribute local cultural goods to the wider market. Finally, there is a need to provide production facilities within the city. Since whilst new works may be conceived in Glasgow at the moment, facilities elsewhere are used to create such goods.

Lessons from Glasgow 1990

It is inappropriate to think of cultural policy merely in terms of the economic benefits that it can induce for a city. Clearly any assessment of gain is contingent upon the definition of culture that is adopted. Concentrating upon the programming of events for 365 days, Glasgow District Festivals Unit assumed the role of cultural impresario rather than policy-maker. The fact that the district council concentrated on the production of a programme of events is significant in terms of evaluating the impact of 1990 on regeneration in the city. It means that the product of £53.5m investment will be most easily measured in ticket sales, satisfied customers and the significant boost to local confidence created by community events.

The long-term impact on the city of 1990 will, like the Garden

Festival in 1988, be hard to measure. Glasgow was improving physically through a series of initiatives, and the economy of the central city was being reinforced by vigorous investment in property development, well before the decision was made to bid for European City of Culture (Boyle, 1990). Nevertheless, there has been a change of perspective within the city brought about by the heightened profile given to culture during the 1990 celebrations. If this is translated into an integrated policy the renewed city could use its improved quality of life to attract inward investment. Moreover, if the city has strengthened its international reputation and widened its artistic basis, the Year of Culture has been the appropriate device to rekindle local forms of creative production and stimulate the broader awareness of its unique qualities. Coupled with this, the community has been animated in such a way as to be capable of responding to the new requirements that may now be placed upon it.

While 1990 was delivered in a policy vacuum, the Festivals Unit and its programme attracted important political support that, crucially, delivered the necessary resources. As throughout the 1980s, Glasgow demonstrated the importance of political consensus for urban regeneration within the dominant, moderate, Labour Party. That consensus was rarely publicly challenged by the left or any other political faction. There was no organised opposition to the district council's role in Year of Culture. Instead, the event was marked by a continuation of amicable relations between the Council and the public, between the different agencies in the city and between the Council and the private sector.

Drawing the different strands of 1990 together leads to the conclusion that culture in Glasgow was successfully employed as a tool of city marketing, like the highly popular Garden Festival two years earlier. The event was given significant political backing and the necessary resources to achieve the desired ends. The success of the programme was built upon a tried formula that combined external marketing alongside the promotion of local activities. As with the 'Miles Better Campaign', the achievements of 1990 can be put down to a skilful balance between satisfying the demands of the local community and extending the possibilities of improving the city's image in the wider world.

In our theoretical framework, it is clear that Glasgow's adaptation of 1990 European City of Culture was primarily concerned with the use of culture for urban marketing and tourist promotion. Those people and agencies charged with urban regeneration in the city, and in particular the staff in the Scottish Development Agency and Glasgow Action consciously and consistently used 1990 to progress their concept of 'Glasgow: A Great European City'. In the same vein as the opening of the Burrell Museum in 1983 and the Garden Festival in 1988, European City of Culture became a 'pacing device', moving the city along a modernising continuum. Indeed, in its final annual report Glasgow Action makes extensive comment on the marketing opportunities of 1990:

> The 1990 Capital of Culture programme itself had an enormous impact on the image of the city – in line with one of the major objectives when bidding for the title. Hours of television programmes have been produced. Thousands of press articles. A vast new collection of literature on the city has been published. Millions of visitors have been attracted, including national and international colleagues of Glasgow business people who were invited to the city to attend various flagship events which took place throughout the year.
>
> (Glasgow Action, 1991: 20)

There is little evidence to support the argument that Year of Culture 1990 made a clear contribution to local economic development. There was extensive rhetorical reference to the economic and social benefits of developing cultural industries and exploiting the possibilities of cultural tourism. But there were few tangible policies, and fewer projects that linked job creation or training to the very successful programme of events mounted in 1990.

Can Year of Culture 1990 be described as 'urban spectacle'? The answer surely is yes. During the year some three thousand events were staged in the city with ten thousand separate performances, attracting an estimated audience of nine million. There is no evidence, however, to support Harvey's thesis that the spectacle was used as a reward for the middle class. The range of events was not divided by class and the scale of the community programme suggests that resources were allocated widely throughout the city. Like the 'Miles Better Campaign' in 1983, Year of Culture 1990 was used, however, as the mechanism for urban unification. The 'Big Day', a free, city-wide, rock concert, television nation-wide, 'Keeping Glasgow in Stitches' and the massed community choral concert were all part of this process. The issue is how this mobilisation of community unity can be employed for the long-term benefit of the city.

In 1990, the citizens of Glasgow, and its visitors, undoubtedly had a good time. As for the long-term benefits to the city, continuing evaluation should provide some answers. Nevertheless, there is a danger of attaching too much importance to marketing the city. Culture, like long-term economic strength, needs to be rooted in the community. The real test of the Year of Culture will be the ability of local groups to sustain its momentum, to channel renewed confidence into economic and social activities and to make full use of the limited physical legacy of 1990. That, in turn, will require a new form of political commitment, continued financial support and the necessary policy instruments to convert the Glasgow interpretation of culture into sustained urban improvement.

— Bristol centre water front focus. Myerse, quote.

References

Baird, Grant and Walker, Jim (1990) 'Glasgow' *Glasgow Herald*, 8 March: 8.

Blake, George (1935) *The Shipbuilders*, London.

Booth, Peter H. (1990) 'The arts as a regenerative force', *The Arts Business*, Southern Arts, summer, 38-9.

Booth, Peter H. and Harding, David (1987) *A Public Art Strategy for Glasgow City Centre*, Glasgow, Glasgow Action.

Boyle, Robin (1990) 'Regeneration in Glasgow: stability, collaboration and inequity', in Dennis Judd and Michael Parkinson (eds) *Leadership and Urban Regeneration*, Urban Affairs Annual Reviews, Newbury Park CA, Sage Publications 109-32.

Boyle, Robin (1989) 'Partnership in practice: an assessment of public–private collaboration in urban regeneration – a case study of Glasgow Action', *Local Government Studies*, March–April, 17-28.

Checkland, S. G. (1981) *The Upas Tree Glasgow 1875–1975 ... And After 1975–1980*, Glasgow, Glasgow University Press.

Council of Europe (1983) *Urban Cultural Life in the 1980s: Reports and Essays from the Council's Twenty One Towns Project*. Strasbourg.

Coveney, Michael (1990) *The City - 21 years of the Glasgow Citizens Theatre*, London, Nick Hern Books.

Daiches, David (1977) *Glasgow*, London, Andre Deutsch.

Damer, Sean (1990a) 'Bill Bryden's Ship – a wallow in Clydeside nostalgia', *ArtWork*, 47, 8-9.

Damer, Sean (1990b) *Glasgow – Going for a Song*, London, Lawrence and Wishart.

Donnison, David D. and Middleton, Alan (eds) (1987) *Regenerating the Inner City: Glasgow's Experience*, London, Routledge & Kegan Paul.

Department of the Environment (1990) *An Evaluation of Garden Festivals*, London, HMSO.

Faley, Jean (1990) *Up Oor Close – Memories of Domestic Life in Glasgow Tenements, 1910-1945*, Wendlebury, Oxon, White Cockade.

Glasgow Action (1987) *Glasgow Action: the First Steps*, Glasgow, Glasgow Action.

Glasgow Action (1991) *Towards a Great European City*, Glasgow, Glasgow Action.

Glasgow District Council (1987a) *European City of Culture 1990*, City of Glasgow District Council, Submission for the United Kingdom Nomination, GDC.

Glasgow District Council(1987b) *European City of Culture 1990*, City of Glasgow District Council,

Supplementary Submission, GDC.

Glasgow District Council (1990) Glasgow Economic Monitor, GDC.

Glasgow District Council Festivals Unit, (1989a) 'The economic importance of the arts in Glasgow', Fact Sheet Number 6, GDC.

Glasgow District Council Festivals Unit (1989b) 'Glasgow 1990 – the background to the submission', Fact Sheet Number 1, GDC.

Glasgow District Council Festivals Unit (1989c) 'Glasgow 1990 – the financial structure' Fact Sheet Number 2, GDC.

Glasgow District Council Festivals Unit (1989d) 'Planning for 1990', Fact Sheet Number 5, GDC.

Glasgow District Council Festivals Unit, (1989e) 'The role of the Festivals Office', Fact Sheet Number 12, GDC.

Hamilton, C. (1990) Keynote speech presented at conference of the Council of Regional Arts Associations, Liverpool.

Harvey, David (ed.) (1989)), The Urban Experience, Baltimore, Johns Hopkins University Press.

Hayton, Keith (1990) 'Culture – economic regeneration or smokescreen?', paper presented at Oulu University seminar: The Relationship between Culture and Regional Development, November.

Horsey, Miles (1990) Tenements and Towers – Glasgow Working-Class Housing 1890–1990, Edinburgh, HMSO.

Keating, Michael (1988) The City That Refused to Die – Glasgow: the Politics of Urban Regeneration, Aberdeen, Aberdeen University.

Keating, Michael and Boyle, Robin (1986) Remaking Urban Scotland, Edinburgh, Edinburgh University Press.

Kemp, David (1990) Glasgow 1990 – the True Story Behind the Hype. Gartocharn, Famedram.

Lever, W. and and Moor, C. (eds.) (1986) The City in Transition: Public Policies and Agencies for the Economic Regeneration of Clydeside, Oxford, Clarendon.

McKinsey and Co. (1984) Glasgow's Service Industries – Current Performance, a Report to the SDA, Glasgow, SDA.

McLay, Farquhar (ed.) (1988) Workers City: the Real Glasgow Stands Up, Glasgow, Clydeside Press.

McMillan, Joyce (1990) 'Nostalgia bows to the new internationalism', Scotland on Sunday, 23 December: 8.

Marcuse, Peter (1989) 'Dual city: a muddy metaphor for a quartered city', International Journal of Urban and Regional Research, 13 (4), 697-708.

Massie, Allan (1989) Glasgow: Portraits of a City, London, Barrie and Jenkins.

Myerscough, John (1988) Economic Importance of the Arts in Glasgow, London, Policy Studies Institute.

Oakley, C. A. (1990) The Second City, fourth edtion, Glasgow, Blackie.

Palmer, Robert (1988) Glasgow 1990 Strategy paper, Glasgow District Council Festivals Unit, unpublished.

Smout, T. C. (1986) A Century of the Scottish People, 1830-1950, London, Collins.

Strathclyde Regional Council (1989) The Development of a Policy by the Council for its Continued Involvement in the 1990 European Year of Culture, Glasgow, Strathclyde Regional Council.

Taggart, J. (1987) Culture and Planning, unpublished dissertation, Glasgow, Glasgow School of Art, Department of Planning.

3

Rotterdam: re-designing the public domain

Maarten A. Hajer

Introduction

For the last fifty years the typical sound of Rotterdam has been the constant hammering of driving piles. Since the traumatic bombardment of May 1940 when Rotterdam lost its entire centre, the city has been permanently under reconstruction. Rotterdam had to start from scratch. Supported by the Marshall Plan, Rotterdam embarked first of all on the construction of a new, modern harbour and subsequently started a period of continuous remodelling and modification of its city centre. The process still continues. Because of its traumatic origins, this process of intensive modernisation has not been accompanied by a sense of public despair. On the contrary, it was accompanied by an almost collective fascination. This partly accounts for the fact that in Rotterdam the 1980s urban regeneration process is, unlike in many other (Dutch) cities, not perceived as a threat, but can rejoice in widespread civic support. Modernisation has become a tradition in the post-war period. This provides a major clue to grasp the role of cultural policy in the social process of urban regeneration in Rotterdam.

By examining various concepts for the development of the city centre over the last forty years you can see how the city council has always aimed to transform the city centre into a real 'public domain'. This effort can be described as a deliberate attempt by the council to generate widespread interest in public activity. A policy to develop a public domain has at least two aims. The first is the almost value-neutral goal of creating an 'interesting' urban environment. This is combined with a normative ethical conviction: the idea that active public life stimulates personal development and is a constitutive element of an urban version of the 'good life'.[1] This chapter will show how the definition of the public domain adopted by Rotterdam

City Council changed over time and will evaluate the urban regeneration process by placing present efforts in an historical context.

This chapter does not aim to show to what extent economic development can be attributed to changes in the cultural climate. Instead it attempts to illustrate how the fact that culture has been identified as a potentially powerful variable in the urban regeneration strategy influenced the character of cultural policy. The chapter focuses especially on the role of architecture and the design of public space, since this has been particularly important in the urban regeneration process in Rotterdam. Other elements of cultural policy, such as the role of music, theatre and dance, are discussed in that context. A short section about the post-war history of Rotterdam is followed by a discussion of the main phases of the urban regeneration process. There is then an account of the remarkable policy style that drives urban regeneration in Rotterdam, which shows that many of the showpieces of the present regeneration strategy were conceptualised during the 1970s, a period that many of those involved in today's regeneration efforts would like to forget.

Although the overall assessment of urban regeneration in Rotterdam presented here is a positive one, the chapter draws attention to two disturbing tendencies. First, the regeneration process in Rotterdam draws heavily on the experience and principles of well known waterfront developments in Toronto, Baltimore and Boston. These American examples are seen as archetypes for urban regeneration. But in this way concepts that were devised to deal with problems that are typical of American cities are transferred to a very specific, and in many respects culturally much richer, Dutch setting. Second, regeneration strategies attempt to bring prosperity back in by targeting the new middle class. Yet creating niches for the better off urban regeneration fails to contribute to the other priority of Rotterdam City Council: the integration of the urban underclass in local social life. The present strategy heavily relies on the possibility of engineering a new social life in clearly marked areas. But it runs the danger of turning against city life as it is: chaotic, ambivalent and unpredictable.

Urban development in the post-war era

Three phases can be distinguished in the process of reconstruction of Rotterdam: the period of the functionalist city (1941-73); the participatory city (1973-84) and the late-modernist city (1984 onwards). Each of these comes with its own ideas about the public domain.

The task of designing the new city centre was immediately begun after the bombardment of 1940. In a long and complex discussion period a group of 'enlightened' industrialists pushed aside a fairly traditional plan for the reconstruction of Rotterdam. They were in favour of a design based on ideas of the Dutch modernist New Building avant garde movement in architecture, which was organised in groups like De Stijl, De Opbouw and de 8. The new plan was totally committed to the functionalist ideals of Le Corbusier and the CIAM movement. According to the Basisplan (1946) the centre was to become the business and shopping district. It was dominated by the central Lijnbaan shopping area (1948-53) (plate 3.1) designed by Bakema and Van Eesteren, themselves leading architects in the CIAM. It provided some of the former inhabitants of the inner-city area with housing in well-designed high-rise modern apartment blocks. Most of them were rehoused in suburban areas according to the prescriptions of a healthy and efficient way of life as formulated by the modern movement at that time. The rational city centre, with its separate pedestrian shopping area and wide boulevards, was meant to restore the sovereignty of the citizens. They could now stroll and shop freely and without the constraints of the medieval city centre. Indeed, the Lijnbaan came to be seen as the international example for the city of the future, hailed by Lewis Mumford as a masterpiece of civic resurgence in his seminal *The City in History*.

During the 1960s the prescriptions of the Basisplan concept were interpreted more loosely and, at a time of great economic prosperity, business increased its presence in the city centre. During the same period the public at large grew dissatisfied with the overly rigid and rational organisation of the city centre. Some community groups openly doubted whether the rational organisation of the public domain was a real improvement on pre-war Rotterdam. This led to a nostalgic re-appreciation of the old 'organic' qualities of Old Rotterdam. As, in 1969, the city council geared itself for another phase of inner-city reconstruction and proposed to clear 30,000 houses for a business district extension, it found itself attacked, to use Berman's phrase, by a 'multitude of passionate shouts from the street'.[2]

The council's proposal functioned as a catalyst. The negative effects of the functionalist model, its scale, its eight-hour economy,

51

Plate 3.1
The functionalist city:
the freedom of the
rational grid (De
Lijnbaan)

Plate 3.2
The participatory city:
let one thousand
flowers bloom (De
Oude Haven)

its spatial division of functions, were becoming only too obvious in the early 1970s. What is more, the rediscovery of the individual, the loss of the 'civic culture' of the post-war decades, and the coming of age of a new generation of citizens resulted in more assertive demands for the development of the city centre into a real public domain. This social concern cleared the way for a new generation of young and ambitious Social Democratic politicians who took office in 1974, determined to make a change. They wanted to move beyond the functionalist city. Rotterdam had to become a 'cosy' city, with a city centre that was to be the domain of the 'Rotterdammers'. For these purposes the planning model of the centre had to be changed from that of a business district into an 'urban intensity model' based on a mix of residential accommodation, recreation, culture and strolling. Pavilions emerged on the central boulevard Coolsingel selling cheap clothing and snacks. Flowers were potted, trees planted and the width of the boulevard was artificially reduced. Identity, differentiation and liveliness became key words. The ideal of the participatory city also implied a commitment to the preservation of urban neighbourhoods and monumental areas and led to a re-appreciation of the role and function of museums in the city. Urban living was to be the alternative to suburban lifestyles, the disadvantages of which had rapidly become more obvious. All this led to a renaissance of urban culture, something that the city had nearly lost over the previous three decades (see plate 3.2). Disused harbour areas that could easily have been converted into a profitable extension of the business district were designated for housing. Old neighbourhoods, spared by the Germans and saved from the functionalists, were to be renovated instead of 'sanitised'.

Behind the political rhetoric the new politicians had a particularly strong drive to surpass the international success of their predecessors. The functionalist Basisplan and De Lijnbaan had given Rotterdam its first presence in the architectural literature. The new political leaders wanted to give the city its second. For this purpose the council started to commission expressive architects to build on major sites in the centre. With the stake dwellings by Piet Blom (1978-84) and the Central Library by Boot (1977-83), this policy achieved remarkable results.

However, as the economic crisis struck in the late 1970s, so Rotterdam had to rethink its policies once more. The social impulse gave way to economic logic. In the early 1980s it became obvious that Rotterdam would need to broaden its economic base. As countries like South Korea and Japan enlarged their share in the traditional shipbuilding market and more European ports started to compete with Rotterdam as centres for trans-shipment, it seemed no longer possible to organise a viable economy around the established harbour activities. In this respect Liverpool functioned as an example of what Rotterdam should avoid: a formerly great port city that had not been able to adapt to change. As an increasing number of economic activities were no longer automatically tied to the harbour, Rotterdam was no longer assured of its economic base. It had to create the preconditions for new economic activities. The promotion of Rotterdam became important to strengthen the links between the city and the growing number of firms that were 'footloose'.

These concerns made the council aware of the discrepancy between the needs and characteristics of the white-collar sunrise industries and its own heavily blue-collar workforce. The uneven composition of the population, and especially the loss of the middle classes was aggravated by the government's 'overspill' policy of the 1960s. According to this policy the government stimulated the public to leave the main Dutch cities for satellite towns. In the same spirit, certain areas on the outskirts of Rotterdam were transformed into independent administrative units. Consequently the population of Rotterdam fluctuated from 619,686 in 1940 to 731,564 in 1965 – an all time high – and then, thanks to the overspill policy, back down to 555,353 in 1984. In 1990 Rotterdam had 579,150 inhabitants of which 68,193 were of nationalities other than Dutch. A total of 48,427 people were registered as unemployed. One of the essential problems was that the city had lost its skilled labour force while the structurally unemployed simply could not move from the inner city. However, since the massive programme of urban renewal was tailored towards the existing inhabitants of the inner city new housing for the new key groups was simply not available.

During the 1980s this discrepancy between the emerging opportunities on the one hand and the facilities both in terms of physical structures, political climate and available human capital on the other, were subject to comprehensive scrutiny. The city council came up with a new policy of which the Binnenstadsplan (1985-87) was the most elaborate expression. What were the key elements of this strategy for urban regeneration and, more specifically, what was the role of cultural policy in the 'New Rotterdam' project?

The analysis and reasoning behind the new policy were familiar enough. The council realised that new employment could be created in the service sector but that new services industries were not being offered an attractive deal. It also realised that employment had to be found for the ever increasing group of unemployed yet often low skilled labourers. In 1985 Rotterdam City Council presented its strategy to create a new Rotterdam. This was an integrated plan that aimed to generate new economic activity in tourism, white-collar services and the cultural industries. It also wanted to change the image of the city to be more competitive in the struggle to attract footloose companies. This city marketing policy meant that Rotterdam began to avoid being associated with the problematic aspects of urban living, whilst the positive side – the cultural climate of the city – became an essential promotional device.

However, the council did not simply embrace every private sector initiative. Refusing to betray its own tradition in the social engineering of change, it wanted to achieve the new economic goals within the context of an elaborate new overall planning strategy. The Binnenstadsplan of 1985 distinguished four inner city areas. The City as centre of government, shopping and leisure; the Kop van Zuid as the new business district; the Green or Cultural Triangle for culture and recreation; and Waterstad for maritime tourism.

Using cultural policy: the main examples

The first example of explicit use of cultural policy in the context of the programme of urban regeneration was the festival *Rotterdam: the City: a Stage* during the summer of 1988. The city council organised a major cultural festival of visual and performing arts. The festival was meant to celebrate the inauguration of the newly built Stads-schouwburg, the main municipal theatre, and was primarily based on the involvement of artists working within the city. The festival aimed at raising cultural awareness and at widening the appreciation of the cultural quality that was locally available.[3] It also had a deep symbolic meaning. It was intended to mark the turn towards a more culturally dynamic era in Rotterdam and was seen as a way of communicating to the citizens the council's decision about the imminent creation of four cultural districts. It was one example in a row of special public space events in the 1980s including free outdoor cinema, an Afro-Caribbean carnival, a two-week outdoor theatre festival – the Teatro Fantastico – the annual Poetry Park and the Boulevard of Broken Dreams. For the purpose of this chapter, two of the four sectors of the Binnenstadsplan, Waterstad and the Cultural Triangle merit special attention.

Rotterdam Waterstad

Following the Binnenstadsplan a triangular area south of the new city centre was developed into a centre for tourist activities taking up all kinds of themes relating to water and the river. Waterstad (or 'city of water') is located where the earliest inhabitants of Rotterdam settled in 1340. The Waterstad project area includes a maritime museum; the Tropicana, a 'sub-tropical pool paradise'; the reconstruction of a traditional harbour; various restaurants; the massive 'special effect' Imax cinema–theatre and a four star hotel.[4] Waterstad also reflects the new 1980s businesslike approach to urban development with the celebrated Willemswerf office block which houses the headquarters of Ned Lloyd, one of the big shipping companies, as well as the three towers with luxurious apartments by Henk Klunder. The council has paid special attention to the design of public space to suggest a sense of unity which is meant to stimulate visitors to further explore the area.

Waterstad aims to attract a regional and even national public but it also forms part of local culture. It not only includes a large residential area but many public facilities such as the central public library and the colleges of art and architecture. Part of the Waterstad development was the reconstruction of the waterfront. What used to be an urban motorway is now a boulevard, which allows people to stroll along the river, and provides ample opportunities for markets and street culture. This area has become a well-integrated part of the public domain.

Looking at the Waterstad project one is struck, first of all, by the elaborate planning of the area. The city council consciously used the design of public space and street furniture to give unity to the area and carefully tried to plan the commercial enterprises to suit its goals. The area around the stake dwellings has become a centre for fashion and design shops. Sometimes the planning is somewhat over-elaborate, as with the special signposts that explain the origin and usage of specific buildings and sites. But in some cases the planners' eye for detail was a key to success. The council even went as far as selecting the type of restaurants – considering their interior design, the menu and their opening hours – to guarantee the right mixture of facilities to match the different target audiences.

Waterstad, it should be clear, is a bureaucratic construction of the 1980s. Not many locals would instantly know which part of the city is meant by it. But this is not to minimise its success. Waterstad today has a national reputation. However, it owes this fame, above all, to the area's architecture, much of which predates the invention of Waterstad. The area contains the symbols of the 1970s in the form of the stake dwellings and the pencil-shaped apartment building by Blom, and the central library by Boot, which is reminiscent of Rogers' and Piano's Centre Pompidou. Furthermore, the area includes the sole jugendstil office block to survive the war which was subsequently saved from demolition in the 1970s. Waterstad thus partly thrives on the icons of the 'participatory city' of the 1970s. Waterstad is widely perceived as a success. Organised as a public–private partnership, so far it has resulted in 400 new jobs, approximately 35 new restaurants or cafes, 2,000 apartments and 100,000 square metres of office space. The Tropicana has had more than one-and-a-half million visitors in the one-and-a-half years of its existence.

The Cultural Triangle

Following the Binnenstadsplan, Rotterdam is actively trying to develop a cultural district in the area around its main museum for contemporary art, the Boymans-Van Beuningen, a new art exhibition hall which is now under construction, and the new National Institute for Architecture, which is also under construction. For this purpose one of the two central boulevards of the post-war Basisplan was designated to be Rotterdam's 'cultural axis'. Again the design and decoration of public space, including many new sculptures, was used to give both unity to the area and to create a sophisticated atmosphere. The Council also actively tried to attract cultural businesses like art galleries and art shops to this district. Various financial and material incentives are available to stimulate the setting up of new art galleries.

A complicating factor with this development is the present character of the neighbourhood. Part of the area is notorious for its night clubs, illegal gambling houses, shoarma bars and drug trade. The council now consciously tries to contain this aspect of city life, primarily through a strict law and order policy. But the creation of a cultural district is obviously also meant to contribute to changing the existing 'sub-cultural' environment. So far the council has subsidised an arts centre and has managed to attract about ten new galleries to the area. This, however, has not been enough to change the character of the district.

The council aims to create a culturally 'interesting' milieu by bringing together elements at various levels, ranging from galleries and artists' workshops to full-size museums. This should be an attractive environment for upmarket entertainment – restaurants, cafes, etc. The character of the Cultural Triangle development is therefore quite different from the goals of the Waterstad area, in two respects. On the one hand, the Cultural Triangle aims to reinforce already existing qualities rather than aiming to create something new from scratch. On the other, it presents us with an example of the dilemmas that are inherent in urban regeneration strategies. One consequence of the implementation of the cultural strategy is to expel those forms of urban life that contradict the optimistic vision of the 'New Rotterdam'.

It is thus difficult to evaluate the Cultural Triangle in the light of its consequences for the public domain. Some of its major elements still have to be completed. It is clear, however, that the area aims to create a special 'milieu' which is meant to attract a restricted 'high culture'-oriented audience. Yet it would be an exaggeration to argue that this reduces the accessibility of the area for other groups. What the Cultural Triangle development does show is the extent to which the council still works with an 'urban intensity' model in mind. Clearly, not all intensity is automatically perceived as 'quality'.

Public design and the entrepreneurial culture

Many aspects of the present strategy for urban regeneration have their origin in the participatory culture of the 1970s. At the heart of the 1970s ideal of the 'participatory city' was the idea that Rotterdam had lost its once vibrant public life. The answer of the new city council was the intensification of activities in order to recreate a dense, popular and democratic city centre. The idea for a new maritime museum, now an essential element in the Waterstad development, dates back to 1976. The international festival of film was first held in 1972 and targeted explicitly at the alternative circuit while the Poetry International festival had started in 1970. Ironically, both are now used to illustrate the 'interesting cultural climate' for the new middle classes. This indicates that some cultural initiatives that are now essential for the international marketing of Rotterdam's image actually predate the conceptualisation and articulation of urban regeneration policies and were, in fact, initiated for quite different purposes.

Especially in the late 1970s the Kunststichting, the Rotterdam Arts Foundation, played a particularly important role in stimulating the role of the arts in urban development. The Arts Foundation is an independent institution which is responsible for both programming cultural events and allocating subsidies to arts bodies. It largely depends on the city council for its funding and sees as its tasks to protect and encourage artistic quality, and stimulate the local debate within and about the arts. The Arts Foundation has special sections responsible for specific arts sectors. The Architecture Section in particular played an important part in urban regeneration in Rotterdam.

The section took an active interest in the evaluation of the 1970s endeavours by the council to give the city back to the citizens. The Arts Foundation started this debate late in the 1970s, criticising especially the dominance of housing and planning considerations and the loss of the overall idea of urban design in the city's development. The participatory mode of policy-making was necessarily piecemeal and dwelling-oriented. The councillor responsible for urban planning at that time, Mentink, had a philosophy that 'anything goes' in architecture as long as it is expressive. Expressive buildings would revitalise the city, not conceptual clarity. The Arts Foundation, on the other hand, was concerned about the dubious quality of some examples of architectural design resulting from this policy, and even more about the general lack of any wider concept of urban design.

The foundation's critique culminated in its organisation of the Architecture International Rotterdam (AIR) festival in 1982. Four international celebrities in urban design presented their visions of how the south bank, the area now known as Kop van Zuid, of Rotterdam could be transformed. At that time this area was destined for social housing. The Arts Foundation questioned the fact that such use was presented by the council as a matter of course and initiated a local debate on future directions for the city. At that time the plans presented by the four experts were refuted as elitist but with hindsight it is clear that they provided the basis of things to come.

In 1979 the Arts Foundation started to organise special trips to other European cities. These annual excursions were meant for local architects, council officials, developers, politicians and the very interested amongst the public at large. After visits to cities such as Prague, Brussels, Berlin, Vienna and Paris the emphasis shifted to 'second cities' such as Milan and to comparisons between 'first' and 'second' cities such as Barcelona and Madrid, Glasgow and Edinburgh, Leningrad and Moscow. The Arts Foundation also organised exhibitions on foreign developments such as the 1984 exhibition on Japanese architecture and the exhibition on Spanish architecture in 1986.

These initiatives stimulated the local debate on architecture and design, introducing foreign concepts and ideas to the city. Consequently, the local elite in planning and design came to realise the importance of Blom's state apartments. They were perhaps the best semantic device to mark the radical departure from the functionalist city. They had been of great symbolic importance but perhaps they were not the way forward after all. The international trips and the general revival of a debate on quality in architecture and design strengthened the conviction amongst the local experts that there were alternative, superior scenarios. They also resulted in the creation of a large international network of contacts on which local actors could draw.

The Arts Foundation not only tried to guide the debate on public design but also initiated a discussion about the protection and development of the impressive architectural heritage of the city. Rotterdam, the city of one of the set pieces of early functionalist architecture, the celebrated Van Nelle factory, had become the city of the New Building movement of the 1930s and especially of J.J.P. Oud who had built many outstanding examples of this greatest moment in Dutch architecture in and around Rotterdam. Later, in 1986, it was decided to rebuild the facade of Oud's cafe, De Unie, and to restore the old working-class areas of the Kiefhoek, which indicates how seriously the task of preservation was taken on.

Apart from the Arts Foundation the Diens Stadsontwikkeling, the city council's department for urban development, played an important role in preparing the ground for the 1985 urban regeneration plans. As it happened, a generation of urban designers retired in the early 1980s to be replaced by a group of young, ambitious architects and designers. This group reinforced the call for a reassessment of the quality of the built environment in Rotterdam. After the old director had been replaced in 1986 by the highly dynamic and powerful Riek Bakker, the institutional norms changed dramatically and the department came to be a key actor in the process of revitalising the city.

In June 1986 the department made an inventory of all the problematic spatial features of the city, which served as a basis for action in the years that followed. One of the main areas of concern was the Kop van Zuid. Under Bakker the Department worked on a new idea for this inner-city harbour district. According to the 1970s local plan the Kop was to be converted into an area for social housing. Bakker, however, thought that given its position in the heart of the city, the Kop should become a highly urban inner-city area, a Manhattan on the River Meuse, as it quickly became known, with 1,500 apartments, 300,000 square metres of office space and 35,000 square metres for recreational purposes. Since this was a break away from the social housing commitment, it was not likely to be a popular idea. In order to avoid having to face protests head on, she invited leaders from the business sector, social workers, ordinary people from the neighbourhood, investors to her private apartment to discuss her plans for this area in small groups. She thus kept politics at arm's length. Only after she had already privately secured the support of leading actors in industry, politics and civil society, did she officially inform the council of her plans.

This bizarre course of affairs perhaps illustrates best the local political culture in which urban regeneration in Rotterdam takes place. The example illustrates a policy style which is at odds with the formal procedural rules of local democracy. The process of urban regeneration depends to a large extent on informal networks; no dramatic changes in the formal organisational structure were made. Clearly, there can be some objections to this political culture. However, it is undoubtedly true that this non-hierarchical, open climate provided a breeding ground for new ideas. It was, at the same time, a means through which a broad consensus could be achieved, and an unusual exercise in post-corporatist bargaining. The community leaders were no longer there to represent an organised interest. They came as knowledgeable and influential individuals and as discussion and sparring partners for Bakker. The fact that the Council could organise sufficient consensus for its plans was thus both the strength and the danger of this policy-making strategy. Once in motion, a coalition of individuals thus formed would be extremely hard to stop.

This technocratic–elitist mode of operating in Rotterdam should be seen as typical of local culture. It is reminiscent of the elitist culture that engineered the amended Basisplan in 1946. It is also clear that the way in which Bakker secured support for her ideas for the Kop van Zuid can only work with the consent of Council leaders and the Mayor. Furthermore, this style of policy-making could only flourish with fairly liberal Directors of local authority departments who were willing to co-operate even when their positions and power were eroded. It would be wrong to regard this as a typically Dutch administrative culture. The culture of a city like Amsterdam, for instance, is exactly the opposite. The somewhat anarchist administrative culture of Amsterdam implies that the publication of any proposals on urban regeneration almost inevitably become the object of scorn and harsh criticism.

The explanation comes from the close and long-standing relationship between the council and the management of the port. More than most other cities, Rotterdam directly experiences the ups and downs in the international economy and recognises it needs to act in an entrepreneurial fashion. Inter-urban competition, recently discovered by city councils all over the country, is not a new phenomenon for a city like Rotterdam. Rotterdam claims to be the world's biggest port since the 1960s and to protect its position it has always had to work hand in hand with business. The council has always played its part in trying to attract contracts, build up liaisons and promote the local business climate and general facilities of the region. In due course, local elites will develop a common framework through which problems are conceptualised. The technocratic–elitist policy style can thus be seen as a strategy to by-pass the problem of persuasion.

The existence of links with the business network also affects the use of cultural instruments in a more direct way. The council heavily draws on its business contacts for the exchange of ideas concerning urban regeneration. Rotterdam has an active relationship with sister-cities like Shanghai and Baltimore. Using the cultural exchanges that came with the establishment of business links, Rotterdam has picked up many ideas from American cities. The city council was also actively involved in the debate at the INTA congress (International Towns Association) about cities as the driving force for economic recovery during the 1980s.

The tragedy of the American inspiration

Rotterdam City Council is much more on top of the urban regeneration process than its counterparts in, for instance, Amsterdam, Utrecht, Amersfoort, Nijmegen or Arnhem.[5] However, there are some disturbing implications and latent problems. Two explicitly relate to the use of public design and architecture in regeneration efforts. It is easy to see why the concept of the participatory city had to make way for the concepts of New Rotterdam. The 1970s policies aimed at the people of the city, not primarily at impressing them with examples of high culture and innovative design, but with understandable, 'humorous' and 'cosy' ideas which would encourage them to use city space again. In the 1980s the council perceived public design and architecture as an instrument which might help to attract the 'sunrise service industry' and bring back the highly skilled middle classes. The design was outward oriented, had to comply with international standards, aimed at an audience that was supposed to be attracted by the new, and renounced the casual everydayness of the city of the 1970s.

The professional quest for quality from the worlds of the arts and design was easily adapted to the city council's initiative for the invention of the 'new Rotterdam'. There is a clear affinity between architectural concerns for the 'city as a work of art' and the marketing-inspired concern about the image of the city. Yet there is an irony to this process. First, much suggests that the public appeal of Rotterdam still largely depends on the symbols of the 1970s, and especially the stake dwellings area. The newly emerging business district schemes of the Weena area are far less striking. This raises the question whether this should be the model for the developments on De Kop van Zuid. The Weena building (see plate 3.3) could be anywhere, there is nothing unique about it, nothing that relates to the specific history and character of Rotterdam. Concern about the cultural image has failed to deliver the goods. On several occasions the council failed to generate the architectural quality which would have added a new and unique dimension to the city. Of course, this is also connected to the limit of any council's power.

A second irony concerns the inspiration for the new Rotterdam projects which primarily came from North America. The use of the American models of urban regeneration with as prime examples Baltimore's Harbor Place, Boston's Quincy Market and South Street Seaport in New York, generated unfortunate side-effects. The American waterfront developments at best produce a parody of urban culture. They all appear terribly neat. But looking at the users, it is obvious that blacks, latinos and hispanics are nearly absent. This is rarely because they are physically excluded but is simply a consequence of what the projects offer. Still, the harbour projects of cities like Boston, Toronto and especially Baltimore, are the archetypes for the regeneration effort in Rotterdam. They have had a visible influence on the overall approach to urban regeneration and on specific design features. Rotterdam's festival 'the City a Stage', for instance, was a direct result of a lesson learned in Baltimore: if you are reorganising the city, let them know. The festival was meant to

Plate 3.3
The alien take-over of the city (Het Weena)

symbolise the new things to come. There are some potentially tragic results. Unlike the American examples, all of which start from the problem that dockland areas had become disused and inhabitable, Rotterdam is making plans for an area which at present is still a lively port. For example, Toronto developed the idea of a harbour museum to suggest at least some activity and dynamism. But Rotterdam does not have that problem. Yet it now has a harbour museum. The plans for Kop van Zuid, however, foresee the clearance of all harbour activity in the area. It is to be transformed into a business district – in many respects simply a different type of monoculture. Many question why the city has not come up with a proposal in which the original harbour activity in the area is maintained, for example by keeping the port-related businesses on one quay of the docks instead of forcing them to move west.

The unique quality of the city of Rotterdam is its river, a fact recognised by the main protagonists of the regeneration debate. As Riek Bakker said, 'the river is the capital of the city'. This is true both in an economic and a cultural sense. The river is the explicit starting point of the new plans. The city should open up to the river again. One of the reasons for the development of the south bank is that it will relocate the centre southward, in the direction of the water. Yet Rotterdam's strength is not so much the mere fact that the river is there, but the fact that the river is full of economic activities. In other words, the perception of the river is not of water but of ships, cranes, hoisted containers, moving bridges and the sound of loading and unloading. Misreading the assumptions underlying urban regeneration strategies in America, Rotterdam failed to recognise the unique, yet un-American, qualities of its riverfront. It is in the process of moving out real activities only to replace them with artificial creations that form a parody on the dynamism of the river as it presently is.

A second source of inspiration, apart from the North American projects, were urban regeneration strategies in Barcelona. Catalan ideas, like using sculptures and the design of street furniture to create a special 'milieu', were used in the 'creation' of a Cultural Triangle around the Museum of Modern Art as well as in the Waterstad area. These ideas built upon existing qualities, and emphasised the characteristics of the area. They are more European in character and scale but also in the sense that they do not start from the assumption of clearance and total design but add elements to the existing complexity of the city.

Urban regeneration and the urban underclass

It is difficult to assess the prospects of the urban regeneration effort in Rotterdam. On the one hand it is clear that Rotterdam has gone up in the urban hierarchy. It still is one of the biggest port cities in the world. But, in addition, it now is The Netherlands' second office city employing over 52,000 people in commercial services. Culturally, the city has certainly become more interesting. The international recognition for the Rotterdam Philharmonic Orchestra, which attracted Covent Garden director Bernard Haitink to work with them, the success of the RO Theatre Company and the construction of several new museums is supported by a widely felt perception that the cultural climate in Rotterdam is rapidly changing for the better. The city has become much more attractive for all those firms whose activity heavily depends on 'human capital' and need a 'culturally interesting' environment to be able to recruit their workforce.

However, although Rotterdam City Council has done its best to create the preconditions to make the dream of a new Rotterdam come true, it still has to face some disturbing realities. First there are doubts about the feasibility of its economic development strategy. Although Table 3.1 indicates that the economic basis of Rotterdam indeed has shifted away from traditional sectors such as industry and trade (sectors 1 to 7) in the direction of commercial services and white-collar employment (sectors 8 to 12), voices can be heard that question the ideal of Rotterdam as an office city.

A strategic study by the Regional Economic Consultation Board, for example, openly questioned whether huge construction plans for more offices are realistic, raising the prospect that a large percentage of the new spaces and buildings would remain empty or would rapidly become disused.

There is a second, even more disturbing, reality. The city struggles to provide accommodation for all the new groups it is trying to attract. But at the same time the problems of the urban underclass do not go away. The philosophy of the council basically projects the urban regeneration effort as a positive sum game in which the affluent centre will pull the periphery and raise the general standards of living. For instance, the Kop van Zuid project is supposed to radiate activity and prosperity to the poor neighbourhoods that surround it. In the 1970s this area was to be redeveloped into a social housing district. Social policy was defined in its own right.

Table 3.1: Number of firms and employment relative to sector

		Number of firms			Employment		
		1984	1988	Change	1984	1988	Change
1	Agriculture/fishery	201	188	−13	549	731	+182
2	Industry	1,385	1,349	−36	42,041	43,001	+960
3	Utility Industry	38	33	−5	3,599	2,759	−840
4	Construction Industry	1,113	1,020	−93	15,451	14,980	−471
5	Trade	7,806	7,302	−504	39,845	37,915	−1,930
6	Maintenance industry	529	467	−62	2,867	2,774	−93
7	Transport	2,092	1,992	−100	53,983	48,498	−5,485
8	Entertainment (restaurants)	1,692	1,672	−20	5,410	5,680	+270
9	Banking/insurance	860	818	−42	15,290	15,864	+574
10	Private sector services	1,859	2,281	+422	19,371	22,397	+3,026
11	Public sector services	3,144	3,001	−143	61,197	63,241	+2,044
12	Other service industry	1,153	1,125	−28	7,396	9,846	+2,450
Total		21,872	21,248	−624	266,999	267,686	+687

Source: *Bedrijven en werkgelegenheid in Rotterdam*, Rotterdam City Council, August 1989.

Now social objectives have been subordinated to economic objectives. It is argued that to bring business to the south bank is a positive move: at present the south bank is a stigmatised area without appeal. The construction of a new bridge, which is primarily meant to improve the accessibility of the new business district, will also benefit the city's neighbourhoods.

The new Rotterdam, in short, is a vision of a sociable city where rich and not so rich live together sharing public space. But what is the prospect of this happening if Rotterdam has now relatively more low skilled workers and less highly skilled workers than the rest of The Netherlands? It is not certain that the city will manage to attract the rich, but the prospect that a solution will be found for the urban underclass is even more doubtful. The story is familiar: a growing part of the population, living in the old inner-city areas, is structurally unemployed. A large part of this group is made up of ethnic minorities. These social groups are low skilled and have no access to the sunrise sectors whilst employment in the traditional sectors does not grow. If new jobs become available in these sectors, they tend to be jobs that require too many skills. In this way, in a period in which many jobs were created in the service sector, overall unemployment in Rotterdam rose from 14,5000 in 1987 to 26,700 in 1981 and 48,880 in 1987. These figures could be worse since The Netherlands' unemployment figures do not list a massive group of people who are 'unfit for further labour'. The rise of 25,000 would then be in the region of 65,000. The picture becomes even more depressing if we add an ethnic dimension to it. Table 3.2 indicates that unemployment is considerably higher for ethnic minorities.

Table 3.2: Unmployment related to country of origin as % of the relative workforce, 1978, 1981 and 1987

	1978	1981	1987
Dutch	6	10	17
Surinam/Dutch Antilles	30	39	45
Mediterranean	11	24	41
Other	13	21	36
Total	7	13	25

Source: Werkloosheid in de Rotterdamse wijken 1987, Rotterdam City Council, December 1987.

The role of cultural policy in designing an urban environment that suits the council's goal to attract firms that are part of the new service economy is well documented. Yet given the above picture, one of the key questions regarding the role of cultural policy in urban regeneration really is how it could contribute not so much to economic development but to the development of society as a whole.

In discussing the main problems facing the city, Rotterdam City Council will always name two: the necessity to anticipate and respond to economic change and the concern about the future of the growing urban underclass. The cultural projects described here might certainly fulfil a role in solving the former. But as they are, they do not contribute to resolving the latter. Like classical music and theatre, architecture and public design are now primarily directed towards the core of the economy. Yet architecture and the design of the public domain are the cultural elements of urban regeneration strategies that can be given universal meaning with the least effort. The challenge to think about design in terms of its cultural and political implications is even more pressing since for a growing group of people, who are structurally unemployed and living in deprived neighbourhoods, the streets, squares and parks of the city are the last remaining links with the rest of society. The council, consciously or unconsciously, keeps the two key problems separate, both on an institutional and a conceptual level. On the one hand there is the project of *stedelijke vernieuwing* (urban renewal) directed towards the core of the city. On the other there is the project of *sociale vernieuwing* (social renewal) directed towards the bottom of the ladder. The former is projected on the city centre whilst the latter concentrates on the inner-city areas in the immediate surroundings of the centre: the problem areas of the city where poverty, unemployment, the drug trade and ethnic unrest accumulate.[6]

Developing the public domain

Is there an alternative to urban regeneration as niche development? Can we develop a model of urban regeneration that does not only focus on the core of the economy, on the specimen of success, beauty and fitness? Could there be a way in which the new heart of the city would be the social centre for the city at large? In a rare contribution on the subject of public design philosopher Michael Walzer distinguishes two sorts of urban space. *Single minded space* is designed with one particular kind of usage in mind. *Open minded space* is designed for 'a variety of uses, including unforeseen and unforseeable uses, and is used by citizens who do different things and are prepared to tolerate, even to take an interest in, things they do not do'.[7]

This is a useful distinction. A city centre is only a democratic space, a public domain, if it is not only accessible for everyone but if it also has something to offer for every citizen or inhabitant. Open minded space is also an environment in which otherness and strangeness are not continuously experienced as a threat but can trigger off interest. An open minded approach is fundamentally different from a single minded one. It emphasises the positive side of urbanity but not in a naive, idealistic way. It accepts that the modern city is the *locus classicus* of incompatible realities. The city is a constant search for a balance between changes, threats and experience. Urban life has pleasures and costs. Whatever we try, the citizen will always have a relationship of love and hate with the city.

It does not follow that we have to tolerate everything simply because it is inherent to urban life. Yet an open-minded approach would emphasise that the negative sides are inherent to the city and warns that strategies to contain 'evil' or to fight chaos do not necessarily improve the situation but might, in many cases, make the situation worse. Of course, it is important to make judgements as to what should be cherished and what should be contained. Yet the city cannot solve its problems by expelling some citizens. The city is made up of various spheres and one should not attempt to rationalise and homogenese their mode of operating. The city centre should be the catalyst for public life, attracting citizens from all spheres. The council should guarantee that the centre can be a place where this life among strangers can be exciting and stimulating rather than dull and destructive.

In this light, we can compare the ideas about the public domain that underlie the various phases of post-war design history. According to the CIAM ideal of the functionalist city the public domain was seen as the freedom of the individual to shop and stroll, without the restrictions of the intensity and confrontation that characterised the traditional city. This functionalist ideal was conceptualised by the professional experts of the CIAM movement, undoubtedly with noble intentions. However, the ideals were lost in the scale in which projects had to be realised in the post-war period. Worse still, the concept of functionally separating activities was meant to create an urban utopia by developing single minded space. Expressionist design was taboo and functionalism was seen as the highest form of beauty. Yet the individual was not as dull as the designers wanted him to be. It would be wrong, however, to put all blame on the designer. Also crucial was the fact that their enlightened ideal of the functional city was in keeping with market forces. With commercialisation, many of the original design criteria went overboard. Yet the embodiment of functionalism in the built form was the opposite of an open minded utopia. 'Rationalisation' came to have negative rather than positive connotations.

In the period that followed, that of the 'participatory city', people defined the public domain for themselves. The political result was the urban intensity model, based on the recognition of the inherent chaos of urban life and the charms of diversity. The aesthetically pleasing, yet intellectually demanding, design features of the functionalist city were dropped. The participatory city was explicitly expressionistic and more open-minded; however, the anti-elitist culture in which it arose often stood in the way of design quality. The present project of urban regeneration is a third attempt which, especially in its early moments, seemed to mark the return of certain assumptions and practices of the functionalist city. There is a renewed appreciation of quality in design. There is a belief in rational planning with a prominent role for the technocratic–elitist mode of policy-making. The layman has to make way for the expert. The citizen's alleged lack of taste and inability to distinguish quality in design from straightforward and superficial effect discredited them as experts of what urban life should be. At the same time, the late-modern city has a much better appreciation of the importance and dynamics of public life. Unfortunately, the threat of commercialisation is looming large. It now seems as if the constraints within which the plans have to be realised threaten the quality of design and bring back the superficial. The project of urban regeneration does not seem to be able to create an environment that is equally accessible and equally interesting for all citizens.

In terms of the appeal of design the expressionistic designs of the 1970s such as the stake dwellings really have met the goal of open mindedness much better. There is evidence to suggest that the ordinary people, and even people from the urban underclass, can relate to these futuristic designs and see them as symbols of the city to which they belong. They are frequently visited, photographed and discussed. The clean, mirror glass architecture that dominates design in the 1980s simply does not have that appeal. It does not relate to people but merely aims to impress. It keeps people at a distance and indeed it often alienates them.

This view should not be interpreted as nostalgia for the 1970s. The aim is to illuminate the unwanted side effects of an almost dialectical development in design priorities that swings, like a pendulum, from one end to another and back again. Urban regeneration could reinforce the open mindedness of the city centre. The problem of this pendular-like development is that the momentum of the present swing now seems to take urban regeneration in Rotterdam in another direction than that which many of its participants aimed at in the first place. An alliance of corporate business and effect-oriented designers of spectacle start to dominate the scene whilst the old aesthetic ideals of the 1982 Architectural International Rotterdam festival, and the even older ideals of developing the centre as a public domain, are rapidly losing influence. The tragedy is that it seems as if the swing of the pendulum always has to be completed before corrections can be made.

The policy-makers working on these issues are driven more by aesthetic considerations and by the wish to create a manageable order than by an appreciation of the democratic virtues of an open minded public life. Should one really try to make shoarma bars and coffee shops leave in order to create a civilised 'museum boulevard'? Only an extremely legalistic perspective would suggest that this would lead to the elimination of unwanted activities. It is more likely that such activities will 'pop up' somewhere outside the immediate city centre, probably in one of the surrounding inner-city areas. There, in more densely populated and far more disadvantaged surroundings, they are likely to cause more structural disruptions than on the 'museum boulevard'. Furthermore, it is not so much a problem of two different audiences meeting involuntarily, since museums and galleries have a day-time economy whilst the shoarma and drug economy tends to peak in the after hours. It seems much more a concern about urban hygiene. Indirectly it would also imply further racial segregation since ethnic minorities do come to visit the fringe activities. But they do not visit the museum of modern art in great numbers, and are unlikely to be attracted to the museum boulevard if it contains galleries alone. The principle certainly contradicts Walzer's ideal of the city centre as a place where one is engaged in a variety of activities, where different people do different things, look at and understand other elements of the city without having to go to a specific area and explicitly look for them. In the city centre everyone has a legitimate presence that allows you to be an onlooker of the urban spectacle without imposing a threat to the other. Segregation reduces the collective experience and restricts our mutual understanding and knowledge of each other. It leads to an unrealistic idea of what is going on in the city and implies a far less tolerant stand towards the other.

The role of culture in present urban regeneration strategies is dominated by a combination of aesthetic, economic and marketing considerations. Yet the deeply felt and seemingly aesthetic concern for clarity and functionality in design is accompanied by a deep-rooted angst about chaos and urbanity. This observation provides both the key to, understanding its success and popularity amongst the urban elite and to grasping the essential threat this scenario for regeneration poses to urban society. In its present form, cultural policy in Rotterdam is still divided in minority policy on the one hand and policies directed towards the core on the other. The development of open minded space, however, provides an alternative cultural strategy that could contribute to both council priorities: the development of the core and the integration of the underclass in public life.

Notes

1 This is evident in the theories of urban visionaries such as Ebenezer Howard, Patrick Geddes, Lewis Mumford and others. Cf. for instance, Peter Hall (1989), Cities of Tomorrow, Blackwell, Oxford.
2 Cf. Marshall Berman (1983), All That Is Solid Melts Into Air: the Experience of Modernity, Verso, London.
3 Part of the 'Second City' syndrome of Rotterdam stems from the fact that a large part of The Netherlands' cultural activities take place in Amsterdam which indeed also receives a very large share of available public subsidies.
4 The plan to develop a 'national econo-centre', a profit-making educational museum which was meant 'to make the economy understandable and exciting', has recently been dropped.
5 Cf. Maarten A. Hajer (1989), De Stad als Publiek Domein, WBS, Amsterdam.
6 It has to be said that the Rotterdam City Council has a set of initiatives meant to address the problems of these old neighbourhoods which, again, serves as an example for many other Dutch cities.
7 Michael Walzer (1986), 'Pleasures and costs of urbanity', Dissent, summer, 470.

4

Bilbao: culture, citizenship and quality of life

Julia M. Gonzalez

When, with the decree of 24 April 1980, the Department of Culture of the Basque government was created, few people could imagine that by December 1990 cultural policy in Bilbao would have become a burning political issue, the object of a controversy over which the mayor of the city would resign his post, and a constant theme in the party politics of the Basque provinces. Bilbao is becoming an example of a city in which cultural policy is the symbol which crystallises contrasting models of development and lifestyles.

This chapter describes the city in its historical, cultural, socio-political and economic contexts. It illustrates the historical development of cultural policy in Bilbao through the interplay of different key actors. Finally, it attempts an analysis of cultural policy objectives and impacts, and of how they relate to wider strategies and initiatives for the city's development.

Bilbao at the crossroads

Bilbao is the core of a metropolitan area of over a million people. It is a city traditionally open to the rest of Europe, with the largest and busiest Spanish port facing the Atlantic. It is the largest city and traditionally the most powerful financial centre of the Basque country and of the north west of Spain. The city, which first established itself as a commercial port, experienced a second phase of economic success based on the industrialisation process of the second half of the nineteenth century. It was the city's ability to create necessary infrastructures, and its social context which encouraged the accumulation of private capital that transformed Bilbao into an industrial magnet for the predominantly rural population of

Spain. 'Cities are hardly ever modelled, or entirely remodelled to catch up with contemporary conditions and trends. Instead, they adapt themselves slowly to such conditions, and shape the trends in their own image' (Glass, 1989: 131). In fact, industrial growth continued in Bilbao well into the 1970s.

By 1975, however, Bilbao's traditional industrial sectors – steel, shipbuilding and chemicals – were collapsing, and there was a considerable increase in unemployment, environmental decay and derelict areas. Bilbao followed the deindustrialisation pattern which was common to many other old industrial cities in Europe which had specialised in labour-intensive and 'heavy' forms of manufacturing. At that time, because of years of neglect, the city's appearance and economic position had deteriorated considerably. The Bilbao metropolitan area lacked technology parks, telecommunication systems, telematic networks and other advanced services, including modern leisure facilities. Its overall external image was poor.

The situation was further complicated by the Basque question. Nationalist opinion was fragmented over the issue of levels of autonomy and self-government for the Basque province, and the means of attaining them. The nationalists had been unable to clarify the different positions within their movement and reach a degree of stability which was necessary to deal with the rise of terrorism, which discouraged further investment into the area.

Bilbao was disadvantaged within its region by the Basque parliament's decision to establish Vitoria as the Basque administrative capital. The city also suffered from competition with San Sebastian, the region's most important tourist centre, and Santander, which was emerging as a magnet with an emphasis on good environmental quality, and from relative peripherality within Europe, lying outside the most important growth corridors. This is the context within which the role of cultural policy in regeneration in Bilbao must be seen.

Developing a cultural policy

By 1980 Bilbao already had an important history of co-operation between the public, private and voluntary sectors in the cultural policy field. The banks of Bilbao and Vizcaya, and other local institutions, traditionally took great pride in sponsoring cultural initiatives. These included support for the Choir, the Society of

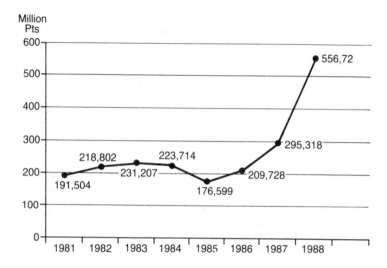

Figure 4.1: Expenditure on culture in Bilbao by the Basque government in 1989
Source: Basque Government, Department of Culture and Tourism.

Friends of the Opera, the Philharmonic Society, and visual arts exhibitions. These institutions were also involved in social activities, mainly targeted at two specific age groups: the young and the elderly.

The city had inherited from the times of the Franco dictatorship a powerful network of church and voluntary groups, which for many years had been the only channel for the free expression of ideas. Particularly relevant, at this level, was the movement for free- time education and socio-cultural animation. The importance of this movement was that it created patterns of understanding and ap- proaching cultural phenomena by emphasising social commitment. This movement educated a large number of the people who would later be active in the local cultural policy-making process.

This is the environment within which the public sector's cultural policy-makers operate. The public sector in Bilbao consists of a complex set of institutions. There are three levels of local govern- ment: the government of the Basque autonomous community, the diputación (provincial government) and the municipality. All three have departments of culture which are financially responsible for some aspects of cultural policy. Co-ordination between these three levels is, therefore, a crucial task.

In the case of the Basque government, despite the fact that in the second half of the period under consideration – 1986-90 – there was a coalition in power between the Nationalist and the Socialist Party, it is significant that the department of culture never changed hands. It was always held by the Nationalist Party. Figure 4.1 shows the range of increases in the Basque government's cultural expenditure in Bilbao throughout our period.

One way of summarising what happened in cultural policy terms in Bilbao in the 1980s is that it was a combination of recurrent themes and changing emphases. The cultural policy of Bilbao and, indeed, of the whole Basque provinces is characterised by very clear constant ingredients. The most important of these is a concern with cultural identity. Basque cultural identity is a political tool, typically embodied in efforts for the protection of the Basque language, as well as in the respect for Basque archaeological heritage. These attitudes are reflected by cultural policy budgets at all levels of public administration.

In fact, the promotion of Euskera, the Basque language, is the primary objective of Basque cultural policy. In Bilbao, in particular, the Basque language is little used, given that the population of the city includes many people who have migrated from other parts of Spain. The awareness of how difficult it is for such an old minority language to survive – with the obvious implications that this has for the survival of Basque culture itself – induced the administration of the Basque country to take a variety of measures to protect and stimulate the use of the Basque language. Expenditure for the promotion of Euskera by the Basque Ministry of Culture has multiplied six-fold over our period.

A further dimension of the effort to rediscover Basque cultural identity and strengthen its presence in contemporary Basque society is the Basque government's emphasis on the protection and enhance-ment of cultural heritage. The culmination of ten years of work by the Basque government is contained in a law on cultural heritage passed on 7 July 1990. The Law states that 'Basque cultural heritage is the principal expression of the identity of the Basque country and the most important witness of the historical contribution of this country to universal culture'.[1]

The Basque government's expenditure increased during the 1980s, reaching its highest point in 1989. Figure 4.2 shows how the budget of the department of culture of the Basque government is spent in specific areas of activity, while figure 4.3 shows how the

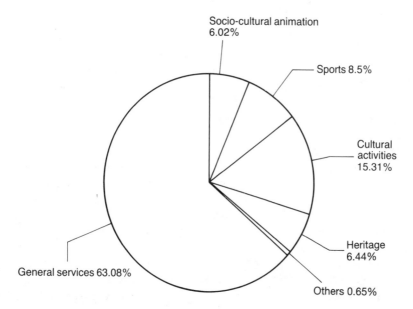

Socio-cultural animation
6.02%

Sports 8.5%

Cultural
activities
15.31%

Heritage
6.44%

Others 0.65%

General services 63.08%

General services: 90% of which is taken up by promotion backing
Basque television and radio channels

Figure 4.2: Distribution of the Basque government's cultural expenditure in 1989
Source: Basque Government, Department of Culture and Tourism.

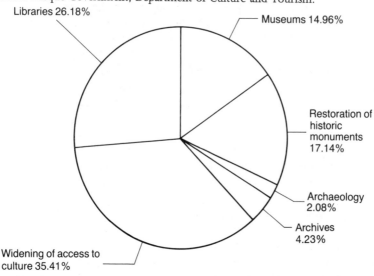

Libraries 26.18%

Museums 14.96%

Restoration of
historic
monuments
17.14%

Archaeology
2.08%

Archives
4.23%

Widening of access to
culture 35.41%

Figure 4.3: Distribution of cultural expenditure by the diputación foral de Vizcaya in
1989
Source: Diputación Foral de Vizcaya, Department of Culture

1989 cultural budget was spent by the *diputación*. The restoration of historic monuments (17 per cent of total cultural expenditure), libraries (26 per cent) and museums (15 per cent) take up more than half of the budget.

Expenditure on Basque television and radio takes up a large share of the cultural budget. This is again related to the political objective of protecting the Basque language.

Figure 4.3 shows that 35.4 per cent of the cultural expenditure of the *diputación* is spent on programmes whose objective is the *difusión cultural*, i.e. the widening of access to culture. The Basque government spends 15.3 per cent of its cultural budget on such programmes.

Programmes aimed at democratising access to culture take by far the largest share of the municipal cultural budget. During the period under consideration this type of expenditure has grown seven-fold. These programmes are characterised by an interest in promoting Basque culture and supporting local artistic creativity, particularly in the case of amateur and young artists.

Expenditure by Bilbao City Council's department of culture in 1986 totalled approximately £9.63 million. The most substantial share of this total was spent on the renovation and maintenance of buildings for cultural uses. This amounted to about 82 per cent, while only 18 per cent was spent on programmes of cultural events and activities.

Within this 18 per cent (a figure close to £1.73 million) 17 per cent was spent on subsidies to music courses, adult education and art workshops, 16 per cent on experimental arts activities and 13.5 per cent on subsidies to cultural groups and associations. Then there were specific allocations of 17.5 per cent for youth activities, of 6 per cent for the revival of the Basque language and of 30 per cent for festivals.

The public sector in Bilbao has created a network of *casas de cultura* which are the most important instruments through which the programme for the democratisation of access to culture is implemented, although there remain problems in terms of the inadequate supply by the municipality to people of information about cultural events and activities in the city. There is also a network of civic centres located in urban districts (the *barrios*) which act as the focus for the cultural life of those neighbourhoods. Voluntary associations, in particular, see the civic centres as a valuable way of encouraging citizens to participate more in local affairs.

This participatory approach is complemented by an attempt to inject dynamism into city life, by organising celebrations, festivals and other cultural animation initiatives. There is a clear intention to rediscover for the city the atmosphere of the fiesta and the vibrancy of celebration, and open air performances which help transmit the feeling of urban liveliness. Expenditure on initiatives of this type is becoming more and more significant in Bilbao. Open-air cinema, festivals in parks and carnivals proliferate.

Two further policy areas have been the object of particular attention by the public sector: sports and youth. They take up 8.5 per cent and 6 per cent of the cultural budget respectively.

The two central goals of sports policy in Bilbao have been to create a network of facilities and services and to concentrate on two different types of campaigns to encourage participation in sports. One is aimed at school and University students and the other, already popular in many countries, is called 'Sports for All'.

The creation of the Municipal Sports Institute (IMD, Instituto Municipal de Deportes), marked the initial point in the attempt to bring sports closer to the life of the barrios. Large sports facilities were designed and built in these areas. They provide a large number of services, from swimming pools to gymnasia, saunas, and courts for playing Basque ball, squash and tennis. These centres soon became popular as venues for a range of other activities, including jazz, dance, aerobics, karate and judo. It was reported that in 1988 a daily average of two thousand people regularly used these facilities.

Despite these efforts, however, the metropolitan area of Bilbao seriously lacks multi-use sports infrastructure. There are very few facilities for specialised sports. In the municipality of Bilbao, in particular, facilities belong to clubs and other private associations.

The picture becomes more complex if trends in popular demand are taken into consideration. An analysis of public demand in the metropolitan area of Bilbao[2] shows that the trend is towards preference for a more diversified pattern of sports activities, in which there is greater scope for practices at individual rather than group level.

Youth policy was characterised during the period under consideration by two different formulas: youth and associationism, from 1982 to 1986, and youth and community action in the second. Concern for youth training was constant during this period, with a shift towards a more communal understanding of the problems and a more all-embracing concern for marginal groups such as women, the elderly or deprived families.

The pattern of expenditure throughout the period shows a marked decrease from 1984. Other themes were gaining momentum. At that time a redefinition of the objectives of the Basque government's cultural department specified the enhancement of the local quality of life as the main objective of cultural policy.

Focusing on urban regeneration

Until the late 1980s the city of Bilbao, and indeed the whole metropolitan area, had lived without a plan and had developed in a chaotic and spontaneous way. In 1986 a revision of the existing plan started. It soon became apparent that a new direction for the city was required. A variety of conferences and symposia to discuss the city's future were initiated. The II World Basque Congress (1987), the conference Bilbao ante su Plan General (March 1988) and the Forum Bilbao on Urban Renewal (February 1989) were especially important in this regard.[3]

The objective of all these initiatives was to discuss what Bilbao could learn from the design and management of programmes for the regeneration of other old industrial cities in Europe and North America. The presentation of the case of Glasgow, for instance, focused attention on the positive contribution cultural policy could give to urban regeneration.

Bilbao realised that it could still be a cultural magnet, attracting large numbers of people. The success of the city's Arriaga Theatre was an indicator of such potential. Bilbao was, at the same time, consolidating its position as a centre for trade fairs and exhibitions. The flows of business visitors to Bilbao in the 1980s increased substantially, due to the success of the city's strategy to market its facilities. The relative success of the city as a centre for international trade fairs and exhibitions provided evidence of how it was possible to tap the potential of local resources through imaginative regeneration strategies. At present the Bilbao fair is being expanded to cope with the increasing number of visitors.

Bilbao's Plan General thus emerged as a global answer to a critical situation. David Harvey (1989: 66) takes post-modernism in the field of architecture and urban design 'broadly to signify a break with the modernist idea that planning and development should focus on large-scale, metropolitan-wide, technologically rational and efficient urban plans'. In contrast, Bilbao has produced a plan as a tool to help the city move from industrial to post-industrial, from modernity to post-modernity.

The three key aspects of cultural policy and urban regeneration in Bilbao which suggest themselves for analysis are the key elements of the plan and the way they relate to cultural policy, the wider role of cultural policy in strategic planning, and the roles of culture and leisure in the transformation of Bilbao from the perspective of people living in the metropolitan area.

Bilbao and the proposals of the Plan General

The plan sets itself a clear objective – to change the image of the city of Bilbao. This was considered as the key requirement for any further action. Bilbao, in common with many other European cities, embarked on a search for an adequate image to market itself as a good location for advanced services, especially banking and insurance, high technology and specialised commerce.

Image is the overall marketing product which should correspond to two major changes: the implicit transformation of the economic base of the city, and the attainment of high levels of quality of life. But, in relation to city image 'the promotional message must be distinctive, yet easily understood and believable' (Ashworth and Goodall, 1989). In this context, the plan's proposal to create a large cultural centre became a powerful symbol of the transformation of the city.

As for the transformation of its economic base, Bilbao is slowly showing signs of a shift away from mass production with a high degree of economies of scale and use of unskilled labour towards a pattern of more flexible production with a more prominent role for information technology and technology parks. There is also clear evidence of the emergence of self-contained, relatively autonomous work groups organised around particular problems, and characterised by flexible patterns of part-time employment. All these signs correspond to a process of change from a Fordist to a post-Fordist economy (Henry and Bramham, 1990).

A central feature of the city's economic fabric is the change in the pattern of employment from manufacturing to services. Employment in the latter increased by 16.9 per cent over the last twenty years.

As far as quality of life issues are concerned, the plan contains elements which appear in many similar documents produced by other west European city governments. The plan's policies include the restoration of buildings, landmarks and facades, the pedestrianisation of the city core for shopping, the reconstruction of city parks, the organisation of public spectacles, the regeneration of the waterfront, the promotion of trade fairs, the establishment of business parks, and even the creation of a Basque mini-Manhattan in the old docks.

Cultural and leisure facilities are important components of the plan in at least four different ways. Firstly, the cultural sector is a growing sector of the economy, able to help solve Bilbao's greatest problem – unemployment. Secondly, it is seen as a significant element of strategies aimed at improving the quality of life of the people living in the city, and as a way of alleviating deprivation in disadvantaged areas. Thirdly, there is the view that it is a key component of the mix of the city's visitor attractions and an ingredient for attracting investment and highly professional, highly specialised personnel.

Finally, leisure and culture are regarded as the symbol of the city's renewed dynamism. In this respect, there was a proposal to build a glass cube higher than the Bilbao–Vizcaya Bank – the city's highest building – on the top of the Alhondiga, a famous and magnificent old wine cellar from the beginning of this century. The cube, which was to house a large cultural centre, was designed by Basque architect Oteiza as a symbol of the new Bilbao. After months of controversy, the project seems forgotten. However, in October 1991 the highest authority in the Basque Country, the Lendakari, signed in New York a pre-agreement for Bilbao to host a branch of the Guggenheim Museum, the second in Europe after that in Venice. The building for the Museum, designed by American architect Frank Gehry, is planned to be constituted by Bilbao's three symbolic elements: stone, steel and water. It would occupy 46,000 square metres in the former docklands in the heart of the city, next to the planned Auditorium, Museum of Science and Technology and Convention Centre.

The most controversial issue in the plan is the notion of quality of life adopted by its authors. If quality of life is an interconnected whole consisting of ecological, social and physical dimensions, it must be concluded that in Bilbao the social dimension is not specifically identified in its development plan. This is becoming a major problem for a considerable number of local citizens.

The transformation of the city and the role of culture for strategic planning

Further proof that the Basque government is aware of the critical situation of the Bilbao metropolitan area is the fact that the Department of Economic Development and Planning, together with the *diputación*, has commissioned a strategic analysis of the revitalisation of metropolitan Bilbao.[4]

The study concentrates on seven critical issues: investment in human resources, the centrality of the services sector for a modern industrial region, physical accessibility, environmental regeneration, urban renewal, the strength of the cultural sector and co-ordination among different levels of government.

In view of the significance of the press and of other commercial cultural industries, the strength of the universities, the city's capacity to organise international conferences and decentralise cultural activities, cultural centrality is considered among the most critical factors capable of influencing the city's progress.

The cultural industries in Spain and in the Basque country in particular have suffered from processes of concentration and above all from internationalisation. They have been neglected by public policy and characterised by a chaotic pattern of development (Bustamante and Zallo, 1988). Internationalisation – with the related risk of homogenisation, added to a growing emphasis on the quality of cultural production, on the development of marketing techniques and strategies, and on the need to project to the outside world national and local cultures – characterised the development of the cultural industries in metropolitan Bilbao.

The key factors affecting the evolution of cultural demand are the increase in the share of leisure time and disposable income for the majority of people, growing mobility, and subsequently a growth in the public's demand for information about cultural events both in Bilbao and in other cities. In this context new models of financial support for culture have emerged in Bilbao. They advocate a pattern of cultural policy-making which attaches more importance to private sponsorship, and to the need to integrate commercial enterprises into their social settings, to promote fiscal incentives for the private sector and to confine the public sector to a more limited role.

The rationale for these developments is to reduce the reliance of the cultural sector on public subsidy, and to allow culture to play a leading role in the regeneration of Bilbao.

The third phase of the strategic plan for the regeneration of Bilbao is now completed. The plan identifies the key poles for the future development of the city's cultural infrastructure. The study has led to the creation of the Bilbao Metropolitano public–private partnership, which is responsible for the future implementation of many of the plan's projects.

Popular attitudes to cultural policy and regeneration

The final part of this chapter examines public opinion in Bilbao about the policies being undertaken in the city. It is based on a survey of citizens and voluntary associations conducted by Bilbao City Council. The following conclusions emerged from the study.

Firstly, images are important, whether they are of the city, cultural development or concepts of culture. These images reveal that there is polarisation of, and confrontation between, different sections in the city's population as cultural themes define people's positions and identify their belonging to particular groups. The implications for a society which is building itself up and looking for new ways ahead are clear – citizens want to participate in the construction of their future.

The survey also identified two scenarios for the future development of Bilbao. According to the first scenario, Bilbao should project itself as a European capital, imitating external models of behaviour. It should attempt to attract investment, tourists and business visitors. It should consolidate its function as a city with good centralised services serving a large region. One of the key symbols of the city's cultural centrality could be the proposed creation of a large cultural district.

In keeping with this view of the city's future, the forms of culture that should be developed would mainly be ephemeral spectacles, aimed at attracting the attention of investors, stimulating cultural consumption and encouraging the development of local cultural industries. Culture, in this context, would be expressed in the language of economics and would serve economic development objectives.

In the second, alternative, scenario citizens felt that Bilbao should look for a model of development based upon indigenous strengths more aimed at meeting the needs of local residents. The main policy objective in this case would be the decentralisation of services so that all citizens share the benefits flowing from the implementation of cultural policies and participate in city development. In particular, there should be greater concern for the deprived areas of the city. Cultural facilities should be small, manageable and well distributed throughout the city's *barrios*.

Cultural policy in this scenario should be closely related to the real conditions of existence and needs of the inhabitants of Bilbao and should primarily be concerned with social and community development objectives. However, the intentions of the early stages of the Bilbao plan suggest that there has been an almost complete lack of communication on these issues so that economic regeneration and social regeneration appear as irreconcilable objectives.

In terms of culture and cultural strategies different goals are advanced in the city of Bilbao. The first is the goal of maintaining a degree of Basque cultural identity. Parallel to this, although it is decreasing as generations integrate in the area, is a demand for a network of centres identified with the cultures of different parts of Spain. These centres attempt to keep alive cultural identities and traditions connected with the places of origin of the older migrants to the city.

Many in the city subscribe to the goal of maintaining a degree of elitism and refinement in a large city with an established bourgeoisie and a tradition of hospitality for wealthy visitors. Along the same line, there are in Bilbao those who seek the democratisation of access to culture, to enable more people to appreciate and enjoy 'high' culture. There are also those who champion the cause of 'cultural democracy' and the right of minority and marginal groups to express themselves and establish their own channels to create their own culture.

Next, there is the cause of culture as an ingredient of the urban quality of life as a factor in the area's economic development, and as a concept actively expressing the fact that all community groups and neighbourhoods in the city are lively and participate in local affairs. Finally, there are the most extreme groups who combine a radical view of Basque cultural identity and nationalist feeling with their struggle against the established order.

All these individuals and groups campaign for different objectives. Most of their requests seem to have been institutionally absorbed by government but it is the solution of this puzzle of diverse interests and pressures which gives a clue as to what the future of cultural policy in the city will be.

Conclusions

At the beginning of the 1990s the city of Bilbao faces a great challenge and it is already running late by the standards of its European competitors. The city has enjoyed ten years of democratic development and autonomous rule, with a serious effort to equip the area with cultural facilities and give it the means to move forward. Awareness of the importance of cultural policy among public sector policy-makers has certainly grown. The coordination of different levels of government and of different party ideologies, however, remains a problem and will be a decisive element for the future.

Also positive is the fact that alliances between the private and the public sector are ideologically accepted and sought, while a less publicly subsidised type of cultural policy seems to be emerging. In parallel with this, the process of identification of resources is underway and the importance of the commercial cultural industries is becoming apparent. The arts are increasingly accepted as part of the local provision of services but there is still a need for strategies aimed at supporting cultural producers and backing research on cultural production and consumption, as well as for legislation regulating the question of private sponsorship.

An integrated vision of economic and social benefits is crucial for the future development of cultural policy in the Bilbao metropolitan area, with a change of perspective towards a future in which arts expenditure can be regarded as investment rather than subsidy. An investment is required which provides economic returns of considerable size, and an investment in the quality of life to be enjoyed by the region's population, for both personal and community development.

If a city is primarily run by its inhabitants then the citizens' desire to participate in local public life and culture is one of the city's greatest assets. It is not only the efforts and the money – at a time when public sector financial resources may be scarce – provided by governmental institutions that can produce the answers to Bilbao's problems. The citizens themselves can put forward solutions through forms of self-organisation that can both express the culture of local communities and help the city as a whole move to progress.

Community initiatives, however, need to be enhanced and backed by a firm awareness of the fact that the social dimension of the local quality of life is absolutely crucial. Since the increasing social polarisation (Castells, 1986) within large cities cannot be denied, it is important to encourage the development within the same city of different systems of production and social organisation which are equally dynamic but very diverse in terms of the kinds of wealth, power and prestige they produce.

For the harmonious development of Bilbao's regeneration, a strategy needs to be developed giving equal emphasis and resources to social, economic, ecological and physical development issues. The process of decentralisation which the municipality has initiated ought to be seen as connected with such a development strategy and given a similar backing from public authorities. It is crucial for the city to gather all its active forces to move forward, but this can only happen with clear evidence that all social groups are taken into consideration and that the gaps between them are not widening.

The local elections of 1990 resulted in the formation of a coalition between the three Nationalist parties which do not support the use of violence. In 1991 one of the Nationalist parties (EA) was replaced by the Socialists. The chapter started with a reference to December 1990, when the former mayor resigned over the issue of the creation of new cultural centre for Bilbao. As we have seen, the idea of building a massive cube-shaped cultural centre on the top of a historic wine cellar has now been abandoned, but the awareness of the importance of investment in culture for the future of Bilbao has grown stronger. Bilbao's river, the Nervión, is seen today as the backbone of the new city. The Nervión used to be a major route for merchant ships. In later years the riverfront became the symbol of Bilbao's industrial landscape of shipyards, iron, steel, and chemical works. With the proposed Museum of the River, the Guggenheim Museum, the Convention Centre, the Arriaga Theatre and many other cultural buildings on its banks, the Nervión could be transformed into a major cultural artery for the new Bilbao.

Cultural policy in Bilbao has evolved rapidly during the last decade. This process combined different expectations and meanings. Cultural policy was seen as a tool for expressing Basque cultural identity, as a vehicle for stimulating the citizens' political participation, and as an element of the quality of life needed for economic revitalisation. It was, in particular, seen as a symbol of the new Bilbao, capable of creating an image of the city's future and consensus to help the regeneration movement go forward.

Notes

1 In *Boletin Oficial del Pais Vasco*, 6 August 1990.
2 *El Ocio como Factor de Transformación Urbana en el Area Metropolitana de Bilbao*, an unpublished study carried out by the Interdisciplinary Research Groups in Leisure Studies at the University of Deusto, Bilbao, published in 1992 by Bilbao City Council as *El Ocio en el Área Metropolitana de Bilbao*.
3 The publication of the proceedings of the II World Basque Congress (1988) covers a variety of issues concerning the development of a society rooted in tradition but moving into modernity and post-modernity. The *Bilbao Ante Su Plan General* conference was held in Bilbao from 22-5 March 1988. The contents were later published by the Oficina Municipal del Plan. *Forum Bilbao: Regeneración Urbana y Transformación de Centros Industriales: Bilbao, Manchester, Boston, Glasgow* took place in Bilbao in February 1989.
4 *Plan Estratégico para la Revitalización del Bilbao Metropolitano*, by Andersen Consulting, 1990-1.

References

Ashworth, G. and Goodall, B. (eds) (1988) *Marketing in the Tourism Industry: the Promotion of Destination Regions*, London, Croom Helm.
Barnes, S.H. (1986) *Politics and Culture*, U.S. Department of State, Ann Arbor Institute for Social Research.
Baudrillard, J. (1981) *For a Critique of the Political Economy of the Sign*, St Louis, Telos Press.
Boyer, R. (1986) *La Theorie de la Regulation: un Analyse Critique*, Paris, Editions de la Couverte.
Bustamante, E. and Zallo, R. (1988) *La Industrias Culturales en España*, Madrid, Akal/Comunicación.
Castells, M. (1986) 'The new urban crisis', in Frick (1986).
Cheshire, P.C. and Hay, D.G. (1989) *Urban Problems in Western Europe: an Economic Analysis*, London, Unwin Hyman.
Frick, D. (ed.) (1986) *The Quality of Urban Life*, Berlin, Walter de Gruyter.
Frick, D. (1986a) 'Overviews' in Frick (1986).
García Merino, L.V. (1987), *La Formación de una Ciudad Industrial. El Despegue Urbano de Bilbao*, Bilbao, Instituto Vasco de Administración Pública.
Glass, R. (1989) *Cliches of Urban Doom*, Oxford, Blackwell.
Harvey, D. (1989) *The Condition of Postmodernity*, Oxford, Blackwell.
Harvey, E. R. (1990) *Politicas Culturales en Iberoamérica y el Mundo*, Madrid, Technos.
Henry, I.P. (1990) 'Leisure, culture and the political economy of European cities: case studies of Leeds, Bilbao and Kalamata – the research framework', Madrid, World

Congress of the International Sociological Association, World Congress, 9-13 July.

Henry, I.P. and Bramham, P. (1990) 'Leisure politics and the state', paper presented at the Leisure Studies Association Conference on Leisure Policy Ideology and Practice, Plymouth, April.

Inglehart, R. (1990) *Cultural Shift in Advanced Industrial Society*, Princeton, Princeton University Press.

Knight, R.V. (1986) 'The advanced industrial metropolis: a new type of world city' in Evers, H.J. *et al.* (eds) *The Future of the Metropolis*, Berlin, Walter de Gruyter.

Lash, S. and Urry, J. (1987) *The End of Organised Capitalism*, Cambridge, Polity Press.

Mennell, S. (1979) 'Social research and the study of cultural needs' in Zuzaneck, J. (ed.) *Social Research and Cultural Policy*, J. Zuzaneck (ed.), Ontario, Otium Publications.

Piore, M. and Sabel, C. (1984) *The Second Industrial Revolution – Possibilities for Prosperity*, New York, Basic Books.

Simpson, J. (1976) *Final Report of the Project on Socio-Cultural Animation: Audit and Legacy*, Strasbourg, Council of Europe.

5

Bologna: a laboratory for cultural enterprise

Jude Bloomfield

Introduction

Unlike the other cities in this book, Bologna did not develop a vigorous cultural policy in response to urban decay, economic decline or competitive pressure to project an image of modernity. On the contrary, Bologna was renowned for its well-preserved urban environment and prosperity even in the recession of the early 1980s, and for its traditional, academic and literary culture which earned the city the nickname of *la dotta*, the learned. The transformation of Bologna's cultural policy occurred under the impetus of a cultural crisis in the 1970s, the rift between socially marginalised and unrepresented young people and the political institutions of the city, which had been dominated since 1946 by the Italian Communist Party (PCI).

The combination of high unemployment among graduates and corporate political institutions which were resilient to generational change and new tendencies in Bolognese society, led to an explosion of alternative and avant-garde culture. In 1977 this expressed itself in support for the *movimento*, a national political revolt of youth against the PCI for supporting the Christian Democrats in its bid to gain power at national level. Although the PCI's reaction to the phenomenon was hostile, demonising it as a violent, even semi-fascist movement, a group of younger intellectuals in the PCI, who shared the ideas of informality of the movement, succeeded to office, setting up separate cultural departments. In particular, under the new councillor in charge of cultural policy (*assessore*), Sandra Soster, cultural policy addressed the city's particular circumstances as a centre for avant-garde and experimental cultural production by alternative youth. The Youth Programme which was adopted in the late 1970s and 1980s as a comprehensive response to the underlying social malaise from which the 1977 *movimento* sprang, developed the production-based cultural policy into a co-ordinated strategy to give young cultural producers a footing in the economic structure of Bolognese society and countered pressures leading to petty crime and drug addiction. Bologna's socio-economic infrastructure of artisan firms offered a ready-made environment for incubating cultural enterprise. Once the mental transition had been made, the alternative culture could be harnessed to economic development purposes and the city transformed into a centre of cultural productivity and diversity.

Bologna's civic culture

Bologna is a medium-sized provincial town, with a population of 420,000 inhabitants, which is declining and ageing every year. The city underwent a crisis in the late 1960s and early 1970s due to the rapid and chaotic character of the post-war boom, the wave of migration and the ensuing unplanned explosion of land and house prices, property speculation and traffic congestion.

The physical fabric of the city has been successfully preserved against the ravages of speculation and gentrification by a regulatory plan, enacted in 1971, which converted old buildings in the city centre to new uses, turning towers and palaces into public theatres, libraries and halls, and retaining the sixteenth, seventeenth and eighteenth century narrow-fronted town houses surrounding courtyards as housing for single people, students and pensioners. This policy bequeathed a plethora of premises and venues for cultural purposes, but also contributed to the high concentration of elderly people in the city centre. Bologna also pioneered neighbourhood councils which were instrumental in conceiving and modifying the city's regulatory plan and were given extensive powers including responsibility for cultural and recreational facilities in 1979 and budgeting in 1983.

The Communist tradition in the city derived not from a modern working class but from the old Socialist heritage of militant rural co-operatives and resistance to fascism, which took a broad, popular form, involving artisans and all members of the family. In the rapid transition to an urban society, artisan skills and management expertise derived from the land were transferred to small firms and co-operatives in the manufacturing sector. In addition, workers, laid off by larger firms, utilised their experience in setting up on their own, encouraged by the PCI which viewed the enhanced autonomy of self-employment positively. Consequently, co-operatives were not confined to agricultural produce, but extended to precision engineering, dental and electrical equipment, office furniture and traditional industries with a high design content like ceramics and footwear.[1] Planning regulations, by discouraging large firms from settling in Bologna, reinforced the economic profile of the city as one of small business and co-operatives, in crafts and high-tech manufacturing.

This structure of small-scale advanced production weathered the recession years of the early 1980s well: Bologna's unemployment rate remained 2 per cent below the national average. While firms employed fewer people, self-employment grew. This system of production, characteristic of the so-called 'third Italy', has important social features. Based on the family as an extended economic unit, it has reinforced social homogeneity and conservatism. The dispersed production units and the spread of small and medium towns throughout the region of Emilia Romagna have ensured territorial balance at the expense of creating a metropolis. An efficient transport system and ease of cycling ensure Bologna's accessibility to the surrounding towns and its functions as a regional capital of culture.[2] This paradoxical co-existence of conservatism and modernism runs through the political culture of the city and has left its mark on cultural policy too.

The city's cultural policy tradition

Renato Zangheri, a university professor of economic history and Communist mayor of the city from 1970 to 1983, invented the post of *assessore* of culture for himself, and from 1957 to 1964 was in charge of cultural policy. But culture formed part of the responsibility of the education and cultural department and had no separate status or budget at that time. Its prestige was closely linked to Zangheri's personality and did not acquire administrative importance until the late 1970s. A strong bias towards experts and institutions, and a distaste for commercial culture, were reflected in the notion of 'cultural quality', which uncritically accepted the canon of high arts as neutral. Zangheri's preferred method was to implement cultural policy through committees of university academics and scholars who determined spending priorities.

The strong institutional orientation also expressed itself in a concern for infrastructure and building-based organisations. The pronounced administrative decentralisation in the city encouraged local cultural facilities – such as libraries and cultural centres – to be set up as an extension of social services. But these were seen primarily as educational channels for raising cultural standards. So while a social need for culture was recognised, civic intervention was directed at enlightening citizens, giving them access to established culture without redefining and remaking culture in popular forms.

Cultural conservatism was reflected also in the university, the oldest in Europe. Despite its long-seated traditions of public learning as spectacle, the university remained a humanist enclave, cut off from modern scientific–technical culture and the mass public. The absence in Bologna of cultural industries, which were based largely in Milan and Rome, prevented pressure on the university to modernise its syllabus. Its faculty of arts, music and entertainment (DAMS) has spawned many of the city's avant-garde theatre and music groups. However, it lacks any applied arts disciplines such as industrial design, film, video and TV production, computer graphics and architecture.[3] The division between fine and applied arts deprived cultural policy of contact with industrial innovation, keeping it as a separate sphere, produced by an isolated intellectual elite. It was conceptually and administratively disconnected from the artisan enterprise, skills and infrastructure of Bologna's productive base.

The Bologna 'model' of fair and efficient local government, showpiece of the PCI nationally, rested on an unprecedented degree of decentralisation, administrative efficiency, social cohesion and a culture of conservation and academic scholarship. The co-option of experts and the close relations between university intellectuals and the city council acted as a source of political legitimation. However, wider social changes were steadily undermining the social cohesion and homogeneity of Bolognese society and exploded with the emergence of the movimento of 1977, a generational revolt against the rather cosy and closed world of the PCI establishment.

The movimento of 1977

Bologna is a highly literate city, with levels of cultural consumption twice the national average (see table 5.1). The pattern of personal expenditure on culture displayed preferences for theatre and performing arts over light entertainment, and a strong commitment to cinema, fostered by the city's numerous cine clubs. The cine clubs were part of the alternative cultural scene which thrived in Bologna after 1968. Under law 285 of 1977, aimed at countering youth unemployment, which was particularly high among graduates, some twenty theatre co-operatives came into being in Bologna between 1977 and 1979.[4]

The city council made no attempt to channel this cultural energy or creatively engage with these new forces. The amorphous character of the movement, its anarchic energy which spilt over into illegality and violence at times offended the PCI's concept of politics as an organised and responsible activity, especially when it was aspiring to become a party of government. The gulf in cultural and political aspirations that had opened up between the council and young people became unbridgeable. All that the Bologna model of Communist government had come to symbolise became the target of ferocious, satirical attack in the upsurge of the movimento of 1977.

Provoked by the PCI's national support for the Christian Democrat government and a policy of austerity in the labour movement, including the loss of seven public holidays, and its ostracising of marginalised social groups, a movement of students, casual and seasonal workers and unemployed youth took shape, including the politically militant and subsequently violent wing Autonomia Operaia. The movement drew imaginatively on historical precedents and parallels of the oppressed and of cultural avant gardes.[5]

The movement established a network of communications over the airwaves, as well as through cartoons, spectacle and signs on the street, mercilessly mocking the local PCI establishment, and its integration into the mainstream of the Italian state. Radio Alice, one of many free radio stations set up in Bologna, gave voice to the style and anger of the movement, mixing 1960s folk and rock heroes with festivity, 'the rediscovery of the body, the new-found dignity of each individual, the acceptance or cult of difference (of all differences including those which are incompatible), the propositions and problems of the new proletariat, the demands of the marginalised.'[6]

Table 5.1: Cultural consumption: average personal expenditure

Year	Sector	Bologna	Emilia–Romagna	Italy
1968	Theatre	440	341	285
	Ballet/opera	354	232	232
	Classical concerts	188	82	72
	Musicals/mime/variety	599	357	275
	Cinema	20,492	16,428	10,539
	Dance	2,436	4,603	1,905
	Entertainment	2,797	2,959	2,117
	Sport	4,182	2,585	1,799
Totals		31,492	27,591	17,227
1973	Theatre	781	406	458
	Ballet/opera	403	278	250
	Classical concerts	551	225	115
	Musicals/mime/variety	689	388	353
	Cinema	23,500	18,958	12,196
	Dance	3,320	5,168	2,178
	Entertainment	4,070	4,273	2,769
	Sport	6,150	3,952	2,448
Totals		39,468	33,650	20,276
1975	Theatre	777	431	419
	Ballet/opera	254	315	243
	Classical concerts	136	128	105
	Musicals/mime/variety	734	481	433
	Cinema	23,299	18,596	11,667
	Dance	3,787	5,576	2,208
	Entertainment	2,951	3,497	2,285
	Sport	5,743	4,102	2,485
Totals		37,684	33,131	19,848
1980	Theatre	799	520	467
	Ballet/Opera	287	237	269
	Classical Concerts	137	159	131
	Musicals/Mime/Variety	993	736	531
	Cinema	12,938	10,819	5,815
	Dance	3,553	7,053	2,816
	Entertainment	2,962	3,770	2,149
	Sport	6,293	3,548	2,241
Totals		27,962	26,842	14,419

Source: Indagine quantitativa sui consumi culturali in Emilia–Romagna (1968-80), pp. 5-7, in lire at constant 1979 values.

Table 5.2: Unemployment rates in Emilia–Romagna region, the north and centre and nationally (%), according to sex, 1977–89

	Emilia–Romagna male/female	m+f(%)	North and centre male/female	m+f(%)	Italy male/female	m+f(%)
1977	2.8/9.4	5.2	3.7/10		4.6/12.5	7.1
1978	2.9/10.4	5.7	3.8/10.4		4.7/12.6	7.2
1979	3.0/10.9	5.9	3.7/11		4.9/13.3	7.6
1980	2.9/11.1	5.7	3.5/10.2		4.8/13.1	7.6
1981	3.3/11.1	6.8	4.0/11.6		5.4/14.4	6.1
1982	4.0/11.1		4.6/12.1		6.1/14.9	
1983	4.8/14.1		5.2/13.2		6.6/16.2	
1984	4.8/12.3		5.3/14.4		6.8/17.1	
1985	N/A		N/A		N/A	
1986	4.5/12.8	7.9	5.3/13.9	8.5	7.4/17.8	11.1
1987	4.1/12.2	7.5	5.2/14.1	8.4	8.2/19.0	12.0
1988	3.4/10.4	6.3	4.7/12.7	7.7	8.1/18.8	12.0
1989	2.9/9.3	5.5	4.3/12.3	7.4	8.1/18.7	12.0

Sources: 1971–80: S. Brusco (1982) 'The Emilian model', Cambridge Journal of Economics, 6: 168; 1981–90: ISTAT, Rilevazione trimestrale delle forze di lavoro; ISTAT (1982) Annuario di statistiche del lavoro, vols 23, 24, 25, p. 31; Statistiche del lavoro (1986) vol. 26, p. 52; Annuario statistico italiano 1987–90.

The movimento spoke the language of the avant garde, of desire, employing irony, graffiti and slogans to subvert order, politics and morality.

The centre of Bologna was first taken over by the movimento in March 1977 and occupied again by 40,000 people in September, during the 'Congress against Repression', protesting at the government's and PCI's over-reaction to the movement, in arbitrarily imprisoning many of its activists. The movement of 1977 highlighted how out of touch the PCI had become with the city's changing social structure and the cultural aspirations of youth. In the outlook of the PCI administrators, the renewal of ideas would come from within institutions, the party, prominent intellectuals, whether left Catholics or Marxist academics. But it would not come through dialogue with social movements.

This conception of cultural change met with opposition from within and outside the PCI in Bologna. The party was accused of fostering a stratum of technical experts on the council, while suppressing the broader, socially critical role of intellectuals. It was also attacked for a narrow, integrationist conception of pluralism which sought to neutralise dissent by institutionalising oppositional demands rather than according them autonomous initiative. This was seen as a cause of the steady cultural migration from Bologna to other cities.

The emergence of a new cultural policy

Only when a new generation of political activists – who shared elements of the cultural formation, humour and casual informality of the movement of 1977 – gained power could the left councils begin to share a common language with young people. In 1975, Bologna was joined by left administrations in all the major metropolises – Rome, Naples, Venice, Turin, Milan, Genoa – and like all the other cities, was influenced by the new cultural policy developed in Rome by Communist *assessore alla cultura*, Renato Nicolini, which aimed to revitalise the city at night, especially in summer when the stifling heat and tourist invasion exposed the cultural desert for those Romans too poor to escape to the seaside.[7] The central aim of these policies was to liven up dead times and dead parts of the city, to recreate the city as a social centre, to bring people together for pleasure, and raise their cultural awareness through the juxtaposition of different forms of entertainment and cultural genre. The policy was pejoratively labelled 'ephemera' by critics, as rubbish art, facile spectacle, as 'increasing impurity' mirroring the trivial nature of the mass market and as sacrilege to the high moral portent and serious-ness of art. Behind the attack, the defensive voice of traditional intellectuals, who felt their role as arbiters of quality and taste was being undermined, could be discerned. Yet the weakness of 'ephem-era' in Rome was not the attempt at social animation, but the failure to link it to a more enduring strategy for cultural production, particularly its divorce from the cultural industries, notably the film industry in Cinecittá. By comparison with Rome, Bologna enjoyed the advantage of a socio-economic environment in which culture, once recognised as a productive activity, could flourish.

However, little of the social crisis of the late 1970s was reflected in Bologna in the cultural policy of the time. Luigi Colombari, *assessore* of culture from 1975 to 1980, who had previously been responsible for town planning with no special expertise in the cultural field, saw himself primarily as an administrator. At first, cultural policy followed a traditional path, concentrating resources on traditional cultural institutions. However, though sharing many traditionalist assumptions, Colombari sought a limited modernisation of cultural services.

Most significantly, he initiated a debate on cultural policy in 1977, in which he recognised the need for greater participation by grassroots cultural groups. Instead of the council's role being conceived administratively as simply providing a quantitative increase in services, he set out an active planning role for the council to reach specific social goals, based on pluralism and an expansion of democracy.

Colombari underlined the overwhelming influence of the cultural industries in constructing popular consensus for the capitalist system. To counteract this influence, cultural policy had to overcome the split between consumption and production by opening up the traditional cultural institutions to the public, and transforming them 'from being a support for the cultural industry' into 'the site of constant critique'.[8] The split between professionals and amateurs was to be bridged through the use of full-time cultural workers in neighbourhood centres. Financial allocations to neighbourhoods for cultural activities began in 1976 at a modest 24 million lire and rose to 84 million lire by 1980.[9]

This approach still bore the hallmarks of pessimism in response to the cultural industries, which perpetuated a negative relationship to mass culture. Cultural policy was directed against the cultural industries and the alternative was to be created through critique alone, rather than stimulating wider engagement in production of artefacts or performances. Inevitably, democratisation in this framework meant enhancing critical appreciation and the city's cultural associations were seen as educational channels rather than as noninstitutional centres for cultural production and experiment.

However, new instruments were developed, such as consultative bodies linking cultural associations, co-operatives and neighbourhoods to the city council. The tradition of relying on committees of experts made up of local notables to vouchsafe the scientific validity of a project and the spending of money was continued, even when trivial sums were involved. No mechanism existed for direct representation of the public's interests. However, the cultural department began to establish permanent relations with other institutions for joint planning of educational courses and cultural activities. In 1976-77, the Institute for the History of Art, the Institute of

Archaeology and a commission on music appreciation, composed of musicologists, ran courses in their relative disciplines.

Cycles of events, such as talks, book presentations and small visual arts and photo exhibitions were held in museums, galleries, and civic and neighbourhood libraries. Initiatives were also taken to retrain library staff in modern methods of organisation, presentation and public relations and a course in cultural animation was set up through the Italo-French Association.

The conventional side of Colombari's policy concentrated efforts and resources on the traditional cultural institutions. The pattern of cultural expenditure confirms this priority as the proportion of expenditure on heritage remained high throughout his period of office. Colombari did not follow the pattern of other left councils in dramatically shifting 'ephemeral' expenditure on *ad hoc* cultural events and services. When Colombari came to office the Medieval Museum was closed, precious collections in the Biblioteca Comunale were in deposit or closed, and the Archiginnasio, a famous history library, was in serious decay. Typically, Colombari set up a scientific commission to oversee it, and recruited students to help reorganise it.

Colombari's intentions to modernise and rationalise were frustrated through lack of funds and the low profile of his cultural policy. However, his innovations were most effective in precisely the area of so-called 'ephemera'. One objective of this policy strand was the revival of theatre in Bologna after years of neglect. The municipal commission on theatre renewed the agreement with the Theatre Association of Emilia Romagna, for the reopening of La Ribalta as an experimental theatre with aspirations of becoming a highly qualified national centre of training in avant-garde drama and research into new theatrical expression.

In response to the increase in demand for theatre by broad social strata in the city and the tendency of musical and folklore festivals to attract Italian and foreign tourists to Bologna, the cultural department set up the Bolognese Committee for Entertainment in June 1976, composed of representatives of the city and provincial administration, as well as the provincial and municipal tourist boards, to put on theatrical, musical and folklore events. It was charged with the explicit adjunct 'of enhancing the public's critical consciousness'. In the summer season the committee put on thirty-one events covering theatre, cabaret, ballet, music, popular choirs, musical festivals and classical concerts, both in the city centre – in the Sala Europa and the courtyard of Palazzo D'Accursio as well as in some of the city's neighbourhoods.

Two clear policy objectives emerge in this period – the promotion of Bologna as a centre for avant-garde theatre nationally and the expansion of cultural tourism. Similar imperatives lay behind the first summer festival in Bologna, Bologna Estate in 1978, organised around the religious festival of Ferragosto (15th August). In addition to attracting tourists, Bologna Estate had the aim of revitalising the historic city centre. The programming began to reflect the mix of classical and contemporary idioms, high and low-brow forms, which had become popularised by Nicolini in Rome. Apart from an international ballet festival, a passion play and jazz concert, the *gran finale* involved both a flute concert with Severino Gazzelloni, a concert of the ironic popular singer Lucio Dalla, and ten mixed shows of drama, mime, puppets, cabaret and recitations, organised in the province.

A production-oriented cultural policy under Sandra Soster

Sandra Soster, Colombari's successor, built on these innovations and achieved a much higher profile for the cultural department and thus for cultural policy within the council's priorities. Her starting point was the changed situation of the city which cultural policy had to address: the growing cultural demand in line with growing levels of literacy, education and information, and the multiplication of social actors engaging in cultural production. She identified the weakness in the council's relationship with the effervescence in the surrounding society in the lack of intermediate and autonomous instances, of responsive filters between a massive institutional presence and society, between publicly provided cultural services and the public, between local authority action and the city.[10]

This called for a new relationship between the council and independent groups of cultural producers, encouraging the most interesting and innovative trends in the city and respecting their artistic autonomy. It was achieved in two ways. Firstly, links were established with youth talent through the summer festival, Bologna Estate and live variety theatres run directly by performers' co-operatives, in collaboration with cultural institutions. Films were shown in courtyards and public places, making live spectacle out of the inanimate screen while maintaining a rigorous arts programme, culminating in a silent movie season in Piazza Maggiore, to live piano accompaniment. Instead of 50-60 film buffs, 300-400 people attended each night for three weeks.[11]

The Magicbus Co-op, which had set up a cultural project in a mountain 40 km from Bologna, was approached by Soster to organise Settimo Cielo (Seventh Heaven), the keystone of the summer festival. This was conceived as a modern, festive, social aggregation outside the home, with the same instantaneous variety, diversity and switch-over potential as television. It took a multi-media form, encompassing cinema, dance, and music appealing to different age groups, aiming to maximise participation.

The summer festival aimed to break down the barrier between the language and forms of high and mass culture and between the cultural institutions as ghettoes of the traditional elite and ordinary people. Such intent was reflected in the very low price of L1,500 (75p) entrance for the evening programme. The festival was 50-60 per cent financed by the council, while the rest was recouped through tickets and fringe sales. The municipality allocated for the event 185 million lire (£92,000) in 1980 and 300 million lire (£150,000) in 1981. Such expenditure was justified by Soster against the criticism of the main opposition party, the Christian Democrats (DC) who argued that there were more important priorities such as the rehabilitation of drug addicts and the care of the elderly. Writing in the 1981 programme of Bologna Estate Soster retorted that 'the problem of life in the big cities is actually, in the first place, a problem of cultural horizons'. The summer months, when there was nothing to do at night, and low prices made cultural events specially accessible, created 'the opportunity to reach precisely those groups which are the weakest and most marginalised'.

The fruitful relationship between the council and young, independent producers was further consolidated by signing conventions which devolved management and artistic control of theatres and events to qualified and competent groups who were to receive an agreed budget and submit accounts at the end of the year. The rolling contracts usually lasted for three years and were then subject to renewal. This also served the cultural objective of nurturing the avant garde which had emerged after 1968 in theatre and cinema and re-emerged so forcefully in 1977.

These innovations revolutionised theatre in the city and formed part of a comprehensive policy for the sector. In 1981, the Teatro Testoni, with its 400-seat capacity, was handed over to the Nuova Scena co-operative who had developed a new kind of theatre, choosing controversial plays, extending the repertoire to unknown and international companies, diversifying forms, mixing dance, prose and music. They were attentive to new authors and texts, held drama workshops with major actors and began to work in theatre-in-education, co-producing plays with schools, and put on a cycle of concerts for people with disabilities. The previous home of Nuova Scena, the San Leonardo Theatre, was turned over in 1982 to La Baracca for a permanent children's theatre for a trial year and then given a two-year rolling contract.

However, Soster's ambitious project to turn the Arena del Sole (Sun Arena) into a multi-media centre for independent groups did not materialise and was instrumental in her political isolation and her eventual downfall. The project was intended to give Bologna a centre for regional theatrical production and performance, jointly financed by ATER, the regional theatre association, and Bologna City Council. But rather than a municipal stage for hosting outside productions, it was conceived as a théâtre d'auteur, based on a strong artistic director with a repertory company.

The project met opposition from the start because of the high price paid for the building – 5.9 billion lire, £3 million, in December 1983 – and the costs of refurbishing it which grew from an initial £3.25 million to £4.12 million by July 1985. The original 12 billion lire (£6 million) acquisition, renovation and conversion costs escalated to a combined figure of £7.1 million. The building proved to be an intractable problem, with running costs exceeding all estimates and, on top of the heavy capital costs, fuelled a bitter controversy with the Socialists and Republicans as well as the DC.

Soster seemed prepared to gamble all on the project against the advice and support of her colleagues, even when it threatened to undermine the objectives of the rest of her cultural policy. Work was stopped on the building in March 1986, on the new cultural assessore Sinisi's orders. However, the growth of theatre subsidy under Soster was matched by the growth of audiences at a time of national decline in theatre attendance.

Soster visualised Bologna as a whole as a cultural laboratory, taking the new practices drawn from the experimental theatre workshops as a paradigm for the city's development. She also extended the concept from 'ephemeral' cultural activities to the traditional cultural institutions, proposing that museums and libraries become 'authentic laboratories of forms, documentation, information in relation to differentiated publics from primary schools to research scholars'.[12] Rather than polarising institutions and ephemeral events, she synthesised the two in her conception of modernity. The museums had to be modernised, bringing them up to date with social and technological change – in live communication with the city. They had to respond by making their collections accessible through modern explanatory and exhibition techniques, by developing audio visual aids, publications and other educational services, and by becoming centres for research in collaboration with the university and other institutes. The Medieval Museum, which was intended as the medieval and modern complement of the Archaeological Museum, had fallen into decay. In the spring of 1985 the museum was reopened in its new premises in Palazzo Fava Ghisilardi in part of the Arena del Sole complex after £3m had been spent on its refurbishment.

The historic library, the Archiginnasio, equally neglected, had outgrown its size, was unable to accommodate the reading public and had expanded haphazardly. This had blurred the identity of its collection. It was decided that it be turned into a specialist research library of scientific and technical culture, with a clear acquisitions policy to enhance these historical strengths, and complement the university library. In addition to the self-managed neighbourhood libraries, support was promised for the specialised libraries which had emerged from the new social movements, and were catering for the needs of more differentiated publics. Support for the library system expanded considerably.

Clearly the characterisation of Soster's cultural policy as ephemeral is one-sided. Her support for non-institutionalised cultural production was combined with a strong commitment to encouraging the collaboration of independent groups with the traditional cultural institutions. Soster called for higher levels of training and closer co-operation with DAMS, introduced proper competitions for posts in the city council's cultural department and cultural institutions, and rejuvenated the advisory commissions of experts, although their role was reduced by devolving management and funds to independent groups. She also pressed for new legislation – for example, for the

Table 5.3: Bologna City Council's cultural expenditure

Year	Total Cult. expend. (bill. lire)	Ratio 407:409 Source: Comune di Bologna	Source: Minardi and Bianchi	Cult. expend. as % of total expend. on on education and cult. Source: Comune di Bologna
1979	5.6	40.5%:59.5%		10.4
1980	7.7	40.2%:59.8%	41.8%:58.1%	12.2
1981	9.4	34.1%:65.9%	25.3%:74.6%	11.9
1982	10.8	32.9%:67.1%	27.9%:72.0%	14.8
1983	13.3	33.2%:66.8%	35.2%:64.7%	15.7
1984	17.0	32.6%:67.4%		
1985	14.9	51.2%:48.8%		
1986	17.1	57.3%:42.7%		12.5
1987	20.2	59.8%:40.2%		13.7
1988	21.9	53.3%:41.7%		14.2
1989	22.0	63.9%:36.1%		13.6

Sources: Comune di Bologna, Bilancio preventivo 1979-89. Minardi, E. and Bianchi, M. 'Le spese culturali dei comuni e delle provincie in Emilia-Romagna', Dipartimento di Sociologia, Università di Bologna, 1986.

revision of the regional law n. 42 on the financing of cultural initiatives by local authorities, and she sought new means of financial intervention such as low-interest credit.

The demarcation between the market and public provision defined the role of the cultural assessore. Cultural policy filled the gaps where the market was insufficient which was why it was directed at supporting experimentation. However, in Soster's view, the objectives of public sector funding were not to support poor initiatives which were bound to fail on the market, but to encourage financial self-sufficiency. The assessore was not an impresario, nor an entrepreneur, but a co-ordinator, making the best possible use of resources, multiplying economic and cultural opportunities and stimulating investment.

Soster's policy innovations met with hostility from the cultural institutions with their traditionalist outlook, and also from PCI colleagues on the council. The relative shift in resources between expenditure on cultural institutions, entry no. 407, and cultural events and services, entry no. 409, reinforced a siege mentality in the cultural institutions, as power was given to outsiders. While the increase in expenditure between 1976 and 1981 as a whole was not marked, the average percentage rate of growth had been 29.7 per cent for cultural expenditure under entry no. 407 and 101 per cent under entry no. 409. Between 1980 and 1981, there was a sharp shift in resources from 407 to 409 and this trend was maintained until the end of Soster's period of office (see table 5.3).

The most enduring feature of Soster's policy was in bridging the gap with the young generation of innovators in the small theatre co-ops and cine clubs that had emerged after the student revolt of 1977, bringing them into the council's remit and giving them space to operate. Throughout Italian local government this became an accepted model for relating to independent groups. Her initiatives also established relationships between cultural policy in the restricted sense and other spheres of council intervention − education, training, science, research and new means of communication and technology. This transformed cultural policy from being one sector among many in the administrative hierarchy into an inter-sectoral concern affecting all departments and all the council's policies.

Cultural policy under a Socialist *assessore*

At the 1985 local elections the Socialists withdrew from their coalition on the council, leaving the Communists to form a minority administration. After Soster moved to the department of social policy, a political stalemate set in with a weak Communist minority council. Riccomini, a university professor and art historian became the *assessore alla cultura*, but he was an interim figure without the political backing or necessary abilities to undertake cultural planning. In 1986 the Socialists re-entered the coalition with the Communists and gained control of the cultural department, reflecting the weakening of the PCI's position. Nicola Sinisi became the new *assessore*.

In the wake of press disquiet about the Arena del Sole, he had published a 'white book', *Cultura e città*, evaluating the weaknesses of cultural policy in the previous two years. The central theme of this debate was how to exploit the full potential of the cultural institutions, by promoting the city's heritage to reach the maximum audience through image-building, marketing and advertising, with the aid of the private sector. The traditional cultural institutions were to be modernised with distinctive logos, signposting, audio visual aids, computerised booking systems and bars, educational and conference facilities. The allocation to culture from the council's total budget was to be raised from 0.85 per cent to 1.5 per cent and cultural funds were to be centralised in the cultural department. Yet while increased funding was envisaged for museums, art galleries and libraries, rationalisation, privatisation and sponsorship were proposed for other sectors, notably theatre. Sinisi did not see sponsorship as a threat to the autonomy of cultural production.

In some ways Sinisi shared Soster's views of culture as an industry and a resource for economic development, and of urban marginalisation and intellectual unemployment as modern forms of poverty. Yet his explicit call for an end to the welfarist tradition of cultural policy-making did not translate into stimulating grassroots cultural production, but rather into reducing the council's commitment to a range of experimental initiatives while concentrating funds on the renovation of the big traditional institutions.

Sinisi developed a new role for the *assessore* as an organiser of funds, drawing in outside sources money from sponsorship, partnerships and advertising. The restoration of the statue of Neptune by Giambologna, a symbol of the city's identity, highlighted the new approach. The Alliance of Bolognese Entrepreneurs, a consortium of seventy-seven businesses, put up 1.5 billion lire (£750,000) for the restoration. At the same time, the restoration work itself became a public spectacle, carried out in a wooden 'House of Neptune', modelled on the outside of a sixteenth-century palace and on the inside of an anatomical theatre. Private sponsorship paid also for the restoration of some parts of the Medieval Museum. The Bolognese Board for Artistic Events was refounded as a private company with public participation to organise art exhibitions and co-ordinate a programme across the individual cultural institutions.

Greater private sector involvement and reduced subsidy also affected theatre. This meant pressure to overlap rehearsal and production times, at the Nuova Scena and La Baracca, but also meant that services were upgraded, particularly provision for children with a crèche at the Testoni and expanded educational and library services at the centre attached to the San Leonardo children's theatre. The solution chosen for Arena del Sole was a variety theatre for multi-media entertainment, particularly light comedy and cabaret, whose private users would fill it at no expense to the council. Although the upward spiral of subsidy for theatre was reversed, some concern for the difficulties of theatre groups starting out was still shown. For example, the former social centre in Via Osoppo in the Savena district was proposed as a rehearsal space for new theatre groups.

Through skilful policy, Sinisi was able to heal the rift between the cultural institutions and council, by holding summer events in the historic courtyards of the Archiginnasio, Palazzo Poggi, the Basilica di San Domenico, with guided tours of the museums and galleries, conducted by famous professors, the curators or the performers themselves, thrown in as part of the performance. Tickets cost L2,500 (c.£1): the normal cost of a museum visit without entertainment. This proved an imaginative way of reducing 'fear of threshold' by breaking down the aura of traditional institutions, and led to increased attendances at the museums in the summer months to around a hundred thousand. Yet while Sinisi continued in some ways the Soster tradition, cultural policy lost sight of the clear cultural objectives of Soster's production-oriented strategy. Emblematic of Sinisi's traditionalist aims, despite his modern marketing and fund-raising techniques, was his characterisation of Bologna in the 'white book', Cultura e città, as 'a great museum, a great theatre, a living museum, which for this reason is in need of restoration, continual works and attention'.

The youth programme

While the economic and social aims of Soster's cultural policy became largely dissipated in the cultural department, they were continued in the youth programme. The social crisis of youth which exploded in 1977 had highlighted the alienation of young people in Bologna from the council. The Progetto Giovani (Youth Programme), established in 1981 on the initiative of Aureliana Alberici, the Communist assessore for education, was set up to address the multiple but inter-related needs of young people. The crisis was caused partly by the disjuncture between school and university, on the one hand, and training and work on the other. In part, the crisis was also seen as urban – the marginalisation of young people on the periphery, without access to the city centre, without local meeting places and prey to the destructive temptation of hard drugs.

To enable the plan to work, it was recognised that it had to be a horizontal organisation cutting across administrative divisions, equipped with its own budget, assessore and staff and able to draw on the technical support of all departments, although it was initially under the auspices of the cultural department until it was transferred to the department of social policies in 1984. Those who initiated the youth programme realised that it could not gain acceptance from young people unless the initiatives were self-managed and not a mechanism of social control as many institutionalised youth clubs had ended up being.[13] Typical forms of intervention which developed were licensing premises for groups of cultural entrepreneurs, establishing a press centre giving groups access to the media, and providing refresher courses for presenters and producers of local private radio, retrieving a relationship with those who had given voice to the revolt in 1977.

The broad-ranging brief of the Progetto Giovani and the new instruments and approach produced a series of novel, if modest, initiatives. The budget started off in 1980 at 800 million Lire (c.£385,000), fell in 1981 and 1982 to 700 million (c.£400,000) but then directed expanded funding to neighbourhoods.[14] Innovations were introduced in work experience of a casual kind for young people who had acquired GCSE equivalent qualifications. The Council offered a three-monthly rotation of 200 jobs, providing casual work between 1979 and 1981, that showed a demand for temporary jobs.

Economic initiatives aimed, on the one hand, literally to capitalise on the skills of the educated, 'giving capital to intelligence' as Mauro Felicori, the officer in charge of the Progetto Giovani from 1980, put it. Policy had been directed to cultivating cultural enterprises and enabling them to become self-sufficient. At the same time, economic policy objectives have always been combined with a social purpose: 'by enabling access to self-employment for young people who possess the skills but are devoid of family resources, these policies are also aimed at equalising opportunity'.[15]

Building on the infrastructure which had grown out of Law 285 of 1977 financing youth enterprises to counteract unemployment amongst youth Botteghe in transizione ('Workshops in transition') was a scheme to support youth artisan enterprises in their initial phase and preserve old crafts which were dying out, such as leatherwork, instrument-making, precious metalwork. The scheme co-ordinated the efforts of the provincial council and the city council, which equipped premises and gave them rent-free to young crafts people until they became economically viable. The ground floor of the Saffi Civic Centre, for example, was converted into goldsmiths, clockmakers and furniture restoration workshops.

Secondly, training initiatives were targeted at those socially marginalised and educationally disadvantaged on the urban periphery, with some of the co-operatives in the knowledge-based/cultural industries themselves providing the training. These initiatives were informed by a sensitivity to both young people's interests and to the requirements of the modern market. These included courses in foreign languages, strip cartoons and computer graphics, information technology, film and video, radio electronics and electronic music in the decentralised youth centres.

The most significant and measurable results of the Progetto Giovani were perhaps obtained from musical initiatives which tapped a vast reservoir of 'underground' culture. The Lame civic centre was equipped with a recording studio and concert hall and a convention signed with a co-operative to run it. They set up a music school with eighty pupils, modelled on the new relationship between independent groups and the council, pioneered by Soster in the theatre field. Some bands emerged from the youth centres and became professional, or financed themselves by providing related services. With the support of the Botteghe in Transizione scheme, over sixty groups came together to form a consortium, Sub Cave, and set up rehearsal rooms and a recording studio in the Caserme Rosse in the Bolognina district, which acted as the hub of a network of grassroots bands, agents and impresarios. Young people from another district, the Navile, initiated Centofiori – a summer cycle of rock concerts which acted as a showcase for new talent. Although Centofiori has not managed to overcome the deficiencies of the Italian rock market, and the lack of a record industry in Bologna, it has facilitated the development of a native idiom in vernacular, and of a regional circuit for live performance throughout Italy.

A hefty commitment was made to renovate and re-equip premises in the neighbourhood recreation centres. In 1980 there were thirteen such centres, which had had an annual budget of a mere 20 million lire (£10,000) and had no training facilities. Sixty new workshops and studios were equipped and nine new centres opened in 1983, offering more specialised services to the whole neighbourhood. They were renamed youth centres, in recognition of their multiple functions, beyond traditional youth club-type activities and given a new statute in November 1984. This reflected the shift in conception from social control or institutional management to autonomous and self-management. The new system legitimated a variety of experimental forms: self-management by young people themselves as in the Morara and Casalone centres, or joint management by youth workers, neighbourhood representatives and youth groups, or by co-operatives renting out facilities to groups in the neighbourhood. While training and economic objectives influenced the transformation of the recreation centres into youth centres, the prevailing ethos was to enhance the personal autonomy, fulfilment and opportunities for socialisation of young people. The social bias remained strong, in positively discriminating in favour of disadvantaged groups – girls, young adolescents aged 11-14, youth living in peripheral areas – in order to distribute opportunities more equitably. Consequently special resources and projects were targeted at children at risk, drug addicts, young people with learning difficulties, truants and those in borstal, co-ordinating efforts with other agencies to provide leisure activities, remedial education, sheltered training and housing to reintegrate them into society. The council's financial commitment matched the social commitment and allocations to youth centres rose three-fold from £45,000 in 1980 to £128,000 in 1984. Thereafter, £150,000 was allocated annually to the neighbourhoods for their running costs.[16]

However, while the allocation to the neighbourhoods has been maintained the substantial funding for the other aspects of the Progetto Giovani in the early 1980s was dramatically curtailed at the end of the decade falling to a mere £50,000, eight times lower than at the start. This makes it all the more pressing to combine funding sources and mobilise external resources, and has increased the entrepreneurial drive of cultural initiatives. The Emilia–Romagna region has been resourceful in utilising European Social Fund allowances to finance training or updating in new technologies. The money has been targeted on particular groups – the under-25s with inadequate qualifications, on women in traditional male jobs, migrant workers and the disabled – and the type of training has also reflected the modern fusion of technology and culture – with electronic data processing for computer graphics, livestock rearing, tourism, robotics and CAD/CAM. In 1986 5,773 people in the region received training from the European Social Fund at a cost of around £30 million.

Although the European dimension in Bologna's cultural policy has been limited, a major international project has been undertaken by the Progetto Giovani: the Biennale of young artists from Mediterranean countries, which goes beyond the boundaries of the European Community, involving France, Spain, Portugal, Greece, Yugoslavia, Cyprus and later Tunisia and Algeria. Run four times during the 1980s, the novelty of the Biennale lies in its efforts to stimulate artistic production as well as offering scope to perform, exhibit work and meet counterparts, and the links it has cultivated with the market and publicity machine, building up a European network of contacts with companies, private galleries, advertising agencies, retailers, cultural centres, television and radio. A number of Bolognese artists who participated in the Biennale have subsequently become well-known nationally and internationally. The city marketed itself at the Biennale as 'the city of training'.

Conclusion

The growth of 'ephemera' in urban cultural policies in Italy in the late 1970s and early 1980s has been attributed to a gap in the market.[17] However, the need which the new-style cultural policy met by focusing on performance art was for social aggregation and urban belonging, a kind of experience which the market could not deliver. In Bologna, the long-term lesson of the 1977 movement that the PCI drew was that it could not continue to control the boundaries and forms of cultural expression or channel them into institutions. It had to give up political control of ideas and allow free range to cultural creativity and artistic autonomy. However, it retained its distinctive political identity in cultural policy by adhering to standards of professionalism across all genres, including those hitherto excluded through prejudice, and by upholding a social dimension in the allocation of resources. Cultural policy was committed to equalising opportunities and positive discrimination in favour of the disadvantaged.

However, these features of Bolognese cultural policy have always been subject to conflicting tendencies which are now growing acute. In the conflict between the council and the movimento, the difference in social status and prospects between unemployed graduates and those marginalised on the urban periphery without higher education, skills or hope was temporarily blurred. It has proved easier to solve the problems of the new middle-class youth by enabling them to become cultural entrepreneurs than that of bridging the gap between them and the poorly skilled and alienated underclass. Social heterogeneity and polarisation are growing, and with them inequality, which new immigrants from Senegal and North Africa, in particular, face.

Such tensions inevitably reproduce the cultural division between city centre and periphery: amateurism and didacticism still prevail at local level, the professional and commercial at the centre. However, the substantial investment in equipping the neighbourhoods to train young people no longer means that they only organise public lectures and conferences, although it remains the case that the council's major initiatives in multi-media and performing arts gravitate towards the city centre as a civic focus.

Financial constraints and legislative mayhem, under which cultural policy has always laboured, will provide the real test for the council's social objectives in this field. The sharp cuts in the youth policy budget and the swallowing up of the youth programme in administrative anonymity indicate the demise of this imaginative policy. In conjunction with the general crisis of local government expenditure, are the wider problems for the Bolognese industrial district, particularly the pressure of take-over on regional lending banks which may lead to the favourable loan terms for small businesses drying up. In addition, Bologna has not overcome its weaknesses as a provincial city, with a restricted market for music and theatres. Cultural migration is still a characteristic of artists who want to reach a wider, national or international market. Its tourism economy also remains marginal at a static level of 700,000 visitors a year.

While these limitations and problems remain unresolved, Bologna has certainly achieved significant successes in cultural policy terms. Through avoiding imitation of metropolitan realities far beyond its capacity, it has capitalised on its strengths. These lay in the realm of highly skilled cultural human resources, small and diversified markets, a strong regional network and infrastructure. It is in the development of cultural flexible specialisation that the success of Bolognese cultural policy acquired legitimacy by treating culture as a field of production, and demonstrating the importance of knowledge-based industries to the economy. It also worked in favour of social cohesion by allowing young people self-expression and harnessing it to work opportunities and open political dialogue. The political impact has been felt in local government where the profile of culture has been heightened and in the form and function of the PCI – which has now become the Democratic Party of the Left (PDS). The autonomy of cultural producers and the diversity of symbolic forms and ideas, along with the wider political decline of the PCI, have undermined the belief in the political party expressing a common language and acting as a social glue.

Notes

1 Jaggi, M., Muller, R. and Schmid, S., *Red Bologna*, London, Writers and Readers Co-operative, 1977, pp. 80-5.

2 Sassi, A. (ed.), *Indagine quantitativa sui consumi culturali in Emilia–Romagna* (1986-80), Istituto Gramsci, sezione dell'Emilia Romagna, 1982, p. 3.

3 Felicori, M. and Vitali, W., 'Il Progetto Giovani del Comune di Bologna', in Montanari, F. and Frabboni, F. (eds), *Politiche giovanili, enti locali e sistemi informativi*, Firenze, La Nuova Italia, 1987.

4 Gallingani, A.M. 'Il tempo e il denaro: spesa pubblica e politica culturale a Bologna e Venezia', Il Mulino, 280, 31, 2, March–April 1982, p. 290.

5 Bianchini, F. 'Cultural policy and urban social movements: the response of the 'New Left' in Rome (1976-85) and London (1981-86)', in Bramham, P. *et al.*, *Leisure and Urban Processes: Critical Studies of Leisure Policy in Western European Countries*, London, Routledge, 1989, pp. 20-1.

6 Eco, U. *La communication subversive neuf ans apres 68'*, in Calvi, F. (ed.), *Le debat intellectuel, Italie 77: le 'mouvement', les intellectuels*, Paris, Le Seouil, 1977, p. 112.

7 Chambers, I. and Curti, L., 'Italian summers', *Marxism Today*, July 1983.

8 Comune di Bologna, Assessorato alla cultura, *Proposte per l'intervento dell'amministrazione comunale nel settore culturale*, April 1977.

9 Gallingani, M. op. cit., p. 279; Comune di Bologna, *Bilancio di previsione 1980-90*.

10 'Il lavoro culturale. Intervista di Pino Petruzzelli a Sandra Soster', *La Società*, 40, April 1981.

11 Bruno Migliaretti, interview with the author, September 1988.

12 'Il lavoro culturale', op. cit., p. 50.

13 Felicori, M. and Tomba, R. *I centri giovanili del Comune di Bologna*, Progetto Giovani, Comune di Bologna, 1987.

14 *Interventi 1980, 1981, 1982, Quadro riassuntivo e impegno di spesa*, Comune di Bologna, Piano Giovani 1983; *Bilancio di previsione*, 1980-90.

15 Regione Emilia-Romagna, Assessorato lavoro e formazione professionale, *Rapporto sull'istruzione e la formazione professionale in Emilia Romagna*, 1987, p. 348.

16 Comune di Bologna, *Bilancio di previsione 1980-90*; Felicori, M. and Tomba, R., op. cit., p. 16.

17 Marchetti, A., 'Le muse e l'assessore. Le spese culturali di quattro comuni metropolitani dal 1974 al 1983', Ikon, 11, 1985, p. 45.

6

Hamburg: culture and urban competition

Jürgen Friedrichs and Jens S. Dangschat

Introduction

Our aim in this chapter is to describe the cultural institutions and cultural policy of Hamburg – the second largest city in Germany, and one of the German states (Länder). In order to place the case study within a wider framework, the chapter compares the experience of Hamburg with that of five other large cities in West Germany: West Berlin, Munich, Cologne, Frankfurt and Stuttgart. The chapter examines the debate about what constitutes 'culture' and assesses the economic impact of cultural resources and the involvement of local politicians, urban planners and architects in the debate about cultural policy.

In view of the enormous dependence of culture on the financial support of state and city governments, the chapter examines the role of investment in cultural institutions in local public policies. Its major assumption is that economic conditions are the foundations of investment in cultural institutions by city administrations. Economic conditions – which affect tax revenues, unemployment rates and expenditure on public welfare – determine the opportunities for and the constraints upon policy-makers' decisions, and affect the cultural budget's share of the total municipal budget. The process of decision-making and the establishment of priorities within city administrations determines the allocation of funds to institutions operating in different cultural forms, such as opera, theatre, museums, public libraries. These decisions are equally important, since they indicate not only the priorities of city governments, but also the relative cultural specialisation of a city in national and international terms.

The term 'culture' is used here in a broad sense. Its meaning encompasses music, the visual arts, literature, theatre, science and the media in which these cultural forms are expressed: newspapers, records, films, architecture, and television programmes. This chapter, however, confines itself to the pre-electronic arts – music, theatre, literature, the visual arts and the crafts.

Economic development and cultural policies in Germany

After the Second World War Germany lost its traditional capital, Berlin, and there was no longer a dominant political, cultural or academic centre in the Federal Republic. Instead, the states (Länder) gained in political power, and cultural policy became their sole responsibility. Under these conditions regional capitals such as Hamburg, Munich, Frankfurt, Dusseldorf, competing with Cologne and Stuttgart, grew in population and economic strength. Under the favourable economic conditions experienced in West Germany for almost thirty years, a well-balanced regional and urban structure evolved. However, with five new Länder constituting the former German Democratic Republic (GDR) added in October 1990, this polycentric structure will become even more complex.

In the mid-1970s the Federal Republic of Germany (FRG) was, as all highly industrialised nations, affected by changes in the global economy. The crises in the textiles, steel and shipbuilding sectors led to plant closures and decentralisation of production to countries with lower wages, including the GDR. In contrast, the rise of computer technology, electronics and of public and private sector company expenditure on research and development, positively affected other regions. The former equilibrium turned into uneven regional development, very broadly described as the 'South–North gradient' (Friedrichs, Häussermann and Siebel, 1986). The decline in mining and steel most affected cities in the Saar and the Rhein-Ruhr region, and the decline in shipbuilding the northern regions, including Hamburg. The growth of the electronics sector boosted the economic fortunes of Bavaria and Baden–Württemberg. Areas hit by economic decline experienced growing unemployment rates – with a subsequent growth in expenditure on public welfare – and shrinking tax revenues. Since public welfare is paid from municipal budgets some municipalities were hit very hard by these transfer payments. Hamburg, for example, spent almost 10 per cent of its entire 1989 budget on social assistance.

Global economic restructuring led to increased competition

among the large cities at both ends of the emerging economic hierarchy. Economically growing cities increasingly competed at a European-wide or even global level, while for declining cities competition became necessary for survival itself. Competition was based partly on the functional specialisation the larger cities in the German urban system had acquired. For example, Hamburg marketed itself as the centre for the media industries and insurance, Frankfurt for banking, Dusseldorf for fashion and trade fairs, Cologne for the visual arts, and Munich for electronics and leisure.

Cultural policy in all these cities developed in response to economic changes after the Second World War. Three periods can be distinguished. The first, from 1945 to the late 1960s, was characterised by economic reconstruction, accompanied by restoring traditional cultural values and institutions and facilities – such as opera houses, theatres and museums – predominantly aimed at middle-class audiences. The following phase, from the late 1960s to the late 1970s, was marked by a reaction against economic prosperity and social differentiation. In particular, the 1968 student revolts had a major impact on urban cultural policies. Terms like 'alternative culture' became popular, while subsidies to large opera houses and theatres were criticised because they came from tax revenues exacted from working-class people who largely were not using these facilities (Hofmann, 1983: 30). In response to pressures to subsidise cultural facilities for the lower-middle and working classes, policies promoting cultural participation emerged. In this way, the meaning of 'culture' was extended to encompass the entire spectrum of urban life. As a result of these processes cultural policy widened its remit to include 'urban district culture': cultural activities and events promoted by emancipatory and grassroots movements, often seeking to counteract urban renewal programmes by advocating the preservation of old, popular urban neighbourhoods.

The last phase since the early 1980s can be characterised as a response to economic competition between large cities. The use of culture increasingly became an element in this competition (Häussermann and Siebel, 1987: 205; Henckel et al., 1986; Sauber-zweig, 1988: p.42). One of the most visible expressions of this trend was the creation of new museum buildings: in Mönchengladbach, Stuttgart, Dusseldorf, Cologne, and especially Frankfurt, where since 1984 at least one new museum was built every year. Particularly in the case of Frankfurt, it was the explicit policy of the municipality to change the city's image from 'Bankfurt' to a major cultural centre by establishing a 'museum quarter' of more than thirty museums (Flagge, 1988: 173; Hauff, 1988).

Less spectacular, but equally important, was the impact on German cities of the publication of the New York–New Jersey study, *The Arts as an Industry* (Port Authority of NY and NJ, 1983). With this report urban cultural departments could finally demonstrate the positive economic and fiscal consequences of public investment in cultural facilities. The methodology of the New York–New Jersey study was applied to studies of the economic importance of culture in Bremen, in Neuss and the entire FRG. (Taubmann and Behrens, 1986; Gerwien and Holzhauser, 1988, 1989; Hummel and Berger, 1988). All these studies demonstrated – as their North American counterparts had done – that investment in cultural facilities such as opera houses, theatres and particularly museums was not a loss of public money, but rather a good investment. Furthermore, culture became an important element in policies aimed at attracting new enterprises – culture as a 'soft' location factor – and tourists, at positively influencing the city's image, and at preventing residents from migrating to other cities.

To document changes in the socio-economic context in Berlin, Hamburg, Munich, Cologne, Frankfurt and Stuttgart, some basic data for the 1980-90 period are provided in tables 6.1 and 6.2.

Arts and media in the six cities

Culture comprises many expressions of art and creativity and the respective institutions through which it is produced, distributed and consumed. This paper restricts its analysis to the mainstream 'classic' domains: theatre, opera and museums. This section discusses the experience of these sectors in our six larger cities. As table 6.3 shows, the number of visitors to municipal and state theatres and opera houses declined in all six cities during the 1980s. While such decline in Cologne and Hamburg was modest, in Munich and particularly Frankfurt it was significant. A second remarkable result is the striking difference in the number of tourists visiting different cities (see table 6.4). These differences are evident not only in terms of absolute figures but much more in terms of the ratios of tourists to the number of inhabitants. Only Stuttgart and Munich have about as many tourists as inhabitants, followed by Hamburg, Cologne,

Table 6.1: Population of selected cities, 1980, 1985 and 1990

City	1980	1985	1990	Pop.Change 1980-90
Berlin	1,902,983	1,848,585	2,088,083	185,100
Hamburg	1,633,043	1,592,447	1,606,600	−26,443
Munich	1,299,693	1,267,451	1,218,269	−81,424
Cologne	976,136	922,286	940,155	−35,981
Frankfurt	628,203	599,634	628,761	558
Stuttgart	581,989	561,567	565,666	−16,323

Sources: Statistiches Jahrbuch Deutscher Gemeinden.

Table 6.2: Selected economic indicators for the six cities, 1988-90

	Unemployment rate (%)	Income Tax revenues DM/inhabitant	Net employ-ment gain 1985-89
Berlin	8.9	781	+ 4.4
Hamburg	11.2	705	+ 2.6
Munich	4.6	665	+ 6.3
Cologne	12.1	566	+ 3.3
Frankfurt	5.2	615	+ 9.3
Stuttgart	4.1	674	+ 5.5

Sources: Hamburg in Zahlen, 7/1990; Amtliche Nachricten der Bundesanstalt für Arbeit, vol. 34, 1986; vol. 38 1989, 1009.

Berlin and Frankfurt. If commercial theatres are also taken into account, Munich, Hamburg and particularly Berlin all improve their positions, as in these cities about half of all seats used are in commercial theatres.

In terms of expenditure on opera houses and theatres, there are again striking differences. High numbers of visitors coincide with high total expenditure but low expenditure per visitor, and vice versa. Hamburg spends over 50m DM more than Frankfurt in absolute terms but Frankfurt spends per visitor more than double what all the other cities spend.

Data on museums are presented in table 6.5. Both absolute numbers and changes over time are different for the six cities. Hamburg started the decade in a middle position and ended it at the bottom. The loss of 7.5% of visitors conceals the growth in numbers of visitors to the city's two major museums. While the Art Museum (Kunsthalle) lost between 1980 and 1989 more than 100,000 visitors a

Table 6.3: Number of visitors to subsidised theatres and opera

City	1980-81[a]	1984-85	1988-89	1988-89 visitors per 1,000 Inh.	% change[b] 1980-89
Berlin	1,103,205	963,882	954,551	0.46	− 13.5%
Hamburg	987,587	1,013,962	957,828	0.60	− 3.0%
Munich	1,391,861	1,404,669	1,074,361	0.88	− 22.8%
Cologne	468,217	445,294	458,241	0.49	− 2.1%
Frankfurt	394,325	384,747	253,150	0.40	− 35.8%
Stuttgart	548,555	427,469	503,195	0.89	− 8.3%

Sources: *Statistisches Jahrbuch Deutscher Gemeinden*, relevant years.
a) Number of visitors for 12 month-periods from September of each year.
b) Change in absolute numbers of visitors.

Table 6.4: Number of visitors, total expenditure and expenditure per visitor for selected subsidised opera houses and theatres, 1988-89

City	Visitors	Expenditure in 000s DM	Expenditure per visitor (DM)
Berlin	632,064	130,024	206
Hamburg	957,827	145,788	152
Munich	941,083	192,266	204
Cologne	458,241	85,332	186
Frankfurt	253,150	94,594	374
Stuttgart	503,195	104,739	208

Source: Information provided by the officer responsible for cultural statistics for the Statistical Yearbook of the Deutscher Gemeinden.

Table 6.5: Museum visitors, 1980, 1985 and 1989 (absolute values and ratio/ visitors/inhabitants)

City	1980 abs. (000s)	1980 ratio visit/inhab.	1985 abs (000s)	1985 ratio visit./inhab.	1988 abs. (000s)	1988 ratio visit./inhab.
Berlin	3,972	2.09	3,998	2.16	5,631	2.77
Hamburg	1,155	0.71	1,319	0.83	1,000	0.63
Munich	4,501	3.47	4.186	3.31	3,362	2.77
Cologne	3,446	3.53	1,424	1.55	1,531	1.64
Frankfurt	895	−	2,813	4.70	3,315	5.29
Stuttgart	922	−	2,139	3.81	2,426	4.33

Sources: City yearbooks for relevant years.

year (−35.9 per cent) the Museum of Arts and Crafts (Museum für Kunst und Gewerbe) gained some 100,000 (+83.1 per cent).

It should be noted, however, that the number of museum visitors depends highly on special exhibitions drawing a national or even international audience. To cite one example, the 1980 data for Cologne are extremely high because the Tutenkhamun exhibition alone attracted 1.3 million visitors.

Figure 6.1 compares the two major Hamburg museums with major museums in Cologne and Stuttgart. The differences are striking − Cologne's Ludwig Museum in 1987 and 1988 attracted about ten times the number of visitors the Hamburg museums had and not because of the organisation of special exhibitions. It is, rather, the larger share of modern paintings and sculpture, and even the quality of the architecture of museum buildings in Cologne and Stuttgart that account for their success. The relative success of the second museum in Hamburg, the Museum für Kunst und Gewerbe can partly be explained in the same way. This museum has over the last five years organised attractive exhibitions − for instance, on the work of the Bugatti brothers, on plastic objects, and on crystal objects by Lalique. Hamburg, however, lacks an architecturally attractive museum building.

The increasing importance of economic considerations in cultural policy-making resulted since the early 1970s in a movement to protect 'cultural' interests from the primacy of economic considerations. With the increasingly footloose nature of capital, 'soft' location factors − quality of housing, environmental quality and the more general notion of 'quality of life' − became more important. Culture, therefore, became a very important part of municipal economic development policies. Moreover, culture itself became a strong, expanding economic sector, with a growing labour force and spin-offs in other parts of the economy, such as tourism, hotels, catering and retailing (Sauberzweig, 1989: 545).

In the mid 1970s cultural policy began to be used within strategies aimed at improving the image of cities. These strategies included, for example, the construction of new museums, theatres and exhibition halls; the creation of new festivals of theatre, music and film, and support for neighbourhood-based culture, theatre workshops, experimental music and low-budget films.

Comparing expenditure on culture as a percentage of municipal budgets raises some problems. Since both the Länder and the municipalities spend on culture, the city states (in our case Berlin and Ham-

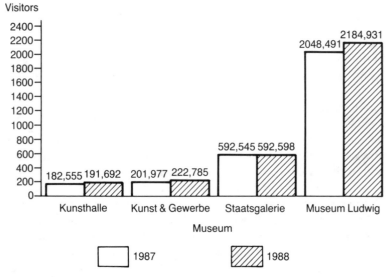

Visitors

Source: Data collected by senior author.

Figure 6.1: Visitors to four selected museums in Hamburg, Stuttgart and Cologne (1987 and 1988)

burg) naturally have a much higher cultural expenditure than other cities. Moreover, the states' capitals (in our case Munich and Stuttgart) house the respective states' theatres and museums and the centralised bureaucracies which are more or less financed by state administrations. Municipalities in non-capital cities (in our case Cologne and Frankfurt) have to finance their cultural policies largely by themselves. Comparisons, therefore, are only possible within the respective three groups. During the period under consideration, Hamburg, Munich, Frankfurt and Stuttgart constantly spent more per capita on culture than the other cities discussed here, but only in Frankfurt did cultural expenditure as a percentage of the municipal budget grow constantly. Moreover, Frankfurt's levels of cultural expenditure per capita were similar to those of the city states. We shall now compare the development of cultural policies in Frankfurt and Hamburg.

Cultural policy in Frankfurt

The different economic functions of large cities in Germany have had an influence on their images. For example, Frankfurt for a long time had the image of an ungovernable, criminal city with always and

everywhere something under construction (Farni, 1985). At the end
of the 1960s the image of Frankfurt worsened: 'Bankfurt' changed to
'Krankfurt' (krank meaning 'sick'), even in the eyes of its own residents.
By the early 1980s, nationwide opinion polls showed that Frankfurt had become a city symbolising all sorts of negative qualities
(Scholz, 1989: 67-8). It was regarded as a cultural desert. The city
seemed to possess a relatively positive image only for younger
upwardly mobile inhabitants. They were impressed by its centrality
within the country, its high salaries and the concentration of banks.
More than 250 banks have their German headquarters in Frankfurt.

The year 1977 was the turning point for municipal policy-making
in Frankfurt. The new lord mayor and prime minister of the state of
Hessen, Walter Wallmann, a member of the former opposition
party, the Christian Democrats, broke away from traditional policies
and adopted a lifestyle very different from that of his predecessor,
the Social Democrat (SPD) Rudi Arndt. The latter was a worker-
oriented, shirt-sleeved politician, while the jurist Wallmann embodied an image of efficiency, dynamism and success. In contrast to
the disastrous traditional image of the city he produced his idea of a
'new Frankfurt'.

To implement this vision he created new symbols, targeted at the
well-educated bourgeoisie. Relying on a wave of sympathy from the
SPD electorate, with the broad support of the media, he launched the
first municipal public–private partnership campaign in the FRG. (The
strategy was later imitated by Lothar Späth, the CDU Prime Minister
of Baden–Württemberg, and Klaus von Dohnanyi, the SPD Lord
Mayor of Hamburg.) An important element of Wallmann's strategy
to 'save' the city of Frankfurt was to create spectacular buildings and
a concentration of cultural facilities right in the city centre. The
reconstruction of the 'Old Opera' was the first step of this programme, acting as an important catalyst to revitalise the city's social
life (Scholz, 1989: 73-82).

The second step was the reconstruction of the eastern side of an
historically prominent location, the Römerberg, which became a
public meeting place and later a tourist attraction. Wallmann's search
for a new image led to a boom in the construction of cultural
buildings. Frankfurt became a German cultural metropolis. In a
synthesis of 'culture and commerce', the city erected between the
Museums Bank on the river Main and the Römerberg an unequalled
concentration of cultural buildings: 22 museums, 80 galleries, 17

theatres and four concert buildings. Such a massive programme of creation of cultural facilities drew the attention of the whole country. The highlights of the programme included: the reconstruction of the Old Opera (1981); the German Museum of Architecture (designed by O.M. Ungers) and the German Museum of Film (by H. Bofinger)(1984); the Museum of Arts and Crafts (by Richard Meier)(1985); the 'Kulturschirn', a building used for international exhibitions (1986); the Jewish Museum (by A. von Kostelac)(1988); the Museum of Anthropology and the Museum of Modern Art (by H. Hollein)(1989) and the Museum of Caricatures (1990) (Schjolz, 1989: 86-7). In 1990 alone, four new museums were opened. Thus Frankfurt began to alter its image from that of an ugly city to a trendsetter of new urban lifestyles (Flagge, 1988: 172).

However, this cultural policy raised political and social opposition and deepened social conflicts. Only the 'new urban middle classes' and wealthy outsiders, not the 'average Frankfurter' benefited from the massive levels of municipal investment in culture and cultural policy. It is doubtful whether Hilmar Hoffmann – Frankfurt City Council's Chief Cultural Policy Officer, with a strong nationwide reputation – reached his goal of avoiding exploiting culture cynically only for the creation of a new image for the city. For example, the budget for neighbourhood-based culture was reorganised and cut back in 1988. The last step in the image improvement campaign was the reformulation of the meaning of the skyline of high rise buildings which distinguishes Frankfurt from other major German cities. International investors and well-known architects entered the scene. Oswald Mathias Ungers' 'Messe-Torhaus' marked a new era of construction and aestheticisation of the fair halls, the latest example of which is the 'Messeturm' by Chicago-based architect Helmut Jahn, with fifty-two storeys and at 254 metres the tallest skyscraper in Europe.

Cultural policy in Hamburg: agencies and goals

Hamburg offers a broad range of facilities covering all kinds of cultural activities and addressing a variety of audiences. It includes amongst its main facilities a state opera and ballet of international reputation; the Schauspielhaus and the Thalia Theatres; several commercial theatres and an 'alternative' stage (the Kampnagel); two children's theatres; seven large history museums; eighty art galleries;

three symphony orchestras; one concert hall and several large and many smaller halls and clubs for popular music concerts; four halls for rock concerts; a 'film house' for young film-makers and producers; a 'media house' for artists working with the electronic media; fifty-six public libraries, in one of the largest systems of urban libraries in the world; two state universities, the University of the Federal Army, and Academies of Economics, Politics, Arts, Music and Architecture; twenty cultural centres at urban district level, aimed at involving local residents in cultural activities.

The most important agency responsible for cultural policy in Hamburg is the Department of Science and Arts (Behörde für Wissenschaft und Kultur). Other agencies include private foundations (e.g., the Körber–Stiftung), several voluntary associations, and many companies and private individuals as sponsors which have sponsored a wide variety of cultural events and activities. The major financial load, however, rests upon the city state. The basic budget figures are given in table 6.7. Between 1980 and 1989 expenditure on culture increased relatively more than the total city budget. However, levels of expenditure were DM96 in 1980 and DM152 in 1989 per capita – a low figure compared with other large cities in Germany.

Given the number and diversity of cultural facilities in the city, cultural policy in Hamburg attempted to cover the full range of cultural institutions and activities. For example, the city state's 1989 policy statement identified a range of ambitious goals which included the following:

- the construction of a new museum for contemporary art at an estimated cost of 50 million DM;
- more financial aid to film producers and financial support for selected cinemas;
- the expansion of the photographic collection of the Museum of Arts and Crafts to make Hamburg the 'capital of photography' in Germany;
- the creation of the Hamburg Cultural Foundation, financed by the public and private sector, to support non-state subsidised cultural activities;
- the creation of a new course in cultural management as a joint venture between the university and arts practitioners;
- new literary prizes and the concentration of subsidies to literary activities on the 'House of Literature', opened in 1989;

Table 6.6: Cultural expenditure by sector in Hamburg, 1985 and 1989 (in thousand DM)

Sector	1985	1989	% Change
Theatre	110,170	132,711	20.15
Public libraries	37,871	40,601	7.2
Museums, planetarium	33,062	38,252	15.7
Music	14,700	15,015	2.1
Film	3,961	7,982	101.5
Landmarks	3,310	4,654	40.6
Urban district culture	4,101	5,613	36.9
Total	218,065	264,516	21.3

Source: Freie und Hansestadt Hamburg, Kulturbehörde, 1989: 58

- the conservation of architectural landmarks;
- the organisation of pop and rock festivals;
- advice and financial aid for the city's three major youth cultural centres (Fabrik, Markthalle, Riekhof);
- the 'Hamburg Summer' – a summer festival comprising all sorts of cultural events, including guest performances in the opera house and the theatres;
- subsidies to twenty neighbourhood-based cultural centres and projects;
- support for women's and ethnic arts groups;
- additional financial support for eight medium-sized cultural centres at urban district level to bring cultural activities to the peripheral housing estates;
- the establishment of the first Cultural Institute of the People's Republic of China in Europe.

This extract from the wide range of cultural policy goals in Hamburg may be impressive. However, no clear priorities were identified for the different spheres or activities. The programme had no time schedule, and almost no cost considerations. As a result, the programme remains vague and vulnerable to political bargaining in the Hamburg parliament.

It is the diversity of activities that characterise the city's cultural policy which prevents Hamburg from coming up with spectacular projects like those of its competitors. Support for the State Opera, the local film industry and for neighbourhood-based culture are the three main features of local cultural policy. They fail, however, to attract tourists.

In short, Hamburg has an attractive cultural profile. However, while Berlin and Munich, as well as Cologne, Dusseldorf, Stuttgart and more recently Frankfurt have attracted much attention, the attractions of Hamburg are relatively little known inside and outside Hamburg itself. Compared with Frankfurt's effort to change the city's image through a broad set of investments in culture, Hamburg may be viewed as the opposite case. The city has an ambivalent attitude and policy towards culture. Economically dominated for a long time by merchants, some of them became significant sponsors of social or cultural facilities, while others distrusted the arts. The latter attitude is documented in the biography of the late Hamburg banker Alvin Münchmeyer *Behind White Facades* (von Viereck, 1988: 57): 'The teachers told us children of merchants to beware of the magic of fine souls as if it were bad magic. The muses remained strange to us. I remember only one member of our school class having a genuine interest in the fine arts – and he did not become a merchant but sought success elsewhere.'

A more recent example of such ambivalence is the conversion of two former flower wholesale market halls into art exhibition halls through the private investment from one of Hamburg's major sponsors, Kurt A. Körber. After the completion of the project in 1989, city officials were worried because they had to pay 1.5m DM per year in upkeep and heating costs. An instructive detail: the name of the sponsor is engraved on a small plate placed in the first building near the door of the toilets. But in front of the building Körber erected a sculpture of the brand mark of his firm.

The chances of developing a clear cultural policy are further reduced by the political goals of factions within both the Social Democrats, the party traditionally governing the city, and the Greens, both arguing against 'establishment' culture, and favouring 'alternative' or urban district cultural facilities. It is perhaps this strange alliance of merchant culture, the left-wing faction of the ruling Social Democrats, and the grassroots movements that prevent Hamburg from developing a distinctive cultural policy.

In 1983, the first lord mayor and prime minister of the city state, Klaus von Dohnanyi – the brother of the conductor of the Philadelphia Orchestra – took up the idea of the city as an enterprise. His concept of 'Enterprise Hamburg' was set forth to push the city into national and European competition. In addition to a shift away from port-oriented industries and new goals for urban planning

Table 6.7: Visitors, total expenditure and expenditure per visitor for selected public opera houses and theatres,[a] 1988–89

City	Visitors	Expenditure in 000s DM	Expenditure per visitor (DM)
Berlin	632,064	129,930	205.6
Hamburg	957,827	145,681	152.1
München	941,083	192,125	204.1
Köln	458,241	85,270	186.1
Frankfurt	253,150	94,525	373.4
Stuttgart	503,195	104,662	208.0

Note: [a] Berlin: State Opera and State Theatres (Deutsche Oper, Staatliches Schauspiel); Hamburg: State Opera and State Theatres (Schauspielhaus, Thalia-Theater); München: State Opera and State Theatres (Staatstheater Gärtnerplatz, Staatsschauspiel, Münchener Kammerspiele); Köln: City Opera and City Theatres (Bühnen der Stadt Köln); Frankfurt: City Opera and City Theatres (Städtische Bühnen), Stuttgart: State Theatre (Staatstheater).

Source: Personal Information provided by the editor of the Statistical Yearbook, published by the Deutscher Stadtetage.

(Dangschat and Ossenbrügge, 1990), he brought into the debate the role of culture as a vehicle for economic growth. Despite high levels of municipal debt the budget for culture was increased (see table 6.7), and a series of arts festivals were organised. Neighbourhood-based events and activities and – as a national niche – the musical were selected as cultural forms particularly worthy of support.

In 1986 the musical Cats, by British composer Andrew Lloyd Webber, had started successfully. Von Dohnanyi, Lloyd Webber, and a German investor decided to establish a second musical theatre for another Webber musical, The Phantom of the Opera. They agreed to choose as the site for a new theatre the Flora, a building that had in the 1920s been a workers' entertainment and variety hall, but at that time was used as a department store. Located within an urban renewal area, it was reconstructed for its new purpose. Protests by neighbourhood residents, craftsmen and shopkeepers fearing gentrification, supported by left-wing grassroot movements, led to a series of harsh and violent clashes between these groups and politicians and urban planners, which were not resolved by the use of the police force to secure the start of the reconstruction work. The investor and the municipal administration finally gave up the plan and constructed a new theatre building several hundred metres away from the initial site. The future use of the old Flora building, n⸴ simply a facade, is still being debated.

Irrespective of the lack of a coherent cultural policy, Hamburg in the last three years has experienced a remarkable economic growth. In the wake of the creation of the single market in 1992 and the 1990 unification of Germany, Hamburg presently has a booming economy, as considerable investment into new buildings demonstrates. The city's leading urban planner, Egbert Kossak, identified architecture as the main factor shaping the city's image. A further spin-off of the new policy of 'Enterprise Hamburg' was the renovation of the fair halls, an impressive enlargement of the system of indoor shopping malls and the construction of various hotels. Economic dynamism is most obvious in the 'City South'. Within only two years all parcels of land in this area turned into sites for the construction of new office space. Empty or run-down parts of the port area and particularly the northern bank of the river are also being re-used.

A specific feature of cultural policy in many large West German cities are neighbourhood-oriented cultural policy programmes, described by the term 'urban district culture' (UDC). Although definitions of UDC vary among city administrations (Kreissig and Grabbe, 1987; Mildenberger, 1987; Sauberzweig, 1974) they have two objectives in common: education and participation. The educational objective is to bring culture to people in an urban neighbourhood, to stimulate the interest of those who otherwise would not visit a 'high' cultural event. The participatory aspect is to encourage people to express their creative and artistic abilities in small groups, with few of the barriers often associated with highbrow culture.

The following quotations from two officials in Cologne and Hamburg respectively are indicative of these objectives:

'in his or her neighbourhood, the citizen is most likely to be interested in participating in cultural activities. Therefore it is in that context that the promotion of cultural development can best be achieved' (Uhlig, 1986: 17).

'Cultural production has to be decentralised to help those people who have for various reasons been excluded from participating in the collectively created richness of culture' (Freie und Hansestadt Hamburg, Kulturbehörde, 1982: 4).

Many German cities have launched UDC programmes and Hamburg was one of the first. Table 6.8 describes the increase in expenditure for UDC and for cultural policy as a whole. The UDC has a small but disproportionately growing percentage of the total cultural policy budget.

Table 6.8: Cultural expenditure by the city-state of Hamburg 1980, 1985 and 1989

	1980	1985	1989
Total budget (in thousand DM)	11,345,010	12,349,247	13,747,330
Cultural policy	173,342	218,365	285,600
% of total budget	1.5%	1.8%	2.1%
DM/inhabitant	105	138	178
Urban district culture	571	4,101	8,232
% of cultural policy budget	0.3%	1.9%	2.9%
DM/inhabitant	0.35	2.58	5.12

Source: Freie und Hansestadt Hamburg, Kulturbehörde, 1989: 57. Information supplied by City-State of Hamburg, Department of Culture, August 1990.

UDC is a sensitive instrument for cultural policy-making. It comprises many activities often excluded from the traditional cultural institutions. They range from meetings of political groups, guitar classes, language courses, belly-dance courses and pottery to research on the history of the urban district or neighbourhood. It is 'culture from the bottom', in contrast with 'highbrow' or 'representative' culture. It is estimated that in 1988 at least 500,000 people participated in UDC activities (Freie und Hansestadt Hamburg, Kulturbehörde, 1989: 49). If we classify organisers and participants by their residence, we arrive at the following matrix:

		Residence of audience	
		Local neighbourhood	Other
Residence of	Local neighbourhood	A	B
organisers	Other	C	D

The political goals of UDC are directed towards activities of type A, but as the facilities grow and become more attractive, the catchment area increases, and the appeal of the facilities moves to cell D. This interpretation is supported by a pilot study carried out in two districts of Hamburg by Mildenburger (1987). Hence, it remains difficult to evaluate the extent to which UDC fulfils its locally directed goals and attracts people who would otherwise not participate in cultural activities.

Conclusion: the impacts of cultural policy

In contrast to many assumptions on the positive effects of cultural policy on the location of companies, its precise impact is not yet clear. Only a few studies in Germany have addressed this question. Henckel et al. (1986) interviewed 140 executives in 110 companies belonging to different industries, while the Kommunalverband Ruhr (Skrodzki, 1989) surveyed 74 managers of companies in the Ruhr area. Three conclusions emerge from these studies.

First, 'culture' – even if it is growing in its significance is not among the location factors given a high priority by the surveyed managers. For example, in the study by Henckel et al. (1986: 143-55) culture was given rank three as a location factor after 'transport accessibility' and 'labour market', but this result is somewhat obscured by the fact that the authors subsumed 'culture' into the broad category 'residential value and leisure quality'.

Second, the range and quality of cultural facilities influence a city's image. In the survey by the Kommunalverband Ruhr, 69 per cent of the managers interviewed regarded urban cultural facilities as an important contribution to the image and quality of life of a city (Skrodzki, 1989: 85).

Third, cultural facilities are judged as important for attracting companies with highly educated and skilled personnel. The more an enterprise has to rely upon the human capital of its employees, the more it depends upon this 'soft' location factor. This conclusion is corroborated by a further finding: 30 per cent of the managers from companies in the secondary sector view 'culture' as an important location factor as opposed to 50 per cent of companies in the services sector (Skrodzki, 1989: 87). The assumption underlying the importance of culture for employees is that companies need skills and creative personnel, and culture is an important source of creativity, innovation and education – a view shared by several authors (Benkert, 1989: 35; Gerwien and Holzhauser, 1989: 105; Henckel et al., 1986; Skrodzki, 1989: 87). Although these findings are based on small samples, we assume that the convergence of their results indicates their validity.

A further dimension of the impacts of cultural policy concerns tourism development. Again, the empirical evidence is insufficient to allow for an exact assessment of the importance of culture to expand tourism and tourist expenditure. We can only attempt to compare

Table 6.9: Number of visitors staying overnight, 1980 and 1989

City	1980 Absolute (000s)	per 1,000 inhab.	1989 abs. (000s)	per 1,000 inhab.	% Change 1980-89 (1,000 inhab.)
Berlin	1,344	707	2,398	1,159	63.9%
Hamburg	1,619	980	1,971	1,230	25.5%
Munich	2,535	1,950	3,302	2,725	39.7%
Cologne	787	806	1,181	1,260	56.3%
Frankfurt	1,594	2,538	1,961	3,136	23.6%
Stuttgart	465	799	562	998	24.9%

Sources: Statistisches Taschenbuch der Freien und Hansestadt Hamburg 1981: 111; 1989: 131.

Table 6.10: Number of overnight stays, 1980 and 1989

City	1980 Absolute (000s)	1,000 inhab.	1989 Absolute (000s)	1,000 inhab.	% Change 1989-90 (1,000 inhab)
Berlin	3,451	1,820	6,581	3,182	74.8%
Hamburg	2,922	1,768	3,787	2,362	33.6%
Munich	5,307	4,083	6,597	5,445	33.3%
Cologne	1,618	1,657	2,367	2,524	52.3%
Frankfurt	2,954	4,702	3,506	5,607	19.2%
Stuttgart	1,176	2,020	1,203	2,137	5.8%

Sources: Statistisches Taschenbuch der Freien und Hansestadt Hamburg 1981: 111; 1989: 131.

the attractiveness of the six cities under consideration. Three indicators are used: the number of visitors staying overnight, the total number of overnight stays, and the hotel occupancy rate (tables 6.9, 6.10 and 6.11).

The average duration of stay (in days) was 2.9 for Berlin, 2.1 for Munich and Stuttgart, 1.9 for Hamburg and Cologne, and 1.8 for Frankfurt. Thus Hamburg was faring better than Frankfurt, but still worse than all the other cities compared here. This is further documented by the data in table 6.11. Although in Hamburg the number of hotel beds increased, the average duration of stay fluctuated and the peak was in 1981 (for a more detailed analysis see Walter, 1989).

We can conclude from these data that Hamburg did attract many tourists, but they stayed for a comparatively short period. Hence, Hamburg seems to be less attractive to tourists than the other five

Table 6.11: Occupancy rate of hotel beds and average duration of stay, Hamburg, 1980-89

Year	No. of available beds	Rate (%)	Average duration of stay (days)
1980	16,597	48.2	1.87
1981	17,240	47.8	1.95
1982	19,393	42.1	1.92
1983	19,007	41.9	1.87
1984	18,758	41.1	1.92
1985	19,378	43.1	1.89
1986	19,208	42.7	1.84
1987	20,046	43.7	1.84
1988	21,172	45.9	1.90
1989	20,861[a]	49.0	1.92

Note: [a]Number of beds available reduced due to occupancy by Germans from Poland and Romania, and by migrants from the GDR.

Sources: Statistisches Taschenbuch für die Freie und Hansestadt Hamburg, 1982: 119, 120; 1984: 110; 1985: 121-3; 1986: 126, 127; 1989: 130, 131; additional information from the Hamburg Statistical Agency.

cities. This fact is well known to municipal officials in Hamburg, but so far has had little consequence in policy terms. The inadequate reorganisation of 'Hamburg Tourism', the major agency for city promotion – is further proof of Hamburg's inertia or, as some describe it, complacency. The city possesses neither a clear marketing concept nor consensus around such a concept. The advantages of Hamburg have yet to be discovered and are not the object of aggressive marketing campaigns such as those mounted by Berlin or Frankfurt.

With respect to the role of culture for urban regeneration, our analysis, and especially the two contrasting examples of Hamburg and Frankfurt, point to three conclusions. First, economic growth can be induced without a clear cultural policy and spectacular new buildings for culture, as the Hamburg case seems to indicate. Second, cultural policy can dramatically improve the image of a city both for its residents and for outside entrepreneurs. Third, most probably investment in culture is not a major factor for the success of urban regeneration strategies. But given fairly equal economic opportunities in many large cities, investment in culture may still be a crucial factor in inter-metropolitan competition.

References

Behr, V., Gnad, F. and Kunzmann, K. R. (eds) (1989) 'Kultur, Wirtschaft, Stadtentwicklung' ('Culture, economy and development'), *Dortmunder Beiträge zur Raumplanung*, 51, Dortmund, IRPUD.

Benkert, W. (1989) *Zur Kritik der Umwegrentabilitätsrechnungen im Kulturbereich* (Towards a Critique of Fiscal Rentability Calculations in the Cultural Sector), pp. 29-36, in Behr *et al.* (1989).

Dangschat, J. S. and Ossenbrüge, J. (1990) 'Hamburg: crisis management, urban regeneration and Social Democrats', in D. Judd and M. Parkinson (eds), *Political Leadership and Urban Regeneration*, Sage, Urban Annual Reviews.

Deutscher Städtetag (ed.) (1973) *Rettet unsere Städte jetzt!* (Save our Cities Now!), Cologne, Deutscher Städtetag.

Farni, K. H. (1985) *Die Pumpe der Republik* (The Pump of the Republic), Frankfurt, Merian.

Flagge, I. (1988) 'Zwischen Moloch Stadt und Stadt als Heimat' ('Between the monster city and the city as a home'), in Hauff (ed.) (1988).

Frey, B. S. and Pomerehne, W. W. (1989) 'Staatliche Föderung von Kunst und Kultur: Eine ökonomische Betrachtung' (Governmental subsidies for arts and culture: an economic view) in Behr *et al.* (1989).

Friedrichs, J., Häussermann, H. and Siebel, W. (eds) (1986) *Süd-Nord Gefälle in der Bundesrepublik?* (South-North Gradient in the FRG?), Opladen, Westdeutscher Verlag.

Gans, H. J. (1974) *Popular Culture and High Culture*, New York, Basic Books.

Gerwien, J. and Holzhauser, I. (1988) *Wirtschaftsfördernde Aspekte kommunaler Kulturangebote am Beispiel der Stadt Neuss* (Aspects of Economic Development through Municipal Cultural Facilities: the Case of Neuss) University of Bremen, Department of Geography.

Gerwien, J. and Holzhauser, I. (1989) *Kultur und Wirtschaftsförderung in Neuss* (Culture and Economic Development in Neuss), in Behr *et al.* (1989).

Hauff, V. (ed.) (1988) *Stadt und Lebenstil. Thema: Stadtkultur* (City and Lifestyle: Theme: Urban Culture), Weinheim & Basel, Bletz.

Häussermann, H. and Siebel, W. (1987) *Neue Urbanität* (New Urbanity), Frankfurt, Suhrkamp.

Henckel, D., Grabow, W., Knopf, C., Raunch, N. and Regitz, W. (1986) *Produktionstechnologien und Raumentwicklung* (Technologies of Production and Regional Development), Stuttgart, Kohlhammer.

Herterich, F. (1988) *Urbanität – Stadtstyling oder Kultur des Widerspruchs?* (Urbanity – Urban Styling or Culture of Contradiction?) in Hauff, V. (ed.) (1988).

Hummel, M. and Berger, M. (1988) *Die volkswirtschaftliche Bedeutung von Kunst und Kultur* (The National Economic Significance of Culture), Berlin-Mühchen: Dunker & Humblot.

Jager, M. (1986) 'Class definition and the esthetics of gentrification: Victoriana in Melbourne', in N. Smith and P. Williams (eds), *Gentrification of the City Boston*, Allen & Unwin.

Koch, H. *et al.* (1986) 'Kultur und Ungleichheit' ('Culture and inequalities'), in H. W. Franz, W. Kruse and H. G. Rolff (eds) (1986) *Neue alte Ungleichheiten* (New Old Inequalities), Opladen, Westdeutscher Verlag.

Kreissig, G. and Grabbe, J. (1987) *Kultur vor Ort* (Local Culture), Stuttgart, Kohlhammer.

Kunzmann, K.R. (1988) 'Kultur – Wirtschaft – Stadtentwicklung: Eine Einführung' ('Culture – economy – urban development: an introduction'), in Behr *et al.* (eds) (1989).

Mildenberger, U. (1987) 'Stadtteilkultur in Hamburg' ('Urban district culture in Hamburg'), Hamburg, Department of Sociology (unpublished diploma thesis).

Port Authority of New York and New Jersey (1983) *The Arts as an Industry: Their Economic Importance to the New York – New Jersey Metropolitan Region* New York, The Port Authority of NY & NJ.

Sauberzweig, D. (1988) 'Die wichtigste Chance überhaupt' ('The main chance'), *Die Deutsche Bühne*, 9.

Sauberzweig, D. (1989) 'Fragen an eine Kulturpolitik der Stadt' ('Problems of an urban cultural policy'), *Universitas* 6.

Scholz, C. (1989) *Frankfurt – eine Stadt wird verkauft (Frankfurt – A City for Sale)*, Frankfurt am Main, ISP–Verlag.

Skrodzki, B. (1989) 'Stadtenwicklung und Kultur im Ruhrgebiet aus der Sicht von Geschäftsführern von Unternehmen' ('Urban Development and Culture in the Ruhr: the Views of Managers and Entrepreneurs'), in Behr *et al.* (1989).

Staatliche Pressestelle der Freien und Hansestadt Hamburg (ed.) (1982) *Stadtteilkultur in Hamburg* ('Urban District Culture in Hamburg'), Hamburg, Staatliche Pressestelle, 27.

Staatliche Pressestelle der Freien und Hansestadt Hamburg (ed.) (1989). *Kulturkonzept '89 (Culture Concept '89)*, Hamburg, Staatliche Pressestelle.

Taubmann, W. and Behrens, F. (1986) *Wirtschaftliche Auswirkungen von Kulturangeboten in Bremen (Economic Impacts of Cultural Facilities in Bremen)*, University of Bremen, Department of Geography.

Uhlig, K.R. (1986) 'Ein neuer Begriff von Kultur' ('A new meaning of culture') *Stadt*, 3, 17-21.

von Viereck, S. (1988) *Hinter weissen Fassaden (Behind White Facades)*, Reinbeck, Rowohlt.

Walter, E. (1989) 'Tourismus in Hamburg' ('Tourism in Hamburg', *Hamburg in Zahlen*, 12.

Whitt, J. A. (1987) 'Mozart in the metropolis: the arts coalition and the urban growth machine', *Urban Affairs Quarterly*, 23.

7

Montpellier: international competition and community access

Emmanuel Negrier

Introduction[1]

The city of Montpellier has grown dramatically both economically and demographically during the past three decades. In the mid 1950s it had a population of about 90,000 inhabitants. By 1990 it had risen to almost 210,000. The metropolitan area experienced an even faster increase, rising from 100,000 to 300,000 in the same period. This was one of the largest demographic increases in western Europe, although it is not all that exceptional for the south of France. This increase is due to large-scale immigration mainly from other regions of France and especially from the Paris region. Eighty per cent of today's inhabitants of Montpellier were not born there.

Apart from the general appeal of the south of France, four factors explain Montpellier's rapid growth. The first was the influx of repatriates from Algeria in 1962 who made a significant contribution to the revival of local business. The second was the process of administrative devolution begun by the reforms of 1964, and followed up between 1982 and 1984 by decentralisation legislation. Montpellier, which until then was hardly distinguishable from the other cities in the Languedoc region, for example, Nîmes and Béziers, was elevated to the rank of regional capital. This allowed the city to attract an important number of tertiary functions often at the expense of its neighbours.

The third factor was the decision taken by IBM in 1965 to set up in Montpellier a factory producing a range of mainframe computers. This had far-reaching consequences, especially in terms of the number of jobs created. Three thousand were directly created and another 2,000 originated from new local firms which dealt with IBM. But above all the alteration of the sociological profile of the town brought about the establishment of a managerial class which was strongly characterised by its allegiance to the 'enterprise culture'. Lastly, Montpellier built upon its university tradition with a rapid expansion in the number of university employees and students from the beginning of the 1960s. There are now over 30,000 students in a population of 300,000. Other cities experienced some of these factors. But Montpellier was one of the few to experience them all at the same time and during such a relatively brief period.

The character of the city has profoundly changed during recent decades. During the Second Empire at the end of the nineteenth century, Montpellier went through a particularly extravagant phase of its economic history as a result of the impetus given to the city by the viticultural monoculture in the Languedoc. This provided high incomes and gave rise to a remarkable sense of financial well-being. However, the crises caused by over-production in the wine sector, as well as by the phylloxera epidemics and the introduction of American plants, became increasingly serious as the decades went by. The city became progressively listless, eking out an existence on the remains of its former viticultural wealth and the memories of its university tradition. Parallel to this, the cultural tradition of the second half of the nineteenth century – especially that of the music-loving *habitués* of the Opera who came not only from the more fortunate classes but also from the ranks of the lower middle classes – was lost.

By the 1960s demand for culture had become rather weak. At this time the cultural policy of the city had two broad strands. The first was to purchase entertainments – touring theatrical performances and concerts, for example – which provided no support for local productions. The second was mainly to organise contemporary visual arts exhibitions, because of the combination of a deputy mayor who was an enlightened amateur of the fine arts and a number of groups amongst the local middle classes who were interested in some of the artists coming out of the Ecole des Beaux-Arts.

During the 1960s the gradual fading of the city's viticultural heritage, the fact that the university was shaken up from top to bottom by the events of May 1968, the rapid increase in the student body and the influx of new population began to change this situation. Amongst those inhabitants of Montpellier who had not been born there, the new managerial class and University lecturers were especially dissatisfied with the type of cultural products on offer. Their frustration stimulated similar responses among the local middle classes.

These cultural disenchantments entered the political domain of Montpellier between 1976 and 1977. As in many other towns across France, 1977 brought in its wake a considerable shift of power, mainly to the advantage of the left. François Delmas, mayor of eighteen years standing, a member of the Government, centre-right, lawyer and excellent representative of the local middle classes, was beaten by Georges Frêche. He was deputy for the Socialists at the head of the list of the Union de la Gauche, a university lecturer, and a local man born in Toulouse. One of the major themes of his campaign, which undoubtedly attracted the votes of the managerial class and of the university lecturers, was his series of widely disseminated proposals for cultural policy.

In fact, this cultural theme was a common feature of the political rhetoric used by the left to attract voters throughout almost every town in France in the 1977 municipal elections.[2] There were, however, significant modifications to the way in which it was used in Montpellier. In addition to the impulse given by the decentralisation of administration and public facilities, there were two related developments: a coherent strategy for image-making and an integrated economic development strategy for the city based on cultural policy.

Decentralisation as the driving force for cultural development

To understand the importance of cultural policy in the strategy of left-wing groups intent on gaining municipal power, it is necessary to understand the political context in which they are situated. Montpellier was at the time of the 1977 local elections in a curious position, in that although the city was classically right-wing, the surrounding area – the Midi Rouge – was strongly left-wing.[3] As in the case of Rennes after 1977,[4] the regional capital was politically atypical of the region. The other towns – Béziers, Nîmes and Sète, for example, the departments (Gard and Aude) and the Etablissement Public Régional were all dominated by the Socialist and Communist parties. The elections of 1983 totally reversed this situation. The city of Montpellier, which was won by the left in 1977, proved the exception in an urban system controlled by the right.

The city has been marked by a significant shift in its population and by the expansion of the new strata of middle-income wage earners. These socio-political elements occurred with slightly different emphases, in both Rennes and Montpellier. The major disparity lies in the role of culture in the two cities' strategies before 1977. As Patrick Le Gales demonstrates[5] in Rennes the Christian Democratic administration developed a 'modernist' cultural policy in keeping with the trajectory of the city's social evolution. The policies pursued in Montpellier by the municipal government before 1977, on the other hand, aimed to achieve respectability without making any attempt at innovation. The municipal representatives, who were mainly representatives of the local establishment, continued to increase the standing of traditional cultural institutions such as the Museum, the Library, the School of Fine Arts, the Academy of Music. In 1977 these institutions accounted for two thirds of the cultural policy budget.

No attempt was made to decentralise amenities into outlying districts. No consideration was given to how to breathe life into local culture. In cultural terms Montpellier began to lag further and further behind other urban centres in France endowed with more imaginative municipal governments, like Rennes or Grenoble. There was a substantial political distance between Montpellier's urban leadership and the demands for reform which stemmed from the left.

Cultural policy: a democratic hotchpotch?

After 1977, the new left municipal government endorsed the construction of an urban cultural strategy in keeping with the demands of its supporters. Relying strongly on numerous theatre groups banded together in an organisation known as *action pour le jeune théâtre* and on movements emphasising regional identity, the new administration developed a cultural policy radically different from that of its predecessors. These new policies were inspired directly by three objectives: the decentralisation of cultural activities and facilities, cultural animation, and the democratisation of cultural policy-making.

The first of these objectives was symbolised by the setting up of the Maisons pour tous. These multi-purpose institutions, of which fifteen were built, were designed to house under one roof a spectrum of neighbourhood-based cultural, sporting and leisure activities. From 1977 to 1981, the total amount allocated to the implementation of this policy was comparable to expenditure on all other cultural amenities. The Maisons pour tous took up a significant

Table 7.1: Montpellier City Council's expenditure on the Maison pour tous as a percentage of its total capital expenditure on culture (FF)

	Maisons pour tous	Other cultural amenities[a]	%
1978	700,000	1,260,000	55.5
1979	2,200,000	2,897,000	75.9
1980	2,551,000	4,390,000	58.1
1981	4,666,000	8,350,000	55.9
1982	2,990,000	16,820,000	17.8
1983	3,790,000	15,310,000	24.8
1984	2,192,000	15,100,000	14.5
1985	885,000	35,960,000	2.5

Note: [a] Museum, library, Academy of Music, Art School, theatre, concert halls.

Source: All data contained in the tables illustrating this chapter have been provided to the author by Montpellier City Council, by the District of the Agglomeration of Montpellier, by the Department of the Hérault and by the Regional Council of Languedoc–Roussillon.

proportion of the total budget set aside for culture. Table 7.1 clearly shows the rapidity with which priorities changed after the 1981. These changes cannot be explained by the fact that the programme of creating new cultural buildings had ended – the number of maisons pour tous increased from eight to fifteen between 1985 and 1990. They indicate a shift in policy objectives.

The second objective, promoting cultural animation, was implemented by increasing municipal support to theatre groups, who had given an important contribution to the victory of the left in the local elections at Montpellier. Another way of implementing this objective was to support the organisation of new cultural events. For example, the first Mediterranean, Jewish and Chinese film and dance festivals, for example, were held in Montpellier. Promoting events such as these, however, takes up only a small proportion of the city's budget.

The third objective, the democratisation of cultural policy-making was, however, rather forgotten. The cultural policy of Montpellier included proposals for the establishment of a Direction Municipale de la Culture to bring together officials, artistic directors and the general public to define the objectives of local cultural policy. However, this Direction never saw the light of day. Similarly, a project designed to allow local people in the city's different districts to participate in making decisions about cultural provision was also abandoned.

In retrospect, the first stages in the development of the new cultural policies were characterised by three elements. Firstly, they

Table 7.2: Theatre groups: subsidies by Montpellier City Council towards running costs

1975	1,179,000 FF
1976	1,256,000 FF
1977	1,400,000 FF
1978	2,536,000 FF
1979	8,529,000 FF
1980	9,941,000 FF
1981	11,652,000 FF
1982	18,965,000 FF
1983	26,486,000 FF
1984	29,100,000 FF
1985	31,372,000 FF

were part of an attempt to implement a political programme which combined a number of different objectives: a significant expansion of the cultural 'menu' on offer, the decentralisation and democratisation of access to culture, and the renaissance of regional identity. The first two goals, in general, have been reached. The last two have largely been left aside. Secondly, cultural policies were aimed at identifying local needs and at attempting to satisfy them on the spot. It was in this spirit that theatre groups received heavy financial support (see table 7.2). Finally, the attention given by the media to cultural policy was relatively poor and no systematic attempt at policy co-ordination was made. The city's mayor, G. Frêche, described this phase of cultural policy-making as one of 'do it yourself'.[6]

The region's institutional resources

The considerable increase in Montpellier's cultural budget required a search for new methods of financing it. In this respect, the previous municipal policy left the new municipal team with considerable room for manoeuvre. The preceding approach, that of the bonus pater familias, which had consisted of an almost obsessional desire to balance the books and a systematic refusal to borrow money, left open the possibility of raising substantial sums on credit. On this basis the size of the budget for culture, like that for other policy sectors, was increased.

The evolution of the cultural budget in Montpellier can be seen in table 7.3.

Table 7.3: Increase in Montpellier City Council's expenditure allocated to culture, 1978-81 (in francs per inhabitant)

	1978	1981	%
Capital expenditure	12.9	65.7	+251.3
Revenue expenditure	112.3	249.7	+ 53.0
Total expenditure	125.2	315.4	+ 64.0
Proportion of budget allocated to culture	7.1%	10.67%	+ 50.3

Table 7.4: Proportion of the regional cultural budget allocated to Montpellier (%)

1975	1976	1977	1978	1979	1980
0	0	27.7	15.6	24.6	35.6

One effect of the change in the composition of the political majority in the municipality was to give the city access to the budget of the Conseil Régional, which was of the same political colour. The financial assistance given by the Conseil Régional, consisting of five departments, was important. Indeed, the proportion of its cultural budget which the Conseil Régional allocated to the city of Montpellier indicates that cultural development in Montpellier was one of their highest priorities (see table 7.4).

The regional priority given to Montpellier was all the more important since the State played no major role in financing the city's cultural policy.

Cultural policy as a communication strategy

In this highly favourable institutional climate, Montpellier undertook a considerable reorientation of its cultural policy. The significant increase in the cultural policy budget has already been identified. Tables 7.1 and 7.2 show the change which occurred in 1982 in the provision of cultural amenities and their funding. They also demonstrate that the proportion spent on decentralising culture continued to decline in favour of more structurally significant cultural facilities. This trend marked the coming of age of the new municipal cultural policy and of the social groups which had brought the new team to power. However, the shifts which took place after 1981 similarly indicate the failure of left-wing groups to establish a strong self-identity and a regionalist dynamic for 'popular culture' in the city.[7] The latter, after having personified a power-wielding alternative, had become – in their own turn – out of touch with the aspirations of the majority of the new urban social strata.

Cultural symbols and their construction

As a result of these changes, cultural policy adopted a dual approach in its search for greater recognition. First of all, this was represented by the recruitment, without discrimination in favour of local people, of leading personalities in their particular specialities to work in the city.[8] Dominique Bagouet in dance, Jérôme Savary in the theatre, and Cyril Diederich in music were all 'stars' before their arrival in Montpellier. With them, culture in Montpellier took on an 'image' aimed as much at the outside world as at the local population. A strategy of public communication including advertisements placed in national and international magazines and posters, which took up 1 per cent of the municipal budget, accompanied cultural policy in the city's effort to refocus its external image.[9]

This change illustrates one of the curious paradoxes of decentralisation in France during the 1980s. The philosophy of devolving power from the centre was accompanied by an inverse tendency to recruit those with specialist talents and abilities from national level, often from Paris itself. The director of Montpellier's Corum Conference Centre was the former director of the Palais des Congrès in Paris. The director of Cultural Affairs in Montpellier came from the Beaubourg cultural centre in Paris.

This decision to exploit the media-worthy dimension of culture explains the astonishing increase in cultural policy expenditure. The cost of these operations was unprecedented. The support given to the *maisons pur tous* was maintained, as was the support given to the smaller arts groups and cultural associations. But the major efforts were directed towards those spectacular events which could be exported and which could distinguish the city in the eyes of the outside world.[10] Initiatives of this kind included: the provision of additional funding for film festivals and a new emphasis on their 'international' character; the birth of international music and dance festivals; the establishment of dance companies and of a theatre of national and

Table 7.5: Budget of the Orchestra Montpellier/Languedoc–Roussillon

Year	Total cost	State contribution	Local contributions (city, department, region)
1980	3,800,000		3,800,000
1981	5,500,000	400,000	5,100,000
1982	12,000,000	2,165,000	9,835,000
1983	17,500,000	3,460,000	14,040,000
1984	19,000,000	6,300,000	12,700,000
1985	21,855,000	7,215,000	14,640,000
1986	22,880,000	7,505,000	15,375,000

Note: Local contributions by Montpellier City Council, the Department de l'Hérault, and the Regional Council of Languedoc–Roussillon

international repute; the expansion of funding for the orchestra of Montpellier/Languedoc–Roussillon. The orchestra's financial stability was guaranteed by a contract whereby the state undertook to provide, together with the city, 50 per cent of the annual budget, with the region providing the other 50 per cent (see table 7.5).

The second aspect of the new strategy concerned the creation of new physical infrastructures. Besides the creation of a new theatre – the Grammont – two other prestigious projects were begun towards the end of this period. The Zenith, a flexible concert hall concept capable of accommodating the largest rock concerts and variety shows, together with other mass spectacles, was copied from the model of the Zenith in Paris. From the moment it was opened, it placed the city of Montpellier on the map as one of the main venues for international entertainments. The Corum Conference Centre and Opera House was built in the heart of the old town. It was designed to fulfil the dual role of accommodating conferences and, with its second hall of 2,000 places, staging operatic and musical perform-ances. It is equipped to accommodate film and music festivals. In contrast with the Opera at the Bastille, which does not have the dual role of the Corum, and which is entirely state financed, Montpellier's conference centre is mainly supported by the municipality.[11]

The city's new cultural policy was closely related to the impera-tives of inter-urban competition. A broader cultural policy provided Montpellier with the ability to offer a larger range of cultural services directed at new social strata. This perspective was the first indication of the link between cultural and economic development strategies. Culture in Montpellier is aimed at managers and economic decision-makers in those industrial sectors which are no longer tied to the proximity of natural resources – service industries, research, computers. The strategy has worked. Besides the natural attractions of the site which included the Mediterranean Sea and the sun, and the presence of a university with 50,000 students, the cultural environment has become one of the principal factors which have induced firms to locate in Montpellier in great numbers in the past decade.

The cabling of the city

In 1985 Montpellier City Council began the process of cabling the city. Superficially, Montpellier's policy towards cable forms part of the provision of a range of purely cultural services: an increase in the number of television programmes and the development of regional productions. But in capital expenditure terms, it was an experiment well in advance of its time. The technology used was highly sophisticated – using optical fibres. Cable formed part of the essential infrastructure for a modern economic environment seeking to attract technologically sophisticated firms.

Montpellier City Council attempted to give its cable policy a social dimension. Cable was targeted at two geographical areas: the Antigone quarter built by Spanish architect Ricardo Bofill, the jewel in the crown of Montpellier's urban renewal, and La Paillade. La Paillade is a zone á urbaniser en priorité (priority zone for urbanisation), created at the beginning of the 1960s in response to the demographic expansion of the city, especially the influx of the repatriates from Algeria. Conceived initially as a relatively small zone, its population considerably increased and is now more than double that originally planned. Isolated from the town, both geographically and socially, it has a large immigrant population, with low incomes and a higher rate of unemployment than the Montpellier average. La Paillade has many of the characteristics of an urban ghetto.

The 'social dimension' of cabling was one aspect of the municipality's desire to break down urban isolation through the adoption of technical policies for public communications, transport and culture. The logic of this policy was also powerful from a commercial point of view. The less economically favoured strata are precisely those which are oriented towards audio visual forms of home-based cultural consumption, rather than live entertainment. The take-up for cable in Montpellier shows the accuracy of this analysis, since La Paillade leads the rest of the city in this regard.

However, the municipal strategy for the social, cultural and economic integration of cable, at least for the moment, has not been entirely successful. The municipality's controversial decision to use France-Telecom, a public utility, and the complex nature of the local authority's relationship with its private partners, have neither allowed the creation of a network accessible to local firms, nor developed a local programme-making industry. Even in terms of the more modest objective of encouraging local subscriptions, the network has stagnated at around 15 per cent of residents. The elected representatives are attempting to overcome this failure by developing a 'Concorde strategy'. Underlying the weakness in the demand for cable, which they hope is only temporary, this strategy is intended to enable Montpellier policy-makers to project the image of a city in the forefront of the new communication technologies.

The creation of the pole Antenna comprising interactive cable TV and other kinds of new media, together with four other poles responds to this objective. For the moment, Antenna has only managed to provide a new base for activities which were already in existence, and for a few small and medium-sized firms specialised in electronic images and telecommunication services. On the other hand, the creation of a Studio International d'Images in 1985, which should have been available to film crews and for post-production work has proved a total failure.

In short, the strategic shifts in communications policy reflect the overall changes in the city's cultural policy. The interaction between local artists and urban cultural movements should have resulted in the development of a local television with a difference, a tool for creativity and local democracy. This objective was quickly abandoned in favour of a 'privatist' and standardised conception of television.[12]

Cultural policy and local economic development

The links between these two kinds of public policy would seem to be a matter of common sense. As the city's Mayor, G. Frêche has written:

The function of the cultural life of a technopolis is to provide a good reason for firms to locate there. European cities are all competing with each other. The rivals of Montpellier are not only Grenoble, Lyons, Toulouse, Aix,

Marseille, Nice, but also Milan, Birmingham, and Munich. At the moment
of deciding where to locate ... a firm will make its choice on the basis of
minor details, such as the quality of urban development, sports facilities and
cultural life.[13]

One definition of local economic development is the mobilisation of
latent resources in the urban social fabric to produce economic
innovation. However, in Montpellier, these resources came mainly
from the outside and had not previously been part of the traditional
urban fabric.[14] But sectors with an essentially symbolic dimension,
such as culture, constitute a possible means of achieving the
integration of the 'new inhabitants of Languedoc' into the urban
fabric. This explains why cultural policy was the first policy area to
be brought to the forefront in the institutional collaboration between
the cities of Nîmes and Montpellier.

The recomposition of institutional alliances

The change of the political majority in the Conseil Régional in 1986
was an event of exceptional importance in cultural policy
development. The shift to the right in the regional government of
Languedoc reopened the issue over the distribution of regional
funding which had characterised earlier periods. The withdrawal of
support from regional government for Montpellier's cultural
policies, although gradual, has been nonetheless striking. Conflicts
over the management of the regional orchestra, its local activities and
its means of finance dominated the local media. The new regional
government believed its predecessor had funded cultural facilities
and activities in Montpellier too extensively at the expense of other
towns and cities in the region. Regional government closed down
the Office Régional de la Culture, discontinued its contribution to
the funding of the Corum and froze funding for the orchestra. This
occurred at exactly the same moment as the municipality's cultural
policies demanded heavier funding.

   This need to raise local funds was one explanation of the recent
privatisation of the city's water supply,[15] when the région received
250 million francs as a buy-in fee from the Compagnie Générale des
Eaux. This example of privatisation revealed a fundamental shift in
municipal politics which can be seen at work, at the same time, in
Nîmes, Grenoble and Toulouse.[16] As they massively develop their
activities in the cultural sphere, French towns often delegate tradi-

Table 7.6: Contribution of the district to Montpellier's 1990 cultural policy programme

Clients	Financial contribution from the city	Financial contribution from the district
Festival de Montpellier–Danse	3,000,000	2,300,000
Compagnie Bagouet (dance)	300,000	1,000,000
Festival Musique Radio France	2,050,000	3,000,000
Orchestra of Montpellier	6,000,000	16,055,000
Théâtre des 13 vents	3,000,000	1,000,000
Cultural Association of the Corum		4,200,000
Association for the Management of the Operas	40,000,000	5,680,000
Montpellier–Photovision	340,000	220,000
Festival of Jewish Israeli Cinema	60,000	50,000
Festival of Mediterranean Cinema	800,000	300,000
Group J. Taffanel (dance)	200,000	200,000
Total	55,750,000 (62%)	34,005,000 (38%)

tional public services to the private sector: catering, public transport, waste disposal, cleaning, etc. The new priorities in municipal policy are culture, sport, urban planning and economic and social policies.[17] The withdrawal of the region from the funding of 'traditional' policies placed the financial equilibrium of this strategy in question.

Montpellier City Council responded to these political developments rapidly, by enhancing the cultural policy functions of the district, an institution for the government of the Montpellier metropolitan area.[18] This process of externalising[19] the subsidy of a proportion of cultural funding has a logic, since the district in the main contributes to expenditure linked to cultural activities the importance of which reaches beyond the city (see table 7.6). This distinction suggests another increasingly marked distinction between the highly expensive cultural policies directed at media-worthy events, and policies which respond to the needs of local cultural organisations.

The cultural policy of the city has clearly created two distinct sectors. The first, which we define as the 'flagship' sector, comprises the Opera, the Philharmonic Orchestra, the Festival International Montpellier-Danse, the Festival International de Musique Montpellier/ Radio France, Montpellier-Photovision, the Festival International du

Table 7.7: Cultural subsidies granted by Montpellier City Council, 1986-90: flagship sector (in thousand Francs)

Clients	1986	1987	1988	1989	1990
Management of the Operas				1,064	40,000
Philharmonic Orchestra	2,275	2,570	2,642	10,170	6,000
Dance Festival	3,270	3,244	3,350	2,550	3,000
Théâtre des 13 Vents	1,365	1,520	2,470	2,790	3,000
Music Festival	897	2,717	1,851	3,029	2,050
Compagnie Bagouet	100	240	863		300
Festival of Med. Cinema	400	400	400	400	800
Journées Int. (Photography)	80	420	329	552	340
Total	8,387	11,111	11,605	20,555	55,490

Table 7.8: Cultural subsidies granted by Montpellier City Council, 1986-90: traditional sector (in thousand Francs)

Activity	1986	1987	1988	1989	1990
Various cultural manifestations (6)	50	505	588	555	570
Théâtre (18 troupes)	877	537	317	383	370
Music (26 assocs.)	114	115	244	113.5	118.5
Dance (8 troupes)	90	80	60	100	400
Literature/philosophy (6 assocs.)	–	55	90	127	128
Visual arts (3 assocs.)	–	5	5	5	70
Miscellaneous (34 assocs.)	318	175.5	206.5	170	122
Total	1,449	1,470	1,510.5	1,453.5	1,778.5

Film Méditerranéen, the Compagnie Bagouet, the Théâtre des 13 Vents.

The 'flagship' sector is relatively homogeneous in nature. The other sector, which we define as traditional, is much more heterogeneous and is largely financed by the city of Montpellier. 'Flagship' institutions are assisted by the state, the Conseil Géneral for the Department of the Hérault, the Conseil Régional for Languedoc–Roussillon, and the private sector through sponsorship. (see tables 7.7, 7.8, 7.9 and 7.10).

These figures take into account only those institutions, projects and activities which are clearly related to Montpellier. However, one of the effects of decentralisation in France has been to create an element of competition between different levels of regional and local governments. The efforts to make municipal policy more media-

Table 7.9: Shift in the relationship between the flagship sector and the traditional sector (traditional sector expenditure expressed as a % of the flagship sector)

1986	1987	1988	1989	1990
17.3	13.2	13.0	7.0	3.2

Table 7.10: The funders of cultural activities in Montpellier: flagship sector 1985-90 (in thousand Francs)

	1985	1986	1987	1988	1989	1990
City	6,150	9,027	10,957	11,436	19,491	55,490
Dist.[a]	2,350	2,500	2,137	3,315	24,160	29,490
CG[a]	1,000	1,640	1,460	1,950	2,500	2,735
Other[a]	135	785	785	785	885	900
CR[a]	13,235	14,860	12,095	13,105	2,000	2,700
State	7,965	15,165	15,745	16,600	17,172	13,696
Spon.	–	–	–	–	6,484	8,584
Total	30,835	43,977	43,179	47,191	72,692	124,010

Note: [a]Key: Dist.=District; CG= Conseil Général du Département de l'Hérault; Other = other departments; CR = Conseil Régional Languedoc–Roussillon; Spon. = Sponsorship.

worthy have created competition in the field of cultural policy. Each level of government prefers to act unilaterally in the cultural field, and produce for example, its own music festival, distinct from that of the capital city. These attitudes inevitably generate duplication and political fragmentation. This is not only due to the traditional antagonisms between left and right. The majority on the department is Socialist, as is the mayor of Montpellier, while the region is conservative. Nor is it clear that the population is aware of political distinctions. The efforts of the region and the department are often concentrated on festivals in Montpellier and on the city's new cultural facilities and buildings, and municipal policies often take the credit for regional cultural expenditure.

A competitive framework of this kind is not peculiar to Montpellier. The same pattern may be found in Nîmes, with competition between the town which is controlled by the UDF and the Conseil Général du Gard which is Socialist-controlled. Its intensity, however, is probably stronger in Montpellier than elsewhere. One of the causes of this can be found in the history of the urban network of Languedoc. It consists of towns of equal importance, without a capital in the real sense of the word and no clear urban hierarchy.[20] The rapid growth of Montpellier has contributed to destabilising this equilibrium and has produced a reaction sharper than elsewhere from other power centres in the region.

Amongst other factors, this contributed to the *rapprochement* between the cities of Nîmes and Montpellier. Both cities experience hostility from the departments as well as a desire to promote economic development through similar 'modernist' political strategies. The Montpellier–Nîmes corridor is by far the most important axis in the region for the establishment of new firms. In 1990 Montpellier and Nîmes signed a draft agreement, with the creation of a mixed working party and the identification of a series of sectors for collaboration.[21] In the cultural policy field, co-operation extends to the joint running of the Academies of Fine Arts and Music, the co-production of operatic works and symphonies, the extension of common invitations to major dance companies, the co-ordination of the programming of concerts, the joint programming of the festival of music of Radio France and the simultaneous staging of the festival of Mediterranean cinema in the two cities.

Integrating cultural policy and economic development in Montpellier

There are three themes in the relationship between cultural and economic development policies in Montpellier. The first is institutional. The development by the district of a cultural policy enables it to create links between cultural policy and Montpellier's 'technopolitan' strategy. The second aspect of the relationship between cultural and economic development policies is the growing participation of the private sector in cultural funding. At present, sponsorship provides a relatively small amount of funding – 6.9 per cent in 1990 for the 'flagship' sector and very little for the rest. Moreover, the use of private sector sponsorship is not systematic and co-ordinated, but remains limited in application and dependent on the goodwill of individual company directors. Its emergence is nonetheless significant.

The third theme is related to the city's communication strategy. The identification of a 'flagship' sector makes the promotion of a city for economic development purposes much easier. The regular coverage of cultural activities in Montpellier by the daily newspapers and nationally distributed magazines forms part of a strategy aimed

Table 7.11: Attendance at the principal cultural events held in Montpellier in 1990 by geographical origin of spectators (%)

Manifestation	Montpellier	Department	Region	Other
Festival Montpellier-Danse (45,000 spectators)	59	–	24	17
Festival of Music (53,000 spectators)	52	–	23	25
Film Festival (28,000 spectators)	68.5	15	–	16.5
Théâtre des 13 Vents (4,200 subscribers, 40,000 spectators)	57	31	–	17

at gaining recognition. In addition, the city's systematic search for prizes and rewards in the field of cultural activity,[22] is itself a successful tool for external propaganda which also create internal legitimacy. Such prizes are regularly advertised in the city on notice boards used for municipal information.

The analysis of attendance figures for the various festivals provides an indication of the geographical remit of the city's cultural initiatives.

More than 50 per cent of those who attended performances were inhabitants of Montpellier, whatever the season – summer for music and dance, autumn for film. The attendance by a significant number of spectators living outside the city and the region, because of the intrinsic attraction of Montpellier, indicates the balance between its internally and externally focused strategies. The social composition of the spectators demonstrates the high rate of attendance by students, teachers, civil servants, professionals and the managerial classes, especially amongst the younger 15-40 age groups. This closely matches the profile of the new inhabitants of Montpellier, confirming that the festivals are a valuable tool for social integration.

The impact of cultural policy in Montpellier

The evaluation of policies is always a delicate matter. Confidence from public opinion surveys is particularly fragile. Nevertheless, one survey, carried out in 1988, indicated that residents' satisfaction with cultural policy in the city: satisfaction with cultural facilities (79 per cent) and animation policies (80 per cent) was higher than in any other area of municipal policy-making.

The evaluation of the relationship between cultural policies and economic policies is even more difficult. The statistics illustrating many new jobs that have been created do not clearly demonstrate the effectiveness of combining cultural policy with an economic development strategy.

Culture may have a special role to play in the competition between European cities and between those of the southern regions of France in particular. Other factors, such as the attraction of the weather and the proximity of the sea, also explain the interest in Montpellier's region shown by firms. The environment, the quality and accessibility of the communications network, together with municipal economic interventionism equally constitute important factors. Recent studies concerning the location of companies show the relative lack of importance of cultural factors taken in isolation from their links with the local industrial fabric and the availability of a well-qualified labour force.[23] The debate is thus shifting towards the question of the potential contribution of cultural policy to the development of local industry.

Notes

1 This introduction was written by M. Lacave.
2 Cf. G. Saez, 'Les politiques de la culture', in M. Grawitz and J. Leca, Traité de science politique, vol.IV, Les politiques publiques, pp. 403-5.
3 Cf. R. Ferras, 'Le Languedoc–Roussillon', in Y. Lacoste (ed.) (1986), Geopolitique des régions françaises, vol. 3, Paris, Fayard.
4 Cf. the contribution by P. Le Gales on Rennes in this book (chapter 9).
5 Ibid.
6 G. Frêche (1986), 'Montpellier: les équipements culturel au coeur de la renaissance urbaine', international conference 'La renaissance des centre-ville', Quebec.
7 N. Gaye (1984), 'Politiques culturelles et collectivités territoriales en Languedoc–Roussillon', D.E.A. dissertation in political science, University of Montpellier I.
8 This process has been analysed in detail, and comparisons made between Grenoble, Lyons and Montpellier, by G. Saez (1990), L'innovation dans les services culturels urbains et la

logique de création artistique locale, Rapport pour le Plan Urbain, Paris, Ministère de l'Equipement et du Logement.

9 Cf. M. Ajar, C. Arpaillance, B. Chikhaoui (1990), 'Politique municipale de communication: la construction identitaire de Montpellier', in *Montpellier: pluralisme institutionnel de gestion du social et contreproductivité de la diffusion d'images urbaines*, CEPEL-ARPES Rapport pour le Plan Urbain, Paris, Ministère de l'Equipement et du Logement.

10 Cf. M. Pongy (1989), 'Politiques culturelles territoriales: une approche en termes de référentiel', in 'Politique culturelle et territoire', *Les Papiers*, 6, Toulouse Presses Universitaires.

11 According to figures supplied by the municipality, which are occasionally attacked as being an under-estimate, the Corum cost 800 million francs, of which the French state provided 50 million, the European Community 20 million, the department of Hérault 50 million, private investors 180 million, the Ville de Montpellier 220 million, the District of Montpellier 280 million. The Regional Council of Languedoc–Roussillon, which had initially offered to fund the operation on its own account, withdrew its offer after the regional elections of 1986. See, for example, F. Edelman (1990), 'Une basilique pour Huguenots', *Le Monde*, 13 Nov.

12 Cf. E. Negrier (1989), 'La maîtrise politiques des réseau de communication. Le cas des politiques publiques de câblage à Metz, Montpellier et Rennes', thesis in political science, University of Montpellier I.

13 G. Frêche (1991), 'Princeps cicèronien', in *L'artiste, le Prince*, Grenoble, Presses Universitaires de Grenoble.

14 Cf. E. Ritaine, 'Territoire: espace de règles du jeu politique', *Quaderni*, 12-13, 'Territoire et communication', Paris, CREDAP, Université de Paris-Dauphine. The author contrasts two models of development: that of Prato, in Tuscany, where development is indeed based on the co-ordinated mobilisation of multiple local resources, and that of Montpellier where development is founded on contributions from the outside.

15 For other hypotheses see E. Negrier (ed.) (1989), *Décentralisation, territoire et nouveaux services de communication. Les politiques publiques de réseau en Languedoc-Roussillon*, Rapport pour le Plan Urbain,Ministère de l'Equipement et du Logement, Paris.

16 For the case of Toulouse, see A. Lefebvre (ed.) (1990), *Les services urbains en quête de modernisation: examples toulousains dans le champ de la culture–loisirs–communication*, Rapport pour le Plan Urbain, Ministère de l'Equipement et du Logement, Paris.

17 The town in the region which was first to illustrate this new formulation was Nîmes, not only through its policy of selective privatisation, but also, with respect to certain high-priority sectors, by returning to direct public control some services which had been given over to private control. Cf. V. Hoffmann-Martinot (1988), 'Gestion moderniste à Nîmes', *Les annales de la recherche urbaine*, 38.

18 The district is a community formed by the city of Montpellier and the fourteen surrounding urban municipalities. Benefiting from an autonomous budget, it has control over a number of highly specific domains, including transportation and economic development. It forms the basis of the Montpellier technopolis. The latter, founded in 1985, includes five poles specialised in different types of industrial research: Euromedicine, Agropolis, Antenna, Heliopolis and Communicatique.

19 It is important to point out that such 'externalisation' is only relative, since the deputy mayor of the city is chairman of the district.

20 Cf. R. Dugrand (1963), *Villes et campagnes en Bas-Languedoc*, Paris, Presses Universitaires de France.

21 The sectors which have so far been identified are: culture, economic development, childcare, employment, tourism, the university, municipal services, urban development, public transport, environment and communications (cable, satellite television, and the joint promotion of the two cities).

22 Montpellier has been awarded the 'best city for culture' title by the magazine MURS-

MURS in 1986, 'the silver broom' award for the cleanliness of the city in 1987, and has been described 'number 1 university town where the living is pleasant' (L'Etudiant magazine, 1987), etc. The eclecticism of this thirst for awards is enormous. A national survey conducted in September 1990 indicated that 66 per cent of Frenchmen would like to live in Montpellier.

23 See, for example, T. Saint-Julien (1984), 'La division interurbaine du travail. La crise et l'évolution de travail dans les villes, Paris, Rapport pour le Plan Urbain–Ministère d'equipement et du Logement; AGURCO (1987), Mutations des services et dynamiques urbaines. Contribution à une étude de la région lyonnaise, Rapport pour le Plan Urbain; CREUSET (1986), Milieux urbains et développement local, Rapport pour le Plan Urbain; C. Courlet, P. Judet (1986), 'Nouveau espaces de production en France et en Italie', Les Annales de la Recherche Urbaine, 29.

8

Liverpool: a tale of missed opportunities?

Michael Parkinson and Franco Bianchini

Liverpool presents a paradox for a book whose theme is the contribution of cultural policy to urban regeneration. In some respects, the city has greater cultural potential and assets than many comparable provincial British cities. Quite apart from being the home of the world's most famous rock group, Liverpool has architecture, heritage, music, art galleries and museums, football teams, television companies, experimental theatres, artists and playwrights in abundance. However, it has done less to exploit them in a strategic way than many less favourably endowed cities. The story of cultural policy and urban regeneration in Liverpool is essentially one of missed opportunities. During the 1970s few British cities recognised the opportunity to exploit the cultural sector. However, in the 1980s many cities – the best example being Glasgow, one of the cities discussed in this volume – aggressively began to explore such strategies. But Liverpool still failed to respond.

Political changes in the city at the end of the decade did lead to the emergence of a series of tentative policy initiatives designed to exploit local cultural resources. By 1992 the arts and the cultural industries had been placed much more firmly on the political agenda of the city. But Liverpool has not yet realised its potential. This chapter provides an analysis of what Liverpool attempted during the 1980s and an assessment of its prospects in the 1990s. In the process the chapter will reconstruct the characteristics and quality of public life in the city during the past two decades.

Liverpool's failure to exploit its opportunities in the cultural policy area must be seen in the larger economic, cultural and political context in which decisions in the city are made. For the past twenty years Liverpool has struggled with intense economic problems which have spilled over into all aspects of its public life. In particular, the city council, the most important economic and political actor in Liverpool, exhibits a set of political and ideological characteristics which have combined to keep cultural issues off the city's policy-making. Since the 1970s the city council has experienced intense polarisation, instability and fiscal stress which has guaranteed that its political priorities lay elsewhere. It failed to either support or lead other actors in the cultural sector in a search for a new strategy.

At the end of the 1980s the council's political priorities changed and cultural resources became part of the political debate in the city. However, a series of political, administrative, economic and fiscal problems still raise questions about Liverpool's ability to enter the competition between provincial cities to market their cultural assets as the spearhead of regeneration. In 1992 Liverpool has yet to clearly demonstrate the political leadership, administrative capacity, financial resources or public commitment required to turn policy intentions into genuine achievements.

Confusion, conflict and culture in civic life (1970–87)

The crucial feature of civic life in Liverpool until the 1990s has been economic and political instability. Since the early 1970s, Liverpool has endured major economic crises caused by the withdrawal of private capital which has in turn created major social problems and continuing political conflict between the political parties which govern the city. Unlike Glasgow, the other British city in this book, and despite its working-class structure and proletarian culture, the city was not a traditional Labour stronghold. For complex social and sectarian reasons, Liverpool was governed throughout much of the twentieth century not by Labour but by the Conservative Party. The Conservatives' control of the city was broken during the 1970s. It was not replaced by a decisive Labour majority, but by a period of weak and divided coalition government between Liberals and Conservatives until the beginning of the 1980s. This political instability meant that the city lacked clear political or administrative leadership through a period of intense economic decline during the 1970s and 1980s. It proved difficult to establish a medium-term strategy for the city's economic future. It was even more problematic to develop an innovative one which embraced cultural policy.

The highly partisan nature of the political debate during this period meant that it was dominated by short-term electoral imperatives and competition for votes in particular over two issues – the level of local taxation and the scope and future role of public housing in the city. By focusing attention and resources on working-class residential areas on the periphery of the city, these priorities prevented the question of the potential role of the city centre getting on the political agenda. This had a crucial impact on the debate about the contribution cultural policy could make to Liverpool's economic future since the bulk of local cultural facilities and activities are concentrated in the city centre. However, there was little political mileage in it and hence little political attention was paid to it. These political preferences were complemented by those of the city's planners. Throughout much of this period professional planning ideology was in favour of slum clearance, 'decanting' people to peripheral areas and minimising traffic congestion in city centres, and Liverpool was no exception. These political and administrative factors prevented the city council from developing a clear vision of the city centre in terms of generating jobs and wealth and enhancing the local quality of life.

There were other reasons why the issues of culture and of its contribution to the local economy failed to emerge during this period. The ideological character of the Liverpool Labour Party was crucial. The party, like the city itself, is dominated by working-class rather than middle-class interests and by blue-collar rather than skilled craft unions. This lack of middle-class interests not merely gave the party a particular leadership structure and policies which were primarily oriented towards the welfare needs of its working-class supporters and members. It also affected the party's internal political culture which became dogmatic, exclusive and workerist in tone. This ensured that the Labour Party was primarily concerned with issues around production and particularly with jobs for manual workers. It was much less interested in or was actively opposed to other policy priorities. For example, the economic potential of activities like leisure, tourism, the arts, shopping or even white-collar services sector jobs which were concentrated in the city centre were regarded with scepticism. These Labour Party priorities also opened a major cultural and political gap with the private sector in the city. The private sector felt Labour was hostile to the interests of business in a general sense. City-centre business interests in particular, felt that Labour focused attention and diverted resources to its power base in the working-class heartlands of the city and failed to support their efforts to develop the downtown area.

This highlights a further important feature of Liverpool which casts a shadow over these issues – the limited contribution which the private sector makes to economic and civic life. The private sector has not emerged as a powerful lobby interest for the city centre and its cultural institutions. This can be explained in a variety of ways. Most obvious is the fact that the decline of the private sector of the economy during the recession of the 1970s meant that the city's largest economic actors are primarily in the public sector. The city council, the health service, the university and the polytechnic are the major employers and the most substantial players. The private sector itself is relatively small. Equally important is the fact that the remaining major private sector interests tend to be large employers, frequently national and multinational corporations, who do not regard themselves primarily as local firms with a direct stake in the local economy. As a result they generally do not play a major part in the city's public life. This has contributed to the fact that there is no powerful private sector group promoting the interests of the city centre.

The dominance by large firms also means that Liverpool has little in the way of a tradition of small firms with local leaders who can provide local leadership. The massive loss of middle-class population from the region and the suburbanisation of many professionals who worked in, but lived outside, the city's boundaries meant that the pool of leaders who are committed to the city and who might promote the city centre and its cultural institutions as a powerful alternative focus for economic development has also remained small. The fact that many middle-class professionals traditionally regarded other more prosperous towns in the region – such as Chester and Southport – as natural retail, entertainment and leisure centres for themselves compounded the lack of political support for a Liverpool city centre development strategy encompassing the formulation of cultural policies.

When, in 1983, the Labour Party eventually took majority control of Liverpool city council, the legacy of the conflicts of the 1970s coloured political debate. Throughout the decade of coalition politics, confusion and paralysis from the early 1970s Labour had increasingly become dominated by an extreme Trotskyist faction, the Militant Tendency. The result was that when Labour took control it was committed to entering into a major political confrontation with the Conservative-controlled national government about the level of financial resources it provided for the city's services and in particular for its public housing programme. From 1983 until 1987, the argument became increasingly vitriolic as the Labour council threatened to bankrupt the city if the Conservative government did not give it more money. At the same time Labour borrowed vast sums of money from foreign banks to support a major public house building programme. The confrontation dominated the national headlines for several years but finally ended in 1987 in ignominy for the Labour council which was disqualified from office by the House of Lords as many of its leaders were expelled from the Labour Party by the national leadership. From that date forward a new Labour administration with different political priorities emerged in the city.

1987 Labour's internal revolution

By the late 1980s political and economic life in Liverpool was in turmoil. The Labour council's confrontation with the government over resources, its commitment to public housing and its reluctance to recognise the significance of the city centre and its economic potential had left relations with the private sector in the city at a nadir. There seemed no obvious way of breaking the impasse since Labour was consistently returned to office during the 1980s with an apparent popular mandate for its policies and tactics. The intervention of external forces, the courts and the national Labour leadership – who expelled from the party the Militant councillors – eventually broke the logjam. But fifteen years of political paralysis and subsequent confrontation by restricting the range of political debate had guaranteed that cultural policy had played virtually no part in the debate about the economic future and civic life of the city. After 1987, different, more moderate, factions in the ruling Labour group emerged into leadership positions. This new leadership spent the next period attempting to develop a new economic strategy for the city and accommodate the local private sector. In the latter part of the decade a series of tentative initiatives and alliances between the public and private sectors emerged in the city. In turn, this encouraged the evolution of a new economic development strategy forum, in which the cultural role of the city centre began to play an important part.

Labour's strategy generated new priorities – focusing upon the new, consumption-oriented as opposed to the traditional, production-oriented functions of the city. In part the new Labour council saw the city centre in a different way from its predecessors, recognising that many opportunities there had not been exploited. Whereas the previous Labour administration had concentrated resources upon municipal services in the city's most deprived areas, the new strategy emphasised the potential of the city centre in terms of retail, culture, leisure, tourism and commercial development. The shift recognised that the council exercised relatively little leverage over the activities of the private sector in the local economy but did have a degree of control over the city centre environment in which over 40 per cent of the city's jobs were concentrated. In the late 1980s a steady stream of strategy documents about the city centre, the arts and cultural industries and tourism emerged from the council advocating the need to diversify the economic base of the city and, in particular, to regenerate the city centre.

The new Labour group's view of the arts and cultural industries was shaped by other less overtly political factors. A crucial one was the achievement of the Merseyside Development Corporation (MDC) in focusing upon the potential of tourism, leisure and heritage in Liverpool. The MDC had been created by the national government in 1981 to lead the regeneration of Liverpool's docklands. Separate from the city council and endowed with substantial government resources and planning powers, the MDC gradually developed a tourism and leisure-led strategy which by the second half of the 1980s had begun to bear fruit.

More importantly, by the end of the decade it had made substantial progress in physically renovating the docks on the city's waterfront. Its jewel in the crown was the Albert Dock, the largest group of Grade 1 listed buildings in the country. Derelict at the beginning of the decade, by 1988 the restored complex housed the Tate Gallery in the North, the Maritime Museum and a regional TV news centre, in addition to shops, restaurants, offices, exhibition spaces and upmarket housing. By 1988 the Albert Dock had become Britain's third most popular free tourist attraction, being preceded only by Blackpool Pleasure Beach and the British Museum (Mellor, 1991). These developments not only transformed parts of the physical core of the city. They placed on the agenda the issues of Liverpool's potential in the tourism and leisure industries and of the relationship between the waterfront and the adjacent city centre. They forced the city council to focus on the regenerative potential of culture, leisure and the city centre. During the period of Militant control in the mid 1980s, the city council had regarded the MDC as a Whitehall-imposed institution which had diverted government resources from the local authority and refused to collaborate with it. The emergence of a new moderate group in 1987 allowed peace to break out and a dialogue about common interests emerged.

A different contribution to the debate about the potential of the cultural industries came in 1986 with the publication by Merseyside Arts, the local Regional Arts Association, of The Economic Importance of the Arts on Merseyside. This major study for the first time identified the size of the contribution to the economic performance of the city that existing arts institutions were making both by appealing to external elites, and creating new jobs and wealth. The report revealed that over 3,000 people worked directly in the arts in Merseyside and that spending by arts organisations and their customers kept in employment a similar number. The report calculated that each job in the arts sector generated 2.8 jobs in the rest of the economy. The arts not only sustained jobs in retailing and other personal services; they also contributed to expanding the tourism industry in the region. The study revealed that almost 30 per cent of tourists came solely to visit cultural amenities and that a further 38 per cent at least partly came for that reason. Equally, middle managers and technologists in the survey recognised the significance of "museums, theatres, concerts and other cultural facilities": 80 per cent thought it was an important factor in deciding where to live and almost 70 per cent regarded it as an important reason for working in the area (Policy Studies Institute, 1986).

A third factor in the emergence of a municipal cultural policy in Liverpool was the fact that the city council absorbed some of the responsibilities in the cultural policy area – as well as some of the strategic thinking and specialist staff resources – of Merseyside County Council, which had been abolished by the Conservative government in 1986.

A cultural strategy for Liverpool

The first significant sign of the impact of this combination of factors came only a few months after the May 1987 local elections, when a new moderate Labour group replaced the Militant councillors who had been disqualified from office. In November 1987 the council published its first strategy document specifically devoted to cultural policy, *An Arts and Cultural Industries Strategy for Liverpool*. This important report located the development of the arts and cultural industries within the council's new overall economic development framework, and related it especially to its strategies for tourism and the redevelopment of the city centre. Linking cultural policy to economic development was an important new departure for the city council. The city council's previous modest initiatives in the cultural policy field had been no exception to the British local government tradition, which traditionally prioritised social integration and democratisation of access to the arts, rather than economic regeneration. The influence on Merseyside County Council of the cultural industries strategies developed by the 1981-86 Greater London Council contributed to effecting this change of attitudes. The key factor, however, was probably the consistent pressure applied by central government through the city's use of Urban Programme resources. Under the Militant regime, the city council had used its funding primarily to support its public house building strategy. After Militant's dismissal from office, the government insisted that the city council should focus these funds less upon social welfare functions than upon initiatives with a clearer economic orientation if it wanted to gain such funds in the future.

An Arts and Cultural Industries Strategy for Liverpool rehearsed the many assets and advantages in the cultural field the city already possessed. For example, there are in Liverpool a number of major firms involved in printing and publishing, electrical engineering and telecommunications which play a significant part in the transmission and distribution of culture. The city is endowed with the country's first professional orchestra, its oldest repertory company, its first lending library and its first arts centre. Its complex of national museums and galleries is perhaps the most important outside London, employing over six hundred people and attracting towards two million visitors. The city's top ten arts and cultural facilities attracted 2.5m tourists in 1986. Liverpool, lastly, is the home of a successful independent television company and the host for many film productions.

The strategy identified four areas in which the cultural industries made a significant contribution to the well-being of the city: the creation of economic activity and wealth; the expansion of community involvement and the development of a common culture; the city's image and reputation, and its tourism appeal. It argued that the arts and cultural industries had the potential to generate new employment since they were labour intensive. They could generate increased income through admission charges, their trading activities and the attraction of private sponsorship. They could release artistic potential within the community and in particular reinvigorate many of those alienated by urban life. A lively arts scene, finally, would boost the city's attraction to tourists and help stimulate private sector investment.

The new strategy attempted to strike a balance between the traditional social welfare concerns of the city council and the imperative to achieve economic development. The former would be protected by attempting to maximise community participation in the arts. The economic development dimension, by contrast, would involve: support for facilities and businesses important to maintaining the city's regional role as a centre for the arts and as an attraction to tourists; support for arts-related businesses with good growth prospects, and the promotion of new arts activities or programmes of artistic excellence from elsewhere. The new strategy had six broad aims:

1. To support arts activities which maintain the city centre's regional role and to help to retain and develop local artistic talent, while enabling residents to experience the best of contemporary and traditional arts.
2. To support the staging of a major annual arts festival which combined the best of the Liverpool experience with the best that other cities offered.
3. To maximise the job creation potential of the arts and cultural industries, by preparing an audit of council resources which could help local arts and business organisations, by developing facilities which could make training, education, distribution and marketing functions available to arts organisations, and by supporting training schemes which provided key arts-related skills.
4. To expand local and external markets for locally generated artistic and cultural material.
5. To ensure that major arts facilities and events are accessible to all and to support the development of community arts.

6. To carry out environmental improvement programmes in the vicinity of major arts attractions and on routes frequently used by large numbers of arts customers.

In sharp contrast to the style of its Militant predecessors, the council recognised that its own resources were limited and that it would have to involve a wide range of organisations: the Arts Council and Merseyside Arts, the European Community, the Department of Employment and its training programmes, the Crafts Council and many other funding agencies and arts organisations.

The report was obviously a significant acknowledgement of the existing and potential cultural assets of the city which could be exploited. Crucially also it marked the first clear recognition by the city council that the city centre – the location of the majority of arts facilities – had to be transformed so that people felt it belonged to them, it was safe to visit, it could be accessed easily and cheaply and its appearance, style and atmosphere attracted people to it. The strategy recognised that this in turn raised crucial questions about the policing, transportation links and general levels of maintenance of the city centre environment.

The city centre on the agenda

The condition of the city centre is a crucial issue for any city seeking to exploit its cultural resources. It was particularly important in Liverpool since the standard of general environmental maintenance by the city council was relatively poor, a result of the broader political factors identified earlier. The decades of paralysis and later confrontation of the 1970s and 1980s had, amongst other problems, created tensions and conflicts between the municipal blue-collar workforce and Labour politicians on the one hand, and city council managers on the other, which had led to a dramatic decline in the efficiency of the council's manual workers. The tight links between this manual workforce, their trade unions and the power structure in the Liverpool Labour Party meant that for over a decade inefficient and antiquated work practices could not be confronted or eliminated by management. As a result, the standards of environmental maintenance and cleaning throughout the city were low and particularly bad in the city centre. Even though the architectural fabric of much of the central commercial and retail quarters were basically good, their routine appearance were not compatible with the attempt to develop and market Liverpool as a tourist destination and as a vibrant, dynamic, creative city. In addition, the links between blue-collar unions and the Labour council which allowed the presence of low-quality street traders throughout the most prestigious shopping areas only compounded the image of Liverpool as a downmarket, low-status retail centre. This impoverished appearance and maintenance of the city centre was in sharp contrast to the adjacent docklands and waterfront areas which the MDC had not only physically renovated but had maintained to very high standards – a factor which at least partly explains the MDC's success in promoting tourism during the 1980s.

Indeed the larger question of the role and status of the city centre as an element of Liverpool's economic development strategy became an increasingly important political issue in the city at the end of the decade. As the council increasingly recognised the potential of the area it spent considerable time attempting to develop a public–private partnership between itself and other key local actors – the MDC, the government's task force and important local business interests – which would focus on the need to renovate, develop and market the city centre as the focus of a campaign to improve Liverpool's image and attract external inward investment as Glasgow had successfully managed to do in the mid 1980s. By the end of the 1980s Liverpool city council had identified the elements of a cultural policy-led regeneration strategy. The real issue was whether the city could deliver the policies.

Implementing the strategy: achievements and problems (1987-92)

Liverpool city council in the autumn of 1987 began an ambitious effort to re-direct cultural policy towards the aims of its broader economic development strategy. This section examines the council's attempts to implement its strategy, and identifies some of the institutional, managerial, financial and political constraints which have slowed down the process of translating the council's strategic objectives into practical policies. The discussion focuses on the council's efforts to: develop the cultural industries; redistribute the benefits generated by a cultural policy-led development strategy; animate the city through the organisation of arts festivals and other cultural events; market Liverpool and develop tourism; exploit the city's physical assets and create a policy-making system which can implement strategic decisions.

Developing the cultural industries

In *An Arts and Cultural Industries Strategy for Liverpool*, the city council adopted a definition of the arts and cultural industries which encompassed the following core activities: the performing arts; advertising; broadcasting; the film, video and photographic industry; the music industry, both live and recorded; the production, distribution and retailing of books, magazines and other printed material, including the library service. Arguably museums and galleries, the visual arts, design and fashion should also be included in any such definition. The council's interventions in the fields of popular music, film, video and broadcasting especially warrant discussion. The council justified its intervention in these sectors as a way of both attracting investors, cultural producers and entrepreneurs from elsewhere to the city and, more importantly, of stemming the constant haemorrhage of cultural talent from the city to London, elsewhere in the UK and abroad, by creating Liverpool-based institutions for the development and commercial exploitation of local creativity.

Film, video and broadcasting

Liverpool's townscape and the unique culture of its people have traditionally provided a rich vein of material for the film and television industries. In recent years TV drama series written by Liverpool authors (*Boys from the Blackstuff, Bread*) and soap operas (Mersey Television's *Brookside*) were set and largely filmed in the city. Similarly, 1980s films set in Liverpool included *Letter to Brezhnev, No Surrender, Distant Voices, Still Lives, Dancing Thru' the Dark* – all by local authors – and *The Dressmaker*. To capitalise on the city's advantage in this field and to promote Liverpool as a location for the film industry, in 1989 the city council appointed Britain's first ever Film Liaison Office (FLO). The post, jointly initiated and funded by Liverpool-based Mersey Television Company, was modelled on the film commissions existing in some American cities and states. The FLO was given a wide remit: to provide location assistance to attract film-makers to the city; to assess the needs of Liverpool's indigenous film industry; to encourage inward investment in film; to co-ordinate the city council's policy on film funding and to assist Liverpool's campaign for Channel 5, a new television channel expected to be on the air by New Year's Eve 1994. Over forty film and TV crews used the services of the FLO during its first twelve months of operation. Crews filming in the city spent about £1m in the local economy in 1989 and £1.5m in 1990, although it is obviously difficult to exactly determine for how many film and TV companies the presence of a municipal film office was a key factor in their decision to use Liverpool as a location.

The council initiated moves in other related areas. For example, it commissioned consultants to investigate which forms of support could be given to non-commercial and independent film and video-makers. In one of its more enterprising ventures, the council was one of the first British local authorities to enter the field of commercial film funding, by agreeing to underwrite for £128,000 the Liverpool Films/BBC production of The Man From the Pru. The campaign for Channel 5 was planned as part of a longer-term film and media campaign, aimed at attracting investors to Merseyside. Most important, the city council in 1992 – jointly with the government's City Action Team, the British Film Institute and North West Arts Board – created the Moving Image Development Agency (MIDA), an independent institution to stimulate the growth all aspects of the moving image sector on Merseyside – film, TV, video, animation, computer graphics. The FLO will operate within the agency which is expected to be funded in the long-term by a public–private partnership.

Popular music

Since the early 1960s Liverpool has been one of the most regular producers of successful rock bands, The Beatles being the best-known and most spectacular example. In the last decade bands like Frankie Goes to Hollywood, Teardrop Explodes, Echo & The Bunnymen and The Christians have all emerged from Liverpool, and have become nationally and internationally famous, often setting trends which have been widely imitated. The concentration of the music industry and related services in London, however, prevents the Liverpool economy from benefiting from the profits generated by local bands. For instance, the council have calculated that none of the

£250m earnings from Frankie Goes to Hollywood's first album was reinvested in Liverpool.

To investigate how to maximise the contribution which popular music could make to the economic and social well-being of the city, the council in 1989 commissioned a consultancy study to examine the state of the Liverpool music industry, in relation to regional, national and international trends; to assess training requirements in the music industry; to develop specific proposals for public and private sector investment, and to formulate a strategy for the promotion of music festivals in the city. The study concluded that the turnover of Liverpool's music industry is approximately £14m, with an equivalent full-time employment of 700. It identified skills shortages in all those areas not directly concerned with ideas generation and performance: administration, organisation and finance, technical and legal services, marketing. The study also assessed the feasibility of creating a local music industry development and advisory service, to identify local talent, provide resources for its effective commercial development, liaise with the local private sector in order to maximise the retention of music industry income within the local economy, and act as a publishing company, training and advisory service. These recommendations, however, have so far not been implemented.

Redistributing the benefits: training, education, access and other equity issues

Experience from cities both in the USA and in western Europe suggests that cultural policy-led regeneration strategies – particularly when they are focused upon city centre-based 'prestige' projects – may bring few benefits to disadvantaged social groups. Cultural policy can indeed sharpen conflicts between city centre and periphery, private and public space, tourists and residents, economic development and quality of life goals. Training, education and access policies are crucial mechanisms to ensure a fairer geographical and social distribution of the benefits of cultural policy-led urban regeneration strategies.

The debate on education and training provision in the cultural field in Liverpool is dominated by two major initiatives. One is the Hope Street Project. The other is the proposed establishment of the Liverpool Institute for the Performing Arts (LIPA, better known locally as the 'Fame' school), initiated by former Beatle Paul

McCartney. The Hope Street Project is the training, community and outreach wing of the Everyman Theatre. Its funding comes from the Urban Programme, the European Social Fund and the Department of Education and Science. It is mainly targeted at unemployed Liverpool-based people, under twenty-five years old, to whom it offers training in a variety of theatre-related skills ranging from performance and stage management to publicity and administration. In early 1992 the project experienced a serious funding crisis which led to the issuing of temporary redundancy notices for its staff.

A feasibility study for the establishment of LIPA was completed in 1990. It recommended that a national and international training centre for all pop music-related skills be created, linked with the provision of a full-time course leading to a 'Music in the Community' diploma, with a resource centre – incorporating facilities for open learning – and an 'international centre for popular musics of the world'. LIPA could become a unique vehicle to develop the skills and attract the investment that an indigenous Liverpool music industry would require.

There is a clear need for co-ordination between the Hope Street Project, LIPA, and Liverpool's other numerous existing or planned education and training schemes in the cultural sector. It is also imperative in these initiatives that the development of the training infrastructure is accompanied by the establishment of local cultural industries able to absorb trained workers so that the city can reap the full benefits generated by its own reservoir of creativity.

The city does face one especially difficult problem. The Black community remains spatially segregated, socially and economically disadvantaged, and in addition culturally mis- or under-represented. The council has responded to the problem by creating a unit to develop the arts in the Black community and ensure that the city's arts organisations take into account the Black perspective in programming, recruitment, education, training and other activities. The unit is responsible for the general development of Black arts, for the visual arts, the performing arts and Black literature respectively. There is also an officer who is establishing within one of the city's libraries an archive documenting the Black experience of life in the city. The unit has been relatively successful in introducing Black arts in inner city schools. However, as argued in a study of cultural life in the Toxteth district, where the Liverpool Black community is concentrated, Black art still faces "the dual disability of unstable funding and the struggle for cultural/artistic recognition in its own right" (Dixon, 1991; 6).

Animating the city

A large array of cultural festivals takes place in Liverpool. They include the Festival of Comedy, the Mersey River Festival funded by the MDC, Earthbeat (a three-day rock and pop concert), the Red Star Brouhaha Festival of youth theatre from eastern Europe, the Caribbean Carnival and 'Video Positive', Britain's largest festival of video art, funded by the city council through the government's Urban Programme. New festivals are planned, including a popular music festival developed in the context of a wider celebration of the city's popular culture. In 1992 the Tall Ships Race returns to Liverpool, celebrating Columbus's discovery of America.

Clearly there is great potential in this area. Some problems, however, remain to be solved to make the cultural animation strategy work. These include the need to provide: better street lighting and late-night public transport; more flexible opening hours for city-centre shops, cafes and other public meeting places; more accurate and widely distributed information about "what's on" in town; a combination of anti-litter drives and environmental facelifts to improve the visual quality of the city-centre environment and greater diversity in the pub and club dominated 'evening economy'.

Marketing Liverpool and developing tourism

Liverpool's image problems are as serious as those experienced by any other city in Britain. Interestingly, however, culture has historically played a positive role in the shaping of Liverpool's image. For instance, in the 1960s, despite its continuing economic decline, the city regained some national and international significance as a centre for street fashion and for youth and popular culture, a swinging provincial alternative to London. The working-class cultural dynamism of 1960s Liverpool, exemplified by The Beatles, the Mersey Beat, and the pop poets of the 'Mersey Sound', was in tune with the national mood of the early years of Harold Wilson's Labour government, a Merseyside member of parliament, and with its promises of an economic renaissance based on class mobility and classlessness. Even Scouse, the often stigmatised local dialect, suddenly became fashionable.

In the 1980s, however, the city – unlike Glasgow, Bradford, Sheffield and Birmingham which are often not as well endowed as Liverpool with cultural resources – has been unable to harness the potential of its considerable cultural vitality for place marketing purposes. One of the problems has been lack of co-ordination between the many agencies responsible for marketing Liverpool. The city has also so far not exploited its international cultural profile by formulating a 'cultural foreign policy', to create fruitful relationships with other cities in western Europe and elsewhere in the world.

Cultural tourism expanded enormously in Liverpool in the 1980s, with events like the 1984 International Garden Festival which attracted about 3.4 million visitors and the launch of new attractions like the Tate Gallery, the Maritime Museum and the Festival of Comedy. In the first two years following its opening in May 1988 the Tate received about 1.4m visitors. The Merseyside Maritime Museum, which applies entrance charges, had over 400,000 paid admissions in 1988, while the Albert Dock as a whole was visited by 5 million people in 1991. One of the outstanding issues to be tackled to consolidate the expansion of tourism is the city centre's environmental quality. This has been the object of a recent urban design study commissioned by the Council jointly with the MDC, the task force and the English Tourist Board.

Exploiting physical assets

Cultural industries strategies can play an important role in exploiting underused physical assets. The debate in Liverpool in this field is dominated by the proposed establishment of a 'creative industries quarter' in the Duke Street conservation area, a section of the city centre which links the central shopping area with the university and polytechnic student quarter, Chinatown, the night-time entertainment area and the city's new tourist focus on the waterfront. London-based developers Charterhouse Estates in 1989 bought the council's freehold interests in the area at a cost of £8.5m, and launched a ten-year strategy for the establishment of a 'cultural district' combining residential, office, 'speciality' shopping, restaurants and cultural uses. The latter would comprise the provision of both arts venues and of facilities for a variety of production-oriented activities in such fields as crafts, design, fashion, electronic music and the media. According to the developers' optimistic estimates the ten-year strategy should bring investment of more than £100m into the area, and create 2,500 jobs.

The developers are working in partnership with the city council who stress the conditions for the success of the development scheme exist. These arguments range from the growth of tourism in Liverpool, the growing interest in the creative industries, and in living in the city centre to the architectural quality, the special character and the suitability for refurbishment for residential, business and cultural uses of many of the buildings in the area. In addition, the council emphasised the relative success of similar schemes in Sheffield (Cultural Industries Quarter), Bradford (Little Germany) and Glasgow (Merchant City), in areas which were in many ways not as attractive as Duke Street. These optimistic considerations, however, have to be set against the realities of low land and property values in the area, the scale of resources needed to refurbish many of its buildings and the contraction of public subsidies for small arts and media enterprises. They will all have an impact on their ability to survive, let alone expand in new premises within the quarter. Progress in the development of the quarter remains limited. But the scheme, which covers about one quarter of the city centre, remains crucial to the council's cultural policy-led regeneration strategy.

Creating effective and well-resourced policy-making bodies

The post-Militant Labour administration which took office in 1987 created Liverpool city council's first ever formal structure for cultural policy-making. An Arts and Cultural Industries Unit was established within the council's Department of Libraries and Arts, employing an assistant director, a film liaison officer and a Black arts development team. Implementing the strategy, however, is not always the highest priority within the local authority. Many remain to be convinced of the important role of cultural policy in urban regeneration. There is no separate arts committee, but only an arts working party within the libraries and arts sub-committee. Inter-departmental co-operation is crucial to the success of the city council's arts and cultural industries strategy and its plans for economic development, tourism development and the revitalisation of the city centre. Such co-ordination, however, has so far not been extensive.

The council's lack of financial resources remains a constraint. The council's revenue budget for the arts is only about £100,000. It obviously pales into insignificance in comparison with many cities in Britain and the rest of western Europe. Liverpool is also victim of the 'parity funding' policy the Arts Council currently adopts for its theatre clients. Under this policy, Arts Council subsidy matches local authority contributions. The city council's fiscal problems limit its ability to contribute; hence the Arts Council is correspondingly reluctant to fund local institutions. The policy caused a major crisis in 1990 as the city's two building-based repertory theatres were threatened with merger or closure. The abolition of the County Council, which had the capacity to fund Liverpool-located institutions from the tax base of the adjacent local authorities, and – despite the creation by Merseyside local authorities of a consortium to fund the arts – the difficulty of developing an effective successor county-wide body in the cultural policy field, only compounds the financial problems of Liverpool's subsidised cultural sector.

Conclusions

At the beginning of the 1990s Liverpool had emerged from the worst of the political and economic storms of the 1980s with a clearer view of where it wished to go and a willingness on the part of the public and private sectors to collaborate to promote the city's long-term interests. The conflicts of the 1980s had been replaced with greater consensus about the agenda for the 1990s. Progress had also been made in the cultural industries sector. The efforts of the MDC and the Merseyside Tourist Board were beginning to show some fruit. Tourism was expanding and the city's waterfront was substantially improved. The city council had recognised the potential of the cultural industries sector. It had an innovative strategy document which recognised the need to develop indigenous cultural industries and create links between cultural policy and other policy areas. It had also made some administrative improvements in its capacity to implement its strategy. It had recognised the crucial importance of the city centre as a focus for economic development and accepted the need to manage and maintain it better and to integrate into it the developing tourist quarter on the waterfront. This was especially confirmed in 1991 when the city successfully won resources in the government's City Challenge initiative to promote major development of the city centre. That event broke the mould of the anti-city centre policies of the 1970s and 1980s. At the same time the city council forged far better working relationships with the Merseyside Development Corporation.

The arts and cultural industries were identified as one of the major sectors of employment growth in the city council's *Economic Development Plan* for 1992-93. An arts and cultural Industries sub-group with officers from different council departments was formed to discuss the potential contribution of the arts and cultural industries to economic development.

Another encouraging sign was the interest in cultural policy shown by the government's Merseyside Task Force, who in 1990 commissioned a report on the economic importance of the cultural industries in Liverpool. The report demonstrated that the city's cultural industries – defined as theatre, music, museums and galleries, libraries, Merseyside arts clients in other cultural sectors, broadcasting, film and video production, exhibition and distribution and excluding the *Liverpool Daily Post & Echo* publishing group – employed about 2,400 people and had a gross income of about £70m in 1989-90. The report also estimated that the indirect employment benefits of these sectors could amount to a further 3,800 jobs in hotels, catering and other ancillary services (Comedia, 1991). Co-operation between the city council, Merseyside Task Force and North West Arts Board in the implementation of the city's cultural policy has improved, with its first product the creation of the Moving Image Development Agency.

The city centre itself had witnessed considerable physical refurbishment of many of its public and private spaces during the latter part of the decade. There was continuing growth in the media and film sectors with more television programmes and movies originating or being made in the city. The major galleries and museums continued to flourish artistically and in audience terms. The Liverpool Institute for Performing Arts, the 'Fame' school, remained a major possibility. The Philharmonic Orchestra had set new musical standards, was developing a serious community outreach programme and organised a successful tour of the USA, in which it effectively acted as an ambassador for the city. It had made major advances in increasing its levels of private sector sponsorship to compensate for declining public subsidy and had begun major redevelopment of its concert hall to double as a conference centre. The Playhouse Theatre had recovered from its financial difficulties and was performing to large audiences.

However, there remained a series of problems. Many of the larger projects like the Merseyside Media Centre, the Fame school and the creative industries quarter required substantial investments that could prove difficult to achieve in the 1990s if the national recession led property developers to be more cautious than they had been in the expansive era of the late 1980s. The city council's continuing fiscal problems and the reduction in Arts Council grant levels meant that the arts and cultural industries in Liverpool in the 1990s would have to be sustained from a shrinking resource base. Although the same problem could be found in other British cities at the beginning of the 1990s, it was obviously more difficult for Liverpool since it had made less progress during the 1980s.

Lying behind the specific problems facing the cultural industries sector were the general ones of Liverpool and the city council itself. The city's economy showed some signs of growth during the last part of the 1980s but its economic base remained relatively fragile and vulnerable. The cultural industries could make a contribution to wealth creation, job creation, the city's image and boosting tourism. But the city's economic and associated social problems remained large. In 1992 unemployment was still 16 per cent and poverty was experienced in some form by 50 per cent of the population. Such problems raised questions about the scale of the local market for cultural consumption which often depends upon relatively high levels of disposable income. Indeed cultural policy, if primarily focused on consumption, could reinforce scepticism about the contribution of the arts and cultural industries to the common good. The implementation of the council's cultural strategy in the 1990s will have to carefully balance its twin objectives of boosting cultural consumption and the consumer service industries associated with it and of developing the local cultural production infrastructure. This strategic choice has implications also for the quality of jobs which could be created. A cultural policy aimed at promoting Liverpool's role as a centre for tourism and retailing – sectors which are often characterised by low skills, low pay and poor levels of job satisfaction – would need to be balanced with job creation strategies in more highly skilled, high value-added sectors like design, electronic music, film and broadcasting. Moreover, a policy which focused exclusively on city centre-based cultural consumption could further alienate from civic life residents of deprived outer estates and inner-city areas, who may find the city centre's cultural provision very difficult to access. All these considerations suggest that concerns about equity and access are likely to be prominent in the cultural policy debate in the city during the 1990s.

The second major problem was the city council itself. The ruling Labour group remained divided about policy and its left wing was suspended in the summer of 1990 by the national Labour Party leadership. Clear political leadership and stability had not yet been achieved. Some of the council services remained inefficient. The city council's basic functions remain at the heart of any regeneration strategy built on the cultural industries. If the basic services – and particularly the environmental services – were clearly inadequate the foundations of a cultural policy-led regeneration strategy remained at best unstable.

More generally, the cities which had successfully developed such strategies had achieved a degree of internal consensus about the nature of the strategy that should be pursued and the means of achieving it. Liverpool had not yet achieved such a consensus, although one was gradually emerging. A partnership between the public and private sectors had been created which was attempting to develop a long-term strategy for the marketing of the city. Relations between the Conservative government and the Labour council had significantly improved since the Militant era. In 1992 the city had many innovative projects planned. But they did not yet form a coherent strategy which linked priorities to resources, agreed goals and actions. Such a strategy remains a necessary, if not a sufficient, condition of success.

Despite these concerns, the feeling nevertheless persists that Liverpool has enormous advantages which could still be capitalised upon. Indeed, in view of the decline of many traditional sectors of its economy, the arts and cultural industries offer one of the greatest opportunities to achieve economic success, despite some potential risks. Liverpool has many of the assets of a great city that many comparable cities do not possess. It has a superb urban seascape. It has extensive Victorian and Georgian architecture and handsome public parks. It has a vibrant cultural scene of artists, playwrights, musicians, popular entertainers. The city has style and authenticity. But those assets need to be exploited if Liverpool is not to fall behind other European cities. The possibility of doing so in the harsher economic climate of the 1990s remains to be tested.

References

Ark Consultants (1990), 'Music information centre and network', Music City Report, 4.

Beck, Antony (1990) 'But where can we find a Heineken? Commercial sponsorship of the arts on Merseyside', Political Quarterly, 61, 4,

Beck, Antony (1991) 'Penny Lane', Local Arts UK, November.

Clark, Gillian and Subhan, Nazreen (1986) Four Hundred Years and Now What?, Liverpool, Merseyside Arts.

Comedia (1991), The Cultural Industries in Liverpool. A Report to Merseyside Task Force, Liverpool.

Corner, John and Harvey, Sylvia (1991) Enterprise and Heritage. Crosscurrents of National Culture, London, Routledge.

Dixon, Ruby M. (1991), Black Arts, Poverty and the Issue of Equity – A Study of Art and Creative Culture Within Toxteth, University of Liverpool, Race and Social Policy Unit.

Harpe, Wendy (1990), A Question of Equity, Liverpool, Merseyside Arts.

Institute of Popular Music (1990), 'Survey of music industries on Merseyside', Music City Report, 2.

ISIS (1990), Merseyside Film and Video Report, Liverpool.

Liverpool City Council (1987a), An Arts and Cultural Industries Strategy for Liverpool. A Framework.

Liverpool City Council (1987b), Liverpool City Centre. Strategy Review.

Liverpool City Council (1987c), A Tourism Strategy for Liverpool. A Framework.

Liverpool City Council (1990), Bold Street/Duke Street Action Plan.

Mellor, Adrian (1991), 'Enterprise and heritage in the dock', in Corner, John and Harvey, Sylvia (eds) (1991).

Myerscough, John (1988), Economic Importance of the Arts on Merseyside, London, Policy Studies Institute.

Policy Studies Institute (1986), The Economic Importance of the Arts on Merseyside, Liverpool, Merseyside Arts.

Schools for Performing Art Trust (1990), The Liverpool Institute for Performing Arts. A Feasibility Study.

The authors wish to thank Dave Abdullah, Dee Hennessy and Paul Mingard, all from Liverpool City Council, for their help in researching this chapter.

9

Rennes: Catholic humanism and urban entrepreneurialism

Patrick Le Galés

The relationship between culture and local economic development is an intriguing one. Indeed, the fact that French cities have probably been involved on a larger scale in cultural policies over the last decade than have their European counterparts, raises questions about the impact of increasing inter-urban competition. In addition, the French Ministry of Culture has pioneered public cultural policies since the 1960s which have had a major spatial impact. During the last decade in particular, the ministry has developed ambitious cultural policy projects which have matched the ambitions of cities. Cultural policy has been an important area of growth and innovation in the 1980s. However, by contrast with some British cities, cultural policies usually have not been seen as a tool of urban regeneration for declining cities. For, with the exceptions of a few industrial cities, most French cities have been economically buoyant through the 1980s and have taken the lead in innovative forms of economic development. The examples of Rennes in Brittany and Montpellier in the southern region of Roussillon are among the best illustrations of this trend.

Rennes's post-war growth: economic development and humanism

Until 1945, Rennes was a rather boring provincial capital. It is today among the most successful, innovative and dynamic urban areas in France. Cultural policy has been an essential component of the transformation of Rennes.

Rennes is the regional capital of Brittany 375 km. west of Paris. It is an *ancien régime* city, as the historian Maurice Agulhon describes it, a city which was a regional capital before the 1789 revolution, had a parliament and an intellectual life, and representatives from the central state, the *intendants* whose role was assumed by the prefect. Rennes, like Grenoble, Toulouse, Aix, Orléans, Strasbourg, or Montpellier endured relative decline during the nineteenth century because it did not experience industrial development. By contrast, growth took place in Saint-Etienne, Le Creusot, and Lille–Roubaix–Tourcoing: cities whose development was largely shaped by nineteenth century industrialisation. In Rennes by contrast, the city was dominated by the church, the army, the railways, the university and regional administration. There were no industrial bourgeoisie or bankers and a weak working class. Since the war, all Rennes's mayors and the main political leaders have been university academics or, occasionally, teachers.

The status of Rennes in Brittany is somewhat ambiguous. On the one hand, it is the regional capital of Brittany, and it has a strong sense of Breton identity. On the other, state representatives are important in Rennes and they use the city to control the region. This cultural ambiguity is a permanent feature of Rennes. There is also ambiguity in the way in which people within Brittany perceive the role of Rennes.

After 1945, *ancien régime* cities had the greatest urban growth in France, at the relative expense of the industrial cities. When Saint Etienne and the others faced a crisis similar to the inner city crisis in Britain, Rennes, Aix and Grenoble flourished doubling their population between the 1950s and the 1970s. These cities are characterised by a young population, good universities, a high level of education, with students representing about 20 per cent of the population in some cases, high-tech firms, a small working class, few inner-city problems and a strong tertiary sector. In the 1980s, these cities were dynamic places which pursued innovative economic and cultural policies in an entrepreneurial way to promote urban development. Rennes is part of this group of cities, although geographically different since most of the other ones are in the south.

A second feature is essential to understand the importance of cultural policies in Rennes: the role of the Christian Democrat elites of the city. Brittany is a Celtic region where catholicism has been a dominant force. The growth of Rennes since the 1950s – from 90,000 to 200,000 inhabitants today, in the city centre itself – was fuelled by emigration from rural parts of Brittany where agriculture was being modernised. Many leaders of various organisations in Rennes were former members of progressive Christian organisations in rural Brittany before coming to Rennes, or worked in the university where the Jeunesses Etudiantes Chrétiennes, or the once Catholic trade union Confédération Française Démocratique du Travail (CFDT) were active. This had two consequences. Local elites constitute a series of inter-related networks and share a global set of values. Rennes's economic development strongly benefited from this situation.

From 1953 to 1977, Rennes City Council was run by a Christian Democrat *grand maire*, Y. Fréville, a professor at the university, and a local grand notable who held numerous offices – *député*, then *sénateur*, chairman of the urban area district, chairman of the *département*. He belonged to the then Catholic political party, the Mouvement des Républicains Populaires (MRP). His election marked a turning point as he was elected as an ally of the Socialists against the local bourgeoisie – mainly shopkeepers and small entrepreneurs whose main concerns were to avoid taxes. Four ideas characterised Fréville's programme: an urban plan to control the expansion of the city, the development of the education system, the strengthening and expansion of urban infrastructures and the establishment of Rennes as an international intellectual and cultural centre. His primary aim, in 1953, was to attract high-technology industries by developing the university and other research institutions. Education and culture, as much as economic development, were part of Fréville's project and characteristic of his era. However, beyond the city council, these values were widely shared by most local key actors. In Rennes any collective project which is based on these sorts of goals is always likely to mobilise the majority of local forces. Since the 1950s there has been in Rennes a broad consensus that the development of culture and education are priorities for the city.

Fréville's programme was, however, very innovative. In it one can trace the humanist Christian Democrat influence in the idea that education and culture for all are the key to the development of an harmonious city. Equally, one can see the regionalist and academic influence in the idea that to promote the international cultural prestige of Rennes against Paris, and to develop the university and research is the key to the development of the city.

A further important point was the nature of the relationship between Rennes's urban elites and the central French State. Rennes

City Council's modernist strategy could only succeed because it was matched by state policies. On the one hand, Fréville and local political leaders were extremely efficient in influencing the government through political connections, and civil servants. On the other, Rennes was one of the first cities to improve the recruitment and increase and the number of local government officers in the 1950s, ten years before other French cities. There is a tradition of very good connections between Rennes and Paris. For example, in the 1960s Rennes City Council was able to benefit on a large scale from the economic decentralisation movement initiated within the government's regional policy and build a second university. This was also an important element in the making of its cultural policy.

Cities and culture in France: some underlying trends

In France there is a powerful tradition of public intervention in cultural policy. For example, in the 1960s De Gaulle appointed the writer André Malraux as Minister for Culture, who created a state cultural policy. The centralisation of power is also a characteristic of France, and it is equally clear that in the cultural field the domination by Paris of the rest of the country has been traditionally extremely important. Cultural values and trends are set in Paris. This tradition of state involvement in the cultural field increased during the 1970s. After 1981, the Socialist minister for Culture Jack Lang dramatically raised the profile of cultural policy. He supported a wide range of initiatives which meant that the budget for culture increased to almost 1 per cent of the total state budget. This is clearly in sharp contrast with the British tradition where culture is less a matter of public policy or of state interventionism.

French local authorities gradually became involved in the cultural policy field, some twenty years after central government. The process was first developed b,y and still mainly involves, the major cities and regional capitals. However, smaller cities and the *départements* and more recently the regions are widening the scope of their interventions in the cultural field. Rennes was the first city in France to formulate and carry out a local cultural policy as early as 1962. Grenoble followed in 1965. They remain today among the most innovative cities in terms of cultural policy.

French local authorities have a long history of cultural spending on local museums, libraries, and local cultural events. But the idea of cultural policy really took substance in the 1970s where many cities followed the original examples set by Rennes and Grenoble. A study by Friedberg and Urfalino (1984) identified the process whereby city councils changed from giving money to a few activities, to implementing 'cultural policies' within a coherent framework, intimately related to the overall strategy of the council. The study demonstrated how wide ranging local authorities' interventions were. They supported activities ranging from professional to amateur arts, from traditional spectacles to elitist ones, from theatre to comics, from opera to avant-garde jazz and rock bands, from dance to photography or museums and libraries. Their work demonstrated that the discourse about culture has hidden considerable variety in terms of cultural forms. In particular, they identify a *jeu du catalogue* – a logic of the list or catalogue. In contrast with official presentations of their cultural policies by local authorities, they showed that local authorities spend money on a whole range of activities in order to have simultaneously a bit of activity in every field – some popular arts, some elitist ones, some prestige events. They found little coherent, rational strategy, except as *a posteriori* reconstruction.

In France cultural policy traditionally has been associated with mass education and social change, both on the left and within Catholic organisations. As a result, cultural policy has often been associated with left politics and ideologies. Because of its role in education and social change, policy evaluation has never been confined to simple measures, for example, size of audience or financial viability. As a result, the audience, is detached from the decision-making process. Professionals in the cultural sector and local authorities officials and councillors are the primary actors in this game. This dual dimension, the *jeu du catalogue* and the restricted actors involved in decision-making, has led to an incrementalist dynamic where cities have been led increasingly towards more actions, more spectacles, a wider variety of cultural activities without real policy control. This led to problems and in turn to efforts to reform cultural policy making in cities. As ever, Rennes piloted this process.

A local cultural policy to educate the people or to develop a cultural metropolis in European inter-urban competition?

The period examined in this chapter can be divided into three parts, even if the role performed by some of the main leaders and managers of local cultural organisations provides a strong element of continuity. However, political events mark some key turning points. In the first period, between 1959 and 1971, the mayor pursued progressive Christian Democrat policies which placed a major emphasis on the role of culture. Between 1971 and 1977 the city council moved more to the right and intense conflicts developed with actors in the cultural field, where the left found most of its growing support. Indeed, the left won the council in 1977. The second period, from 1971 to 1981, therefore, was characterised by uncertainty and discontinuity. In the third period after 1981, with the Socialist government in power, Rennes City Council was able to search for a policy to implement its ambitious programme.

Education, culture and the harmonious development of the city (1959-71)

Rennes's voluntary sector has been extremely powerful since the Second World War. Catholic influence was exercised through a network of voluntary associations involved in sports, culture, leisure and social activities. Two major organisations unite this series of voluntary societies and associations. The first is the Cercle Paul Bert, which unites non-religious societies, and the network of Union des Patronages which brings together societies connected to the Catholic church.

Fréville's ambition for Rennes was to modernise it through a cultural development programme. He appointed Michel Le Roux a *maire-adjoint*, a sort of committee chairman for cultural affairs, as early as 1962. It was the first such appointment in France and started the tradition of Rennes being a leader in urban cultural policies. Michel Le Roux was a Catholic activist who had been involved in the student Catholic movement and in the popular education movement close to progressive Christian Democrat organisations. He was also a journalist in the local newspaper *Ouest-France* and personally involved in many voluntary organisation. Culture, like housing, was seen as necessary for the harmonious, balanced, development of the city. In fact, social and cultural activities were dealt with together in a common policy sector known as *socio-culturel*.

Fréville created a structure which became a model for other cities in France, the Office Social et Culturel (OSC). This was formed in partnership with the city council, the body in charge of social housing (HLM), and a government agency responsible for allocating various social benefits, la Caisse d'Allocations Familiales (CAF). The CAF and HLM had become interested in the principle that the city council should invest in social and cultural centres in partnership with representatives from a wide range of voluntary associations. In this way, for the first time, decisions to invest in social and cultural facilities and activities were taken in co-operation with the voluntary sector. This, in turn, gave a tremendous boost to the development of voluntary organisations which were already active in the cultural sector in Rennes. The management of a number of facilities was negotiated between the main associations using them. For the first time in France, a genuine form of co-management was able to exist because the council allocated a general sum of money for cultural activities and then delegated to the OSC responsibility for allocating the funds and making decisions about infrastructure investment. A strategy for the establishment of cultural facilities and new cultural programmes planned for each neighbourhood, particularly working-class areas, often in conjunction with new social housing schemes. The facat that the city council normally accepted the proposals made by the OSC demonstrates the level of mutual trust between the two organisations. The whole process was an early example of decentralisation of a local authority's cultural policy-making.

At the same time one of the Maisons de la Culture, which had been created all over the country by Culture Minister André Malraux to decentralise provision from Paris was also established in Rennes.

Culture as an instrument for political change: the ideological crisis and the rise of the left.

During the 1970s, culture was one of the terrains of confrontation between social and political forces in Rennes. The cultural policy consensus of the 1960s collapsed. The events of 1968 brought considerable change to the Rennes political scene. On the right, the Mayor Fréville had shown signs of sympathy for some ideas brought forward in 1968 and he tried to defend the university. Partly as a result he lost his seat in Pparliament to a right-winger. More generally, in the municipal election of 1971 major changes occurred within the council. Fréville failed to maintain his alliance with the progressive wing of the former Christian Democrats. He lost the support of major local politicians such as Le Roux and other former Catholic trade union leaders who had been the driving forces behind the development of the 1960s culture and education programme and shifted to the right by allying himself with politicians closer to business interests, in the process distancing himself from the Catholic activist working in popular education.

On the left, May 1968 radicalised many individuals and groups and all the organisations of the left were strengthened, from the Communists to the Trotskyists and especially the Maoïsts who were quite influential in Rennes. Many former Catholic trade union leaders, members of the Catholic rural, working class or student societies moved to the far left, often becoming the leaders of leftist organisations. These political groups became quite influential in the cultural sector. Simultaneously, along with the new social movements, a new generation of Socialist leaders emerged who in the 1980s would benefit from the support of the state.

Culture became a point of ideological confrontation between the left and the right, the council and the voluntary sector. On the one hand, the city council demonstrated a growing distrust towards actors in the cultural field who they regarded as leftist. However, the council had no strategy except to regain a tight control over this sector and spend less money on it. The ideologies and ideas which grew after 1968 led many actors operating in the cultural field to feel that they were being manipulated by dominant interests. They wanted to use culture to denounce exploitation and alienation and as an instrument to change society and life. To be more radical and attack the interests of the bourgeoisie they believed they had to obtain more autonomy from the council and its financial priorities.

This inevitably led to conflicts. Many people involved in the cultural sector – managers, chairmen of cultural associations, teachers and people from the university, important users of these activities – were on the left. This permanent opposition between the council and the actors in the cultural field was used by the Socialist party as a base to recruit its militants and elites. The leftist groups also went for confrontation. This made the OSC's policies a permanent source of conflict. The council divided responsibilities for culture among several councillors and obtained direct control over some facilities.

In this period culture and economic development were regarded as antagonistic. Trying to link culture with economic development was seen by most actors in the cultural field as establishing an alliance with the devil. In this respect, it is revealing to look at the party manifestoes for the 1977 local elections. The left, led by the Socialists, attacked local business. Speeches and writings by left-wing politicians used the idea of culture to help people understand their social and economic position in society and bring about social and political change. During the economic crises of the 1970s and 1980s both the left and the right rejected the progressive Christian compromise and vision of the city. On the one hand, the right-wing council tried to instigate and accelerate the modernisation of the city in partnership with business interests, often by promoting prestigious urban development projects. Rennes had to become close to business interests to acquire international status. Culture had to bring prestige. On the other hand, actors in the cultural field and groups on the left saw in the economic crises the sign of the coming end of capitalism. They contrasted the mayor's ambitious prestige projects with a policy based on people's needs which was hostile to the interests of the bourgeoisie. This ideological view of the world hindered the development of cultural policy in Rennes. However, despite radicalisation on both sides, many institutions and societies pursued interesting initiatives. The Maison de la Culture, for instance, appointed a new director, who raised its profile with new policies on theatre and third world culture.

The left gained control of Rennes City Council in 1977, with a clear commitment to develop a cultural policy. They produced two documents about the aims of cultural policy which reflected both the prevailing left ideology of the time and the lack of a coherent strategy for the city. In a context where culture professionals had supported the left, the incrementalist logic of the *jeu du catalogue* played a major part. Everybody in the cultural field took the opportunity to ask for substantial increases in funding. It took two years for the new council to be able to accommodate all the new demands which were placed upon it. The decision-making process was dominated by actors in the cultural field. In fact, the council mainly increased its involvement in a wider range of activities and increased consistently the overall budget from 8 per cent of total municipal expenditure in 1977 to 12 per cent in 1982. This was presented as a 'catch up' policy because during the 1970s Rennes has lost ground to other

French cities – most obviously Grenoble.

Culture was given a high profile in institutional terms with the appointment within the local authority of a director for cultural development. A teacher, Martial Gabillard, was appointed as *maire-adjoint* for culture. He had been involved in the former OSC, was a leading figure within the council and was very close to the mayor. Reforms of the OSC which had been planned in 1973 were introduced. The OSC was reorganised as the OSCR, Office Social et Culturel Rennais. Despite this, the original principle of the OSC was maintained and the OSCR was still supposed to play the role of mediator between the city council and the voluntary sector. The staff was renewed with most of the new appointments politically in tune with the council. The OSCR had less management responsibilities since the council imposed certain policy decisions. The OSCR was supposed to become more a forum for local associations, which would encourage innovations and suggest ideas for policy-making. Finally, the new council, and specifically people working in the cultural field, were very sensitive to the question of regional identity. An effort was made to encourage local and regional cultural production with the emphasis placed on "Rennes in Brittany", as one municipal logo said.

The growth of local cultural policy (1981–83)

The year 1981 marks a turning point in Rennes. Until then, the new council had adopted a rather cautious strategy on cultural policy. The councillors had to adapt to their new position of power. They had held the view that economic and social changes derived from the control of the state. An effective local policy was impossible without the implementation of changes at the centre. They had believed that the crisis of capitalism, the consequences of which were apparent in Rennes, could only be tackled by a Socialist strategy implemented at state level. As a result, they had been reluctant to formulate economic development strategies mobilising the city's cultural resources. In 1981, a Socialist president was elected and the left won the parliamentary elections. This changed the context for local economic development and cultural policies. The mayor of Rennes was appointed Minister. He became a *grand notable*, able to mobilise state resources in Paris to finance his strategy. It also meant he was committed to the success of government policy and that Rennes would be at the forefront in the implementation of policies designed by the government. Rennes had to take the opportunity to respond quickly to the priorities set by the government and to take advantage of the funding which would follow. In parallel, the decentralisation reforms and the creation of a system of decentralised regional planning gave Rennes an opportunity to work out its strategy. After four years in power, the mayor felt confident enough to develop ambitious plans for his city. Because of his privileged position within French government, he had the opportunity to identify the key issues for the future of cities. And he made sure that Rennes was among the first cities to exploit new opportunities.

Between 1981 and 1983 Rennes City Council launched an expansionist economic development programme to create jobs locally and to take full advantage of state subsidies. The political and economic elites, under the guidance of the mayor and his advisers, took advantage of the decentralisation reforms to work out a new urban development strategy.

Cultural policy in Rennes was significantly influenced by the changes in central government after 1981. Jack Lang, the new Minister for Culture, had many ambitious plans. As early as the summer of 1981, advisers and councillors from Rennes were in Paris negotiating programmes for their city. In the view of civil servants, Grenoble and Rennes were the most dynamic cities which could take advantage of the change in government. In fact, some Minister's advisers came from Grenoble. Once in Paris, they tried to get money for a variety of projects which had been designed locally in line with the priorities set by the Ministry. As already discussed, Rennes's elites have a tradition of being good at developing schemes falling into line with central government priorities. Rennes's mayors have always been surrounded by officers and advisers who once worked for central government or for agencies in Paris and so know the networks. This proved to be particularly effective in the case of cultural policy.

In October 1982, Rennes City Council and the Ministry of Culture signed an agreement – a *convention* – in which the state gave 4.7 millions francs to Rennes City Council for interventions in the cultural field, plus 1 million francs between 1982 and 1983. This direct agreement between the city and the government, which bypassed regional government, demonstrated the new role that regional cities were given. Indeed, the agreement was justified by the decentralisation process and also by the fact that cities of regional importance like Rennes, which had supported a cultural policy for a long time, would benefit from state support.

A number of projects which were supported both by the state and by the city, justify the earlier assertion that a *jeu du catalgoue* was operating in Rennes. By analysing the contents of the *convention*, it is possible to gain an idea of the elements of Rennes's cultural policy and identify shifts in policy priorities. The first priority was developing artistic creativity. In the field of music, the government supported opera and the establishment of a regional symphonic orchestra. In the field of dance, a dance theatre was created in 1978, financed by both the government and the city council. The Theatre Chorégraphique de Rennes has created various new shows and was supported to tour to other cities. It received about 700,000 FF from the council and 700,000 from the state each year. In the case of drama, the council contributes 300,000 FF a year. In 1982, however, in order to contribute to the foundation of the Centre Dramatique National/Comédie de Rennes, the state increased its subsidies to nearly 6 million FF. The city and the Ministry also supported youth theatre companies based in different parts of the city and theatrical training schemes. In the relatively under-developed field of the visual arts, the council and the Ministry multiplied their efforts and initiatives, with exhibitions, museums and public. The Ministry provided 250,000 FF for this sector.

The second priority was to develop the professionalisation of cultural policy. The Minister wanted to create a network of professionals in the cultural field and go beyond the range of voluntary associations which had traditionally been involved. This applied not only to theatre but also to popular music, film and video, with the provision of premises and equipment.

Widening the audience for cultural activities was an important objective of the *convention*. A variety of measures were taken, for example developing libraries in every neighbourhood, and supporting a cultural centre for Islamic students. Training for the film sector and the development of initiatives to promote popular reading were also included. These received a total state contribution of 850,000 FF. The promotion of Breton culture and the opening of Rennes to cultures from all over the world were other priorities. These included the creation of a museum and of an eco-museum in a farm to document the rural civilisation of Brittany, support regional cultural production, and keep specialised archives in music and dance. The Ministry contributed 850,000 FF in 1982 towards the support of 'old' and 'new' regional culture. The city council also decided to create an ambitious cultural centre in a popular neighbourhood in the south of the city, which cost several millions FF.

Three points about the *convention* are particularly worth highlighting. First, the growth in cultural policy budgets. In 1981-82 the major French cities spent on average 12 per cent of their municipal budget on culture. Grenoble and some cities with a more recent involvement in the field spent a higher percentage. The figure was about 8 per cent in 1977-78. By 1990 it was close to 15 per cent. The *jeu du catalogue*, the development of regional capitals at the expense of smaller cities and rural areas, the pressure from the state to go for professionalisation in the cultural sector and the growing inter-urban competition all contributed to a dramatic increase in the costs of cultural policy.

Second, in the 1982 *convention* one can find both traditional types of policies and more ambitious ones. On the one hand, the city council wanted to offer people more opportunities for more cultural consumption facilities and jobs. It also wanted to create training and to support regional culture. On the other hand, the city council promoted prestigious programmes of cultural events where the quality of theatre, popular music and dance had to be nationally, or even internationally, recognised to enhance the prestige of the city. Now Rennes has the most important rock festival in France, les Transmusicales.

The second major change during the 1981-83 period concerned the internal dynamics of the city. Under the new institutional framework following the decentralisation reforms, the regions were supposed to prepare a regional development plan and sign a contract with the state specifying how the plan would be implemented. The regional plan was supposed to be drawn up once every tier of government, from the *communes* to the *départements*, had set its own priorities. It did not work this way as regions did not have enough interest or political legitimacy to pursue this process. Rennes decided to play the new game and to formulate a *plan de développement* for its urban area. The city council, and the council for the whole urban area which was dominated by Rennes, created a new organisation in partnership with the Chamber of Commerce and the trade unions. For a period of six months, some four hundred people from every kind of local voluntary group and public and private sector institutions sat on committees to establish a strategy for the following five years. Le plan de développement du pays de Rennes was an interesting mixture of political principles, economic analysis, and forty-five initiatives for which money had to be found through negotiations between local elites and the state. It presented a view of the economic development of the area which was accepted by most local actors. The major theme of the document was that job creation in Rennes could be achieved by the development and exploitation of the scientific research capability which had been built up in the area during the previous twenty years. The document created the principle that for Rennes's development to occur the city had to encourage advanced research and promote the integration of research, training, production and marketing. It was subsequently decided to create a science park, one of the first institutions of its kind in France. Rennes also had to develop its international relations by taking into account its economic development priorities. It was decided that an integrated policy linking economic development projects, the showcase science park, a place marketing strategy, cultural events and innovations would increase the city's chances in the developing economic competition between cities at a European level.

Culture and new technologies to become a European metropolis (1983–90)

The plan de développement for the Rennes urban area changed the position of cultural policy in urban policy-making. To a certain extent, local elites had returned to the strategy designed by Fréville in the 1950s. The context of the 1980s implied increased competition between urban areas. Instead of using education and culture to sustain modernisation – as in the 1950s – in the 1980s advanced research and the 'knowledge industries' were put at the core of the process of economic development.

The priorities of cultural policy changed. The main innovations of the 1980s were in relation to the economic development and image building strategies which led to radical modifications in the relationship between cultural and economic policies. In the new local context for culture, several points must be highlighted. First, the science park, Rennes Atalante, which was successful and became the shop window of Rennes's economic development strategy. The main research centres in the science park work in the fields of image recording, telecommunications and electronics. After 1983, in parallel with the new economic strategy, the city council developed its new place marketing strategy, based on research, new technologies, history and culture. The city developed the ambition of becoming a European metropolis. In contrast with the previous three decades, when its regional dimension had been consciously projected to the outside world, Rennes chose to present itself to the world as a modernist, ambitious city linked with other French and European cities through systems of networks. In keeping with this strategy, Rennes was the first municipality to set up a cable television system, enhancing its profile as a modernist city. The council also launched a national awards scheme for the most innovative firms which became an opportunity for journalists to see how Rennes had transformed itself into an innovative and dynamic city. Within the space of a few years, Rennes built an image of itself as a modern and enterprising place, with the success of its science park and its cultural policy as a key element in the process.

Rennes's priority, in cultural terms, became to promote the city as a cultural capital, building on its tradition as city of innovation. On the one hand, it developed cultural events related to new technologies and the future; on the other, it planned to increase the prestige of its 'traditional' cultural events. The first direction was to develop cultural forms related to new technologies. Since this was also a central government priority, Rennes was quick to seize upon the proposals made by the Ministry of Culture to create a cultural centre for new technologies (CCSTI), similar to the Science Park at La Villette in Paris. Rennes was one of the first cities in France to have a CCSTI and through its network of dynamic cultural associations, to publish a regular newsletter and develop cultural animation initiatives around the centre. All this fitted nicely with the promotion of the city's science park. The council also launched a Festival for Electronics Arts with artists working on computer graphics and applications of electronics to buildings in the city. The festival was a national cultural event which suited the city promoting the association between arts, the city and technological innovation in public consciousness. The council organised an exhibition called Rennes au Future showing aspects of life in the city in the future and the impact of new technologies. The exhibition attracted 50,000 visitors, a considerable number for a city of 200,000. In short, the synergy of cultural policy and new technologies, within the framework of the city's economic strategy, was successful in promoting and projecting a coherent external image of the city. The marketing of Rennes was built on the science park, the research centres, its young, educated and dynamic population which had 3,000 academics or researchers and 40,000 students. The city could claim to possess the most advanced technologies in computer graphics, small high-tech firms, the Festival for Electronic Arts and an important rock festival. It emphasised both the modernity of its science park and the beauty of its renovated historic city centre. Local elites took the view that the success of the city depended on its ability to be modern and innovative in all sectors. New programmes in the social, education and cultural fields were opportunities to demonstrate that the modernity of Rennes was not confined to its science park.

The second element of Rennes's cultural strategy was to raise the profile of the local cultural institutions. The convention with central government was an essential part of this strategy as it allowed the development of important cultural facilities. Until 1981, the city had adopted a cautious approach towards its Maison de la Culture. A director was appointed from 1982 to 1985 to promote an ambitious programme. However, ambiguities remained about the real profile of this institution and the extent to which it should respond to the needs of local residents or create spectacles which would obtain national or international recognition. A new, prestigious director was appointed in 1986, who reorganised the Maison and obtained money to renovate its facilities. A detailed analysis of the Maison's programme reveals that it followed national trends and that many individual events were the same which could be found in other regional capitals or Paris, in dance, music or theatre. Rennes followed the trend towards the homogenisation of cultural programming which is observable in most French regional capitals.

While it pursued these new priorities for cultural policy, the council did not give up its traditional involvement in other areas. Support for Breton culture, although it was not really reduced, did not benefit to the same extent, since it did not fit the image of 'modernity' the city wanted to project.

The *jeu du catalogue* led to a financial crisis in Rennes City Council's cultural policy. Indeed, it is remarkable at the end of the 1980s, how many cities – Orleans and Angoulême, for instance – went through a financial crisis caused in part by the high costs of cultural and economic development programmes. The high costs of cultural policy-making attracted criticism from both the right and left. In

1983, after the local elections, some newly-elected right-wing mayors in French cities closed their cultural centres since they viewed them as too expensive, or too elitist, or too leftist. In 1987, French regions spent 770 million FF on culture, or 16 francs per inhabitant, an increase of 30 per cent since 1984. French *départments* spent 2,688 million FF on culture in 1987, 5.15 francs per inhabitant, an increase of 44 per cent since 1984. Cities over 150,000 inhabitants spent 601 francs per head on culture in 1981, 789 francs per head in 1984, and 905 francs per head in 1987. Rennes's expenditure is slightly above these averages. In recent years, as cultural expenditure in some cases reached 15 per cent of municipal budgets, many local authorities have faced a financial crisis and have started to question the allocations of funds for culture. Rennes is no exception to this process. For example, the Maison de la Culture went bankrupt. This is surprising since the Rennes Maison de la Culture was one of the most successful in France as the following data reveal.

Table 9.1: Number of subscriptions, total audience and public funding for the Maisons de la Culture in Grenoble, Le Havre and Rennes

1987	Grenoble	Le Havre	Rennes
Subscriptions	7,000	7,000	16,000
Audience (per year)	74,000	97,000	165,000
Subsidy (million FF)	24	21	15.8
from State	11	10.5	7.5
from City Council	9	9.5	7.9

If the audiences is the yardstick against which the Maison should be judged, Rennes' Maison de la Culture works well. However, since 1982, it has regularly faced financial crises which led to the departure of its director and left the city council and central government to find extra money for it. This inevitably created political conflicts. It was observed before that the decision-making process was dominated by players in the cultural sector. Each time there was a conflict, the culture professionals pretended that the councillors were stubborn politicians who did not understand the reality of culture and had a narrow, finance-driven view of the world. Since 1985 the expansionist trend in cultural expenditure has been stopped. However, the management of cultural organisations has not always been efficient and this has provoked a new financial crisis. The city council has tried to diversity the sources of finance for cultural facilities at neighbourhood level, even by attracting money from the private sector. This is in tune with the council's new economic strategy but was seen by many in the cultural field as intolerable.

The Maison de la Culture and its ambitious director faced another major financial crisis in 1989. There were rumours that it could face a deficit of between 2 and 8 million francs. An audit was carried out by the council and they discovered that the deficit created in three years from 1986 was 23 million francs on an annual 1989 budget of 34 million francs. The Maison's financial situation became a major political issue and the city council and central government had to intervene heavily. The Maison was saved because the council contributed 36 million francs. But of its 68 employees 36 were sacked and the 1990 budget was reduced to 20 million francs. A semi-public body was created to manage it consisting of the city council, a public sector-owned bank for local authorities and private sector partners. Such restructuring is not peculiar to Rennes. Since 1989, Grenoble and Le Havre had to reorganise their Maisons de la Culture for similar reasons and La Rochelle had to close its Maison down altogether. Central government has, at the same time, reduced its financial contribution. For instance, the Ministry of Culture reduced its subsidies to cultural institutions when the Chirac government was in power between 1986 and 1988 and the city council had to go to the courts to get the money which it had been promised.

For the first time because of its financial problems, the city council has launched an extensive review of its funding for cultural groups, in partnership with the OSCR and other local actors. This audit, conducted by research groups Lares, is a pilot experience in France. It has attracted considerable interest in other French cities. The city council also launched a committee with outsiders from the city council to make proposals for a new cultural policy. The key words have become management, assessment, cost control, organisation. This may open a new period for Rennes's cultural policy.

Conclusions

These conclusions focus on the major points in the relationship between economic trends and culture and the notion of local cultural policy. The 1980s may be seen in the future as the golden years of urban cultural policies. French cities expanded as economic trends and state policies favoured regional capitals at the expense of rural areas and small cities. The Ministry of Culture played an important role in this process by encouraging and financing many new cultural developments. City councils also had the financial resources to strengthen their involvement in the cultural field, both in qualitative and quantitative terms.

In France competition between cities has clearly given a major impetus in the mid 1980s to create prestigious cultural events and festivals or to attract world-famous architects. This is increasingly a constraint for cities which use culture as an element in inter-urban competition. It is also widely used by local politicians to improve their legitimacy and their own image. Beyond the logic of competition, there is also a social logic of distinction between different cities. As far as competition is concerned, many French cities have yet to realise that they are quite small in European terms and that in comparison with German cities, for instance, their aspirations seem very ambitious.

From the French perspective, there has been an important trend at work in major cities in the past decade. Culture has received more and more attention. But at the same time, it has had to be closely related to the main priorities of the local authority. This articulation was well designed in the case of Montpellier or Rennes. If city councils develop strategic planning, cultural policies may become more and more integrated within overall urban development strategies. The financial constraint which will be a key issue for French cities in the 1990s will also force adjustments. Hard choices will have to be made. The facts observed in Rennes suggest that cities may try to organise their cultural policies in a different way in order to control the incrementalist *jeu du catalogue* trend. In the immediate future, financial crises are likely to occur in several cities. Creating a new festival will, for instance, become an increasingly high-risk strategy as so many exist already.

Thus far, this chapter has assumed that urban cultural policies do indeed exist. However, it can be argued that the diverse actions in the area of culture by local authorities do not constitute a policy. The future of cultural policy is at stake now in many French cities which cannot afford the costs incurred during recent years. Cultural policies require to be controlled by the local authority. However, a new trend is emerging which could prevent this. In the last three years, the private sector has played an increasing role in financing cultural events. This is in line with cities' attempts to diversify resources put into culture and to share the cost of these events. However, privatisation of cultural interventions is now increasingly common. In some cities facing financial difficulties, in Avignon for instance, the management of events has been transferred to a private company. A new set of companies has been created from consultant to cultural entrepreneur to take charge of cultural activities and events. Some belong to companies like Générale des Eaux which are a key actor in the provision of urban services such as water, garbage or cable television for local authorities. Local public–private partnerships are also becoming more important in the cultural field. Privatisation or development of a public sector-led urban cultural policy? It is not yet clear in France. But it is difficult to see how culture can be an exception to the general trend towards growing privatisation of the local public sector.

Referances

Balme, Richard (1985), 'L'Action Culturelle et ses Incideance sûr les Sistems Politiques Municipaux', doctoral thesis, Bordeaux, Institut d'Etudes Politiques.

Beaunez, Roger (1985), Politiques culturelles et municipalités, Paris, Editions Ouvrières.

Boure, Robert (1989), 'La ville on risque de la communication', Les papiers du GRESE, 6, autumn.

D'Angelo, Mario, et al., (1989), Les politiques culturelles et les administrateurs, Paris, La Documentation Française.

Developpement Culturel, nos 55, April 1983; 64, September 1985; 65, March 1986; 69, March 1987; 73, February 1988; 81, July 1989; 82, July 1989; 85, May 1990.

Estebe, Philippe and Remond, Emmanuel (1983), Les communes au rendez-vous de la culture, Paris, Syros.

Friedberg, E. and Urfalino, P. (1984), Le jeu du catalogue, Paris, La Documentation Française.

Friedberg, E. and Urfalino, P. (1984a), 'Les municipalités et la culture', in Esprit, 1667, mars, p.45-110.

Friedberg, E. and Urfalino, P. (1984b), 'La gestion des politiques culturelles municipales', in Politique et management public, 1, 2, 3-26.

Gasquy-Resche, Yannick (1990), Marseille, Montreal Centres Culturels Cosmopolites, Paris, L'Harmattan.

Herscovici, Alain (1989), 'Demandes culturelles et politique communale', Les papiers du GRESE, 6, autumn.

Lefebvre, Alain (1989), 'Privatisation ou tutelle partagée? Examples Toulousains dans le Domaine des Loisire et de la Television Locale', Les papiers du GRESE., 6, autumn.

Mazet, Pierre (1989), 'Les collectivites locales et les festival: Logiques emblematiques, logiques territoriales', Les papiers du GRESE, 6, autumn.

Ministère de la Culture, Direction du Développement Cuturel (1984), Rock et politique culturelle: l'exemple de Rennes, Paris.

Ministère de la Culture et de la Communication, Secretariat National à la Culture (1989),

L'etat, les villes, la culture et les socialistes, Paris.

Negrier, Emmanuel (1989), 'Nouveaux reseaux de communication et territoire', *Les papiers du GRESE*, 6, Autumn.

Padioleau, Jean G. (1989), 'Un mouvement de rationalisation de l'action publique urbaine, le planning strategique', in Wachter, Serge (ed.), *Politiques publiques et territoires*, Paris, L'Harmattan.

Pongy, Mireille (1989), 'Politiques culturelles territoriales: Une approche en termes de referentiel', *Les papiers du GRESE*, 6, autumn.

Pontier, J. M., (1986), 'Les regions et la culture', in *Revue Française de droit administratif*, 4.

Rizzardo, René (1988), 'Cooperation des collectivités publiques et action culturelle', contribution to a colloquium held in Grenoble, 1-2 December.

Saez, Guy (1983), 'Politique de style, politique de ville (Grenoble et Rennes devent la culture)', *Les cahiers de l'animation*, 3, 41.

Saez, Guy (1989), 'De l'autonomie des politiques culturelles territoriales', *Les papiers du GRESE*, 6, autumn.

Saez, Guy (1990), 'Le niveau de la politique culturelle metropolitaine: Coherence ou Fragmentation', in Gasquy-Resche (1990).

Saez, Guy (1990a), *Les villes en recomposition. Les politiques culturelles à Grenoble et Montpellier*, Grenoble, CERAT.

Ville de Rennes (1979), *La vie culturelle à Rennes*, Rennes.

Ville de Rennes (1985), *La politique culturelle dans les equipements de quartier*, Rennes, 19 February.

Ville de Rennes (1987), *La vie culturelle à Rennes*, Rennes.

10

Culture, conflict and cities: issues and prospects for the 1990s

Franco Bianchini

Introduction

This book is not intended to be the last word on the topic of urban cultural policy in western Europe, but rather the beginning of a debate. This final chapter attempts to explore the controversial implications arising from the adoption of cultural policies as strategies for urban regeneration, to provide tentative answers to some of the questions raised by other chapters and to point to a future agenda for both policy-makers and researchers. The use of cultural policy as an element of urban regeneration strategies is increasingly an uncontested issue. Yet this consensus masks serious dilemmas regarding strategic choices in economic, cultural and community development. The chapter discusses the possibility of developing cultural policies based on the recognition of these dilemmas, which attempt to reconcile social and cultural with economic development priorities.

The chapter also examines wider themes concerning cultural policy and the future of cities as public realms and political communities. In particular, it focuses on the question of the extent to which cultural policies can help cities function once again as genuinely democratic public domains and catalysts for public social life. The debate on cultural policy and the future of cities as public realms in the 1990s is linked with the debate on the future of citizenship and local democracy in western Europe. Two key problems in this area are the increasing social, spatial and cultural segregation of low-income groups in west European cities and the need to make ethnic and racial minorities an integral part of the civic network. The evidence is that the latter task will be particularly hard to accomplish. Can cultural policy-makers encourage immigrant communities and other disadvantaged social groups to demonstrate the relevance of their ideas, aspirations, skills and resources to the city's overall development? Will post-1992 Europe be imbued with a triumphalistic, civilisational notion of European culture and identity, emphasising 'high' art and national cultures, rather than popular, local and ethnic cultures? Or could something more modern, dynamic, inclusive and democratic emerge from the cultural policies of European cities? In the 1970s and 1980s city cultural policies have in may cases been more innovative and based on broader definitions of 'culture' than national policies. City governments have often been more effective than national governments in promoting multiculturalism.

The concluding sections of the chapter outline a way forward for urban cultural policies in western Europe. It starts from the recognition that municipal governments will have a central and irreplaceable role in urban cultural policy-making, but it asks what forms of support a supranational institution like the European Community could provide to make the task of city administrations easier. Despite the considerable financial, political and legislative constraints on city governments, the chapter argues that there is much European cities could do to improve the effectiveness of their cultural policies, simply by learning from the experience of successful cities and by reconceptualising their strategic interventions. Three broad areas in which a change in perspectives would be beneficial are identified: the need for organic links between policies on culture and policies on training, education, research and development; the importance of adopting broader definitions of 'urban regeneration' and 'quality of life' as bases for policy-making; and, most importantly, the adoption of a 'cultural planning' perspective, with significant implications for the training of policy-makers and the corporate working of city governments.

Three dilemmas in urban cultural policy development

In most cities cultural policies aimed at fostering local economic development and at supporting city marketing strategies enjoyed in the course of the 1980s a remarkable degree of political consensus, at both national and local government level. Cultural policies, however, can have controversial cultural, economic, social and spatial implications, which can be seen in the form of strategic dilemmas. For example, conflicts can arise between cultural provision in the city centre and in peripheral areas, between consumption-oriented strategies and support for local cultural production, and between investment in buildings and support for local cultural production. These are not the only dilemmas policy-makers face; we highlight them here because they have been faced by many of the cities in this collection.

Spatial dilemmas: city centre–periphery tensions, and the risk of gentrification

Economic inequities have clear spatial manifestations in many major European cities. New conflicts emerged in the 1980s between affluent city-centre and suburban residents, and low-income citizens living in run-down inner-city areas and outer housing estates, whose opportunities for participation in the city centre's cultural renaissance were undermined by a number of factors. The most important of these was probably the further deterioration in the relative economic position of these social groups, who were the main victims of the growth in long-term unemployment and of the deskilling process related to economic restructuring. Rising fear of crime, and the rapid escalation in the cost of out-of-home cultural consumption compared with its domestic equivalents contributed to the growth in home-based leisure, and to reducing participation by low-income groups in more 'public' forms of cultural activities.

How can the growing divide between lively, convivial city centres in which cultural activities are flourishing and increasingly marginalised peripheries be bridged? One way of addressing such conflicts in the spatial distribution of cultural provision is to create neighbourhood-based arts facilities, as demonstrated by the experiences of two of the cities discussed in this book, Hamburg and Bologna. The city state of Hamburg created a system of neighbourhood cultural centres which are used by about half a million people every year for activities ranging from language classes to rock concerts and political meetings. In Bologna, the city council's 1981 'Youth Programme' re-equipped and renovated the city's neighbourhood youth centres, and stimulated – with the provision of training courses, loans, premises and technical facilities – the flourishing of enterprises in electronic music, video, computer graphics, crafts and other cultural sectors. As shown by Jude Bloomfield's chapter, the new youth centres contributed to enhancing social cohesion in the city. They helped reintegrate many young people into the local economy, and created opportunities for political dialogue between them, the local authority and the rest of civil society.

The establishment of neighbourhood-based cultural centres and the support given to grassroots activities can be effectively combined with strategies aimed at democratising access to city centre-based cultural provision. The introduction of 'town cards' to easily access cultural facilities at discount prices for local residents, the wider distribution of accurate information about city centre-based attractions and activities, as well as better policing, street lighting, late-night public transport and car-park safety would make a significant contribution in most cities to enhancing accessibility.

On their own, however, interventions of this kind are not sufficient to bridge the gap between the city centre and deprived peripheral areas. Urban policy-makers need to recognise the importance of developing what Michael Walzer describes as 'open-minded space', which is "designed for a variety of uses, including unforeseen and unforeseeable uses, and used by citizens who do different things and are prepared to tolerate, even take an interest in, things they don't do" (1986: 470). Maarten Hajer suggests in his chapter that the development of urban design and city planning strategies based on the concept of open-minded space could form the basis for an effective cultural strategy, which would contribute to the revitalisation of the city centre and the integration of the underclass in public life.

A second type of spatial dilemma in urban cultural policy-making is the need to respond to the fact that, as one graffiti in Montreal proclaimed, in many cases "artists are the storm-troopers of gentrification" (Toronto Arts Council, 1988). The establishment of certain areas of cities as 'cultural districts' in some cases – as in Frankfurt's new Museum Quarter (Simor, 1988) – has generated gentrification, displaced local residents and facilities, and increased land values, rents, and the local cost of living, as measured – for example – by the prices charged by local shops. These processes can drive out of the district artists and other cultural producers who survive on relatively low incomes. Such cases clearly demonstrate the inadequacies of unrestrained property-led regeneration strategies, and raise important issues for policy-making in the 1990s.

Economic development dilemmas: consumption v. production

In cultural policy-making there is often a clear separation, which can generate tensions and conflicts, between consumption and production-oriented strategies. The first develop and promote urban cultural attractions and activities as magnets for tourism, retailing, hotel and catering. The second provide strategic support for publishing, film, TV, electronic music, design, fashion and other cultural industries which require specialised skills and infrastructures.

It can be risky in the long term for cities to rely on consumption-oriented models of cultural policy-led economic development, even if they may be profitable in the short term, by creating visibility and political returns. The success of strategies that use cultural policy to boost retailing and consumer services industries, expand tourism and attract external investment increasingly depends on factors over which cities have very limited control, ranging from airfare prices to changes in the level of the residents' and visitors' disposable income. A related problem concerns the quality of the jobs created by consumerist approaches to cultural policy-led regeneration. Booth and Boyle in this volume demonstrate that the cultural revitalisation of Glasgow contributed to the growth of employment in the city's tourism and leisure industries from 14,785 in 1985 to 25,000 in 1989. However, the employment generated by the 'customer effect' of cultural policies – which is particularly strong in sectors such as retailing and hotel and catering – is frequently low-paid, part-time, and characterised by deskilling and poor levels of job satisfaction, legal rights and working conditions. Precisely for these reasons, it is important for cities to combine a policy aimed at boosting cultural consumption with local cultural industries strategies, which have the potential of creating skilled jobs in high value-added sectors of the economy. Initiatives like Bologna's Biennale of young artists from Mediterranean countries, described in Bloomfield's chapter, demonstrate how festivals can imaginatively combine support for innovation in cultural production with the widening of opportunities for cultural consumption.

Cultural funding dilemmas: 'ephemeral' v. 'permanent'

The case studies have raised the argument about the extent to which cultural policy-makers must choose between 'ephemeral' programmes of events and activities – like festivals and other cultural animation initiatives – and investment in 'permanent' facilities such as concert halls, libraries, museums and arts centres. This juxtaposition – which was common among critics of the summer cultural animation policies of Rome City Council in the late 1970s and early 1980s – is in many ways artificial. Apparently 'ephemeral' events, if coherently organised and repeated, can become 'permanent' features of a city's cultural landscape, producing long-term benefits in terms of image, tourism and support for local cultural production.

The 'ephemeral–permanent' dichotomy, however, does allow us to focus on the problem that maintenance costs and loan charges on cultural buildings are often so high that they absorb most of the resources available. For example, Julia Gonzalez in this volume observes that over 80% of the cultural budget of Bilbao City Council in 1986 was spent on the renovation and maintenance of buildings for cultural use, which left relatively little for the funding and programming of cultural activities. The same criticism has been made of many of the Maisons de la Culture, the large multi-purpose arts centres built during the 1960s in a number of French provincial cities (Ardagh, 1990).

In times of financial stringency city administrations are more likely to curtail revenue funding for those activities which are seen as 'marginal', often aimed at disadvantaged social groups or innovative and experimental in character, than to withdraw money invested in theatres, concert halls and other physical facilities (Challans, 1991). In this context, greater use of public and open spaces, temporary structures and buildings combining culture with other types of uses could liberate resources to fund events, activities and new cultural production.

Cultural policy and the future of cities as public domains and democratic communities

Policy-makers increasingly have to deal with anti-urban tendencies which can be characterised as monofunctionalism, cultural standardisation and the erosion of urbanity. These processes – as the European Commission recently recognised in its *Green Paper on the Urban Environment* (1990) – are driven by a range of factors. They include the gentrification of historic city centres by affluent professionals, the segregation of low-income residents in run-down peripheral housing estates, the continuing influence of the functionalist tradition of zoning in European planning philosophy and practice, the mushrooming of out-of-town shopping malls, the related gradual disappearance of facilities for everyday shopping in city centres, the banality of the international style of much contemporary corporate architecture, the growing commercialisation and privatisation of public space, and the introduction of new forms of policing designed to rid central city shopping areas of 'undesirables'. One of the results of these pressures is that our experiences of urban public life are less diverse, as they increasingly take place within a more socially homogenous environment.

The participation of disadvantaged ethnic and racial communities in public and cultural life in European cities is particularly problematic. Many working people belonging to Asian, African, Afro-Caribbean, Turkish and more recently East European ethnic communities are trapped in the unskilled sectors of urban labour markets, with limited prospects for mobility, or, worse still, are being ruthlessly exploited as illegal workers in the informal economy. They are frequently discriminated against in housing, education, policing and the provision of other urban services, and suffer from the growing influence of implicitly or explicitly racist parties and movements, from the French National Front to the Italian Lombard League, which have established strong bases in many European cities.

The range and scale of the problems we have identified suggest that linking the debate on the future of cities as physical and economic entities to that on the future of citizenship and local democracy will be one of the most important critical tasks for the 1990s. Cultural policy is one of the instruments through which such linkage could be created. There were, however, contradictory trends in the cultural policy experience of urban Europe in the 1980s. On the one hand, the political consensus about the value of cultural policy as a vehicle for social as well as economic development led to a depoliticisation of the debate about cultural policy, particularly in comparison with the 1970s. On the other hand, many city governments tried to make the cultural policy-making process more responsive to the demands, aspirations and ideas of citizens, community groups and local business, with a new emphasis on partnerships between the public, private and voluntary sectors. They drew up 'cultural plans' auditing their cultural resources and identifying the needs of of the local community. Public consultation, and the devolution of decision-making powers to community groups also ensured in some cities a degree of democratic control over cultural policy-making. However, these efforts to involve the citizens in the policy-making process and in the debate about the future of the city should be widened and deepened in the 1990s. Urban cultural policies in the 1990s should be driven by a new 'civic' inspiration. They could then become one of the key instruments to trigger off a broader politicisation process and create stronger links between civil and political society.

Cultural policies should recognise and respect the rights of urban grassroots movements to autonomy and self-organisation, and to express and celebrate the distinctiveness of their identities. However, to counteract the trend towards increasing social polarisation and fragmentation within European cities, cultural policy-makers ought to encourage the urban social movements to contribute their energies, resources and ideas to the debate about the future of the city and to improving the quality of life of the wider community. Creative inputs and perspectives from disadvantaged ethnic and geographical communities, organisations representing disabled people, feminist and environmentalist groups could help democratise and enrich the city's cultural policy and could raise important questions about the way the city functions and is designed.

The role of municipal government

The book illustrates a wide range of achievements by European cities in the cultural policy field. They demonstrate how local government can be innovative, imaginative and dynamic, and how it can respond to changing economic conditions and the changing needs of the community. The case studies highlight the fact that the success of cultural policy as a regeneration strategy in cities endowed with similar resources is crucially aided by a variety of factors. They include: the presence of solid partnerships between local government and the private and voluntary sectors, the quality of urban leadership, the ability of strategic policy-makers to formulate practical action plans, and their awareness of the city's position within national and international urban cultural hierarchies. It is instructive to compare, in this respect, the success of Glasgow with Liverpool's relative failure. The case studies also show that cultural policies have an impact on all other areas of policy-making, and are most effective when they are part of integrated development strategies. There is certainly scope in cultural policy-making for partnerships between different agencies, ranging from central and local government to the private sector and arts organisations. It is clear, however, that locally accountable and democratically elected multi-purpose agencies such as municipal governments are much better placed than either national governments or the private sector to make cultural policies work effectively.

The role of the European Community

Our emphasis on the centrality of municipal government does not mean that European Community institutions cannot play a useful role in support of city cultural policies. Discussions of cultural policy in western Europe still overwhelmingly concentrate on the national dimension. There is a serious dearth of comparative knowledge and research on the richness of policy-making experiences and traditions at city level. There are, for instance, no standardised definitions of the remit of urban cultural policies. The lack of reliable comparative statistics obviously hinders the development of meaningful debate and comparative research. There may be a role for European Community institutions here. The Commission could support staff and best practice exchanges for west European cultural policy-makers, as well as the creation of a clearing house for research, a network for sharing information on west European urban cultural policy issues, and an urban cultural co-operation fund. These initiatives would be valuable since cities in different European countries have different specialisations. For example, the development of local strategies for the media industries (Wynne et al., 1989; Cornford and Robins, 1990; Barnett, 1991; Bianchini, 1991b) and of cultural policies targeted at ethnic and racial minorities (Owusu, 1986; Khan, 1991) is more common in Britain than in other European countries. However, French cities have a rich experience in the promotion of innovative architecture and new telecommunication technologies such as telematics and cable (see Medias Pouvoirs, 18, 1990, and 22, 1991), while Italian cities tend to excel in the organisation of film and performing arts festivals and art exhibitions. The Commission could also encourage cultural co-operation agreements between cities like that signed by the municipalities of Montpellier and Nîmes and described by Emmanuel Negrier in this book. Co-operation agreements between neighbouring cities of regional importance are arguably one of the most important preconditions for the success of urban cultural policies at national and international level.

The European Commission's cultural policy at present pays relatively little attention to the potential contribution of cultural resources to urban and regional development. Some of the Commission's initiatives, however, already give a significant contribution to facilitating access to the European market for small-scale, independent cultural producers – for example, through the packages of measures in support of the European audiovisual industry known as MEDIA '92 and MEDIA '95. Independent cultural production is often based in provincial cities, away from the major concentrations of commercial cultural industries, and is often closer than commercial culture to the experience of marginalised social and political groups. In short, initiatives within MEDIA '92 such as the European Film Distribution Office – which provides financial support for the distribution to European cinemas of low-budget films – may not be able to create viable regional alternatives to the nerve centres of the European cultural economy. They could, however, encourage the Commission in the 1990s to support the creation of Europe-wide networks of 'independent' cultural industries based in different cities – for instance, Black publishing, electronic music and film industries – which have an important contribution to make to the development of cultural pluralism and diversity, and of a democratic European civil society.

Towards a cultural planning approach?

A recognition of the strategic dilemmas raised by the experience of the 1980s should inform the process of urban cultural policy-making in the Europe of the 1990s. In the 1980s urban cultures were energetically exploited by politicians and policy-makers to assist the transformation of local economies from 'old' to 'new' functions, and to soften the social impact of restructuring. Urban leaders in western Europe, as many of their counterparts in the USA had done in the 1970s, encouraged the development of cultural policies to enhance the reputation of their cities, assist the physical regeneration of city centres, boost tourism and other 'sunrise' service industries and help generate local consensus at a time of economic and social change when many controversial decisions had to be made. There is no doubt that this emphasis on the importance of consumption, property assets and image was an important addition to the battery of arguments for urban cultural policy-making. The 1980s perspective, however, is too narrow to provide a sound basis for policy development in the present decade. We would argue that in the 1990s cities should move towards a more holistic 'cultural planning' approach, which puts a cultural perspective centre stage when formulating urban development strategies.

The notion of cultural planning, already widely used in the USA and Australia (Von Eckhardt, 1980; McNulty, 1991; Mercer, 1991), is still uncommon among west European policy-makers. Its central characteristics are that it rests on a very broad, anthropological definition of 'culture' as 'a way of life', and that it integrates the arts into other aspects of local culture and into the texture and routines of daily life in the city. Its field of action ranges from the arts, the media, the crafts, fashion and design to sports, recreation, architecture and townscape, heritage, tourism, eating and entertainment, local history, and the characteristics of the city's public realm and social life, its identity and external image. Cultural planning can help urban governments identify the city's cultural resources and think strategically about their applications, to achieve key objectives in areas as diverse as physical planning, townscape design, tourism, industrial development, retailing, place marketing, community development, education and training.

Policy-makers in west European cities are still not sufficiently aware of the potential of their cultural resources. Aesthetic definitions of 'culture' as 'art' still tend to prevail, and policies for the arts are rarely co-ordinated with policies on sports, the media and other elements of local culture. The result of this lack of integration is the failure to exploit potential synergies and strategic development opportunities. By its nature cultural planning cuts across the divides between the public, private and voluntary sectors, different institutional concerns, and different professional disciplines. To implement cultural planning strategies, city governments will have to move towards a more corporate approach to policy-making. This is already common in Germany, where since the mid 1970s a number of cities have established cultural development plans which connect cultural policy with other areas of municipal policy-making (Ismayr, 1987: 62-3).

The movement towards the development of corporate cultural policies is gaining strength also in Britain. Birmingham City Council, for example, in 1989 merged the cultural functions of five of its committees in one new, cross-departmental Arts, Culture and Economy (ACE) Sub-Committee. Before its establishment, the Finance and Management Committee was exclusively responsible for grants to major arts organisations, while festivals and community arts came under Leisure Services, the media industries under Economic Development, public art under Planning and arts education under the Education Committee (Sargent, 1991).

The cultural planning approach also reveals the inadequacy of narrowly based professional specialisations, which may make it more difficult for policy-makers to capitalise creatively on their cultural resources. At present formal training is basically rooted in the traditions of arts administration for arts policy-makers, of marketing studies for tourism development officers and city marketers, and of land use planning for physical planners. There is a clear need for broadly based forms of training in cultural planning, which can be shared by policy-makers with different remits and professional backgrounds. Training should provide knowledge of urban and regional economics, history, sociology, politics, geography and planning, as well as of European Community institutions and of models of urban cultural policy in different European countries. The aim of this type of training would be to create a shared language to enable policy-makers to make imaginative connections between their respective areas of work, thereby producing richer and more effective urban development strategies.

Conclusions

Making the advancement of local democracy and citizenship rights a central priority for cultural policies in the 1990s and adopting a cultural planning perspective would involve the rethinking of many of the assumptions upon which the policy-making process was based during the last decade. To start with, as Julia Gonzalez observes in this book, there would have to be a change in the notion of 'quality of life' adopted by policy-makers, from that as a commodity to be marketed as an element of urban competitiveness, to quality of life determined by how residents relate to their city as a collective entity, and how they participate in its public life.

More generally, it would be necessary to rethink what the regenerative potential of cultural policy can be. 'Urban regeneration' is a composite concept, encompassing economic, environmental, social, cultural, symbolic and political dimensions. Cultural policies, in order to be truly regenerative, should have a positive impact on all of them. As we have seen in the book, the experience of the 1980s was innovative in the symbolic and economic spheres because it linked cultural policy with the 'marketing' of cities and with strategies aimed at expanding tourism and other consumer service industries. Urban economic success in the 1990s, however, will depend on advanced industries and services which make intensive use of high-quality 'human capital' and specialised skills and knowledge. To maintain an important position within future economic development strategies, policies on culture will have to be linked with policies on education, training, research and development.

The chapter about Bologna in this book shows that an integrated cultural and training strategy can help create local networks of firms working in highly skilled, high value-added services and manufacturing industry sectors. The same chapter also highlights the importance of strategies encouraging self-managed forms of training which can build on informal skills and bridge the gap between amateurism and professionalism. These strategies can contribute to reintegrating into the local economy geographically and socially marginalised groups within European cities, whose skills and potential are often overlooked by the professional cultural sector and mainstream educational institutions. A number of cities in Britain have adopted strategies to strengthen local cultural industries such as fashion, design, film, broadcasting and popular music. In some cases – such as Rennes and Montpellier among the cities discussed in this book – links have been made between the cultural sector and institutions engaged in advanced research on media and telecommunication technologies. Lastly, towns in the 'Third Italy' (Bianchini, 1990; Pyke et al., 1990) demonstrate the importance of the contribution of craftspeople, designers and visual artists to the success of small firms operating in the clothing, glass-making, furniture, shoes, pottery and tiles sectors.

City marketing in the future could be a celebration of local cultural production and of its applications to the development of a modern economy. This potential can already be glimpsed in initiatives like the Biennale of young artists in Bologna, the Media Park in Cologne or the International Festival of Science and Technology in Edinburgh.

In conclusion, a cultural planning perspective rooted in an understanding of local cultural resources and of cities as *cultural entities* – as places where people meet talk, share ideas and desires, and where identities and lifestyles are formed – could help planners assess the needs of the community, ensure cultural pluralism and conceptualise essential strategic questions about the city's future. According to this perspective, an explicit commitment to revitalise the cultural, social and political life of local residents should precede and sustain the formulation of physical and economic regeneration strategies.

The 1980s saw a flourishing of studies on the economic importance of the cultural sector in different cities, and of the direct and indirect economic impacts of cultural activities and policies on employment and wealth creation (Behr *et al.*, 1989; Hummel and Berger, 1988; Myerscough, 1988). This tradition of studies was undoubtedly important to raise the profile of cultural policies and to advocate for increased public and private sector investment in culture. In the 1990s, however, new methodologies and indicators will be needed to measure the impact of cultural policies and activities in terms of quality of life, social cohesion and commmunity development. They should provide evidence upon which stronger arguments for the cultural planning approach could be built. Such arguments would be one of the most effective ways of placing cultural policies in a leading position within urban development strategies, and of creating more humane, balanced and civilised cities for the 1990s.

References

Ardagh, John (1990) *France Today*, Harmondsworth, Penguin.

Barnett, Steven (1991) 'Selling us short? Cities, culture and economic development', in Fisher and Owen (eds) (1991).

Behr, V. Gnad, F. and Kunzmann, K.R. (eds) (1989) 'Kultur, Wirtschaft, Stadtenwicklung', *Dortmunder Beiträge zur Raumplanung*, 51, Dortmund, IRPUD.

Bianchini, Franco (1990) 'The third Italy: model or myth?', thematic study within *Urbanisation and the Functions of Cities in the European Community*, Centre for Urban Studies, University of Liverpool, October.

Bianchini, Franco (1991a) 'Urban cultural policy', *National Arts and Media Strategy Discussion Documents*, 40, London, Arts Council.

Bianchini, Franco (1991b) 'Models of cultural policies and planning in west European cities', in The Cultural Planning Conference, Mornington, Victoria, Australia, EIT.

Blanchard, Simon (ed.) (1990) The Challenge of Channel Five, London, British Film Institute.

Challans, Tim (1991) 'Local authorities and the arts', in National Arts and Media Strategy Discussion Documents, 16, London, Arts Council.

Cornford, James and Robins, Kevin (1990) 'Questions of geography', in Blanchard (ed.) (1990).

Cummings, Milton and Katz, Richard (eds) (1987), The Patron State. Government and the Arts in Europe, North America and Japan, Oxford, Oxford University Press.

Fisher, Mark and Owen, Ursula (eds) (1991) Whose Cities?, Harmondsworth, Penguin.

Hummel, M. and Berger, M. (1988) Die volkwirtschaftliche Bedeutung von Kunst und Kultur, Berlin–Munich, Dunker & Humblot).

Ismayr, Wolfgang (1987) 'Cultural federalism and public support for the arts in the Federal Republic of Germany', in Cummings and Katz (eds) (1987).

Khan, Naseem (1991) 'Asian arts', in Fisher and Owen (eds) (1991).

McNulty, Robert (1991) 'Cultural planning: a movement for civic progress', in The Cultural Planning Conference, op. cit.

Mercer, Colin (1991) 'Brisbane's cultural development strategy: the process, the politics and the products', in The Cultural Planning Conference, op. cit.

Myerscough, John (1988) The Economic Importance of the Arts in Britain, London, Policy Studies Institute.

Owusu, Kwesi (1986) The Struggle for Black Arts in Britain, London, Comedia.

Porter, Robert (ed.) (1980) The Arts and City Planning, New York, American Council for the Arts.

Pyke, F. Becattini, G. and Sengenberger, W. (1990) Industrial Districts and Inter-firm Co-operation in Italy, Geneva, International Institute of Labour studies.

Sargent, Anthony (1991) 'Views from a big city', in National Arts and Media Strategy Discussion Documents, 16, London, Arts Council.

Simor, Anne (ed.) (1988) The Role of the Arts in Urban Regeneration, proceedings of a symposium organized by the America–European Community Association Trust at Leeds Castle, Kent, 28-30 October.

Toronto Arts Council (1988) No Vacancy. A Cultural Facilities Policy for the City of Toronto.

Von Eckhardt, Wolf (1980) 'Synopsis', in Porter (ed.) (1980).

Walzer, Michael (1986) 'Pleasures and costs of urbanity', Dissent, summer.

Wynne, Derek et al. (eds) (1989) The Culture Industry, Manchester, Greater Manchester Economic Development Ltd. and North West Arts.

Index